القول السديد في مقاصد التوحيد

شرح كتاب التوحيد

An Explanation of Muḥammad Ibn ʿAbd al-Wahhāb's *Kitāb al-Tawḥīd*

by *ʿAllāmah* ʿAbd al-Raḥmān al-Saʿdī

Translated by

Abu Khaliyl

ISBN 1 898649 61 8

British Library Cataloguing in Publication Data.
A catalogue record for this book is available from the British Library.

Published: Al-Hidāyah Publishing and Distribution

Distributed by: Al-Hidāyah Publishing and Distribution
P.O. Box 3332
Birmingham
United Kingdom
B10 0UH

Tel: 0121 753 1889
Fax: 0121 753 2422
Website: www.al-hidaayah.co.uk
Email: mail@al-hidaayah.co.uk

القَوْلُ السَّدِيدُ فِي مَقَاصِدِ التَّوحِيدِ

شَرْح

كِتَابِ التَّوْحِيدِ

An Explanation of
Muḥammad Ibn ʿAbd al-Wahhāb's
Kitāb al-Tawḥīd

Contents

Transliteration Table

Consonants,

ء	’	د	d	ض	ḍ	ك	k
ب	b	ذ	dh	ط	ṭ	ل	l
ت	t	ر	r	ظ	ẓ	م	m
ث	th	ز	z	ع	‘	ن	n
ج	j	س	s	غ	gh	ه	h
ح	ḥ	ش	sh	ف	f	و	w
خ	kh	ص	ṣ	ق	q	ي	y

Vowels, diphthongs, etc.

Short:	ـَ	a	ـِ	i	ـُ	u
Long:	ـَا	ā	ـِي	ī	ـُو	ū
diphthongs:			ـَيْ	ay	ـَوْ	aw

Introduction to the translation of *al-Qawl al-Sadīd*

All praise is due to Allāh, and may He send peace and blessings upon His Messenger. This is the beneficial commentary of Shaykh ʿAbd al-Raḥmān bin Nāṣir al-Saʿdī on Shaykh Muḥammad Ibn ʿAbd al-Wahhāb's, monumental book, *Kitāb al Tawḥīd*. This commentary, *al-Qawl al-Sadīd*, is brief but concise, bringing helpful points to the reader regarding these important discussions on the subject of *tawḥīd* and *shirk*.

Here it should be noted that all of the footnotes are the translator's. An attempt was made to provide useful information about the condition and recording of the ḥadīths and reports where possible. For the additional explanatory comments in the footnotes, the following titles are often referenced: *Taysīr al-ʿAzīz al-Ḥamīd fī Sharḥ Kitāb al-Tawḥīd* by Shaykh Sulymān bin ʿAbdullāh bin Muḥammad bin ʿAbd al-Wahhāb (Eighth Edition, Beirut 1409). This is the earlier commentary whose author was only able to complete up to chapter 49; *Fatḥ al-Majīd bi Sharḥ Kitāb al-Tawḥīd*, by Shaykh ʿAbd al-Raḥmān bin Ḥasan bin Muḥammad bin ʿAbd al-Wahhāb (Third Edition Riyādh 1413). His source for referencing and editing was the previous mentioned title. Additionally, quotes are often cited from ʿAbd al-Qādir al-Arnā'ūṭ's notes on *Fatḥ al-Majīd* (Third Edition Damascus-Beirut 1414). Other references are noted.

ʿ*Allāmah* al-Saʿdī's introduction

From the pen of Shaykh ʿAbd al-Raḥmān bin Nāṣir bin Saʿdī, being an abridgement and summary of the pure creed of *Ahl al-Sunnah*, as derived from the Book and the *Sunnah*.

All praise is due to Allāh. We praise Him, we seek His help, we seek His forgiveness, we turn in repentance to Him.

We seek refuge in Allāh from the evils of ourselves and the mischief of our deeds. Whomever Allāh guides, none can misguide him, and whomever He allows to stray, there is no guidance for him.

I testify that there is none worthy of worship but Allāh alone without partners, and I testify that Muḥammad is His worshipper and Messenger.

We previously published these helpful notes on the subjects of *Kitāb al-Tawḥīd* by Shaykh al-Islām Muḥammad bin ʿAbd al-Wahhāb, may Allāh bless his soul. This resulted in some benefit and help for the average people, and brought assistance for those in the field of knowledge, since it contains beneficial details with some comprehensive explanation. It was published by the publishing house of the Imām, then it ran out of stock due to the many requests for it. So the urgent need to reprint and distribute it arose, but this time it occurred to me to preface it with a brief discussion of some points from the creed of *Ahl al-Sunnah*, both in its foundations and branches. So I say, while it is Allāh alone whose help we seek;

They believe in Allāh, His angels, His books, His messengers, the Last Day, and in the Divine Will, its good and its bad.

They bear witness that Allāh is the Lord, the worshipped God, the one who is alone in all perfection. They worship Him alone, practising religion sincerely for Him.

They say that Allāh is the Creator, the Originator the Fashioner, the Provider, the Giver, the Withholder, the Arranger of all matters.

That He is the one to be deified, the one worshipped, the sole goal. That He is the First; before whom there was nothing, the Last; after whom there is nothing, the *al-Ẓāhir*, the *al-Bāṭin*.

That He is the Exalted Most High in every meaning and sense; exalted in His essence, exalted in His ability, and exalted in His power.

That He is ascended above *istawā* His Throne, an *istawā* befitting His Honour, His Majesty, His unlimited Exaltedness, and His absolute Aboveness. His Knowledge encompasses all externals and internals, a Knowledge of the heights and the lows. He is with His worshippers in His Knowledge, knowing their every condition, and He is the Near, the Respondent.

That He in His entire self is independent of the entire creation, all are in need of Him in every way, be it in their origination, or in the origination of what they are in need of in every circumstance. None is in any sense independent of Him.

He is the Generous, the Merciful. There is no temporal favour, nor religious blessing nor defence against trouble for the worshippers except by Allāh, so He is the cause of all favours, the defence against all woes.

Out of His Mercy He descends every night to the lowest heaven to answer the needs of the worshipper when the last third of the night remains. He says, "My worshippers do not ask from other than Me. Who is it that calls Me so that I may respond to him, who is it that asks of Me so that I may give him, who is it that seeks My forgiveness so that I may forgive him." Until *fajr* begins. He descends as He wills and He does what He intends, "There is nothing similar to Him, and He is the Hearing the Seeing."(*al-Shūrā* 42:11)

They believe that He is the Wise, the one whose judgement in legislating and decreeing is complete. So He did not create anything uselessly, nor does He institute legislation, except that it is beneficial and wise.

He is the One turned to, the Pardoner, the Forgiving; accepting repentance from his worshippers, and pardoning their faults, forgiving the grave sins of the repentant, those seeking forgiveness, and those who turn penitently.

He is the Grateful, the one who appreciates the small deed and increases the thankful by His blessings.

They describe Him as He describes Himself, and as Allāh's Messenger described Him. With all of His attributes of being; like living, perfection, hearing, seeing, omnipotence, honour and greatness. He is the Majestic, the Glorious, the Beautiful, and the Praised absolute.

And [they describe Him] with the attributes of action related to His will and power; like mercy, pleasure, anger, and speech. He speaks as He wills, how He wills, His words are not alterable, nor perishable. And that the Qur'ān is Allāh's words, un-created, originating with Him, and returning to Him.

That He is unending, and never ceases to be able to do as He intends, speaking as He wills, and ruling by His rules of decree for His worshippers,

His legislative rules, and rule overall. So He is the Ruler and the King, any king other than Him is ruled over by Him. There is no escape for the people from His sovereignty nor from His rule.

They believe in what is mentioned about Him in the Book and what is reported in well known form in the *sunnah*; that the believers will see their Lord (ﷻ) with their eyes, and that the favour of seeing Him, and the reward of His pleasure, are the greatest of favours and delights.

And that whoever dies upon other than faith and *tawḥīd*, then he will be punished in the fire of *Jahannam* forever, and that those who perform the major sins when they die without repenting - if they have not had their sins erased, nor are they interceded for - then they enter the Fire. But they will not remain in it eternally, for no one remains in the Fire whose heart has the weight of a mustard seed worth of faith, except that he will eventually be removed from it.

And that faith comprises the creed of the hearts and their actions, as well as the physical deeds and sayings of the tongues. So whoever abides in these with the most complete intention, then he is the real believer, the one deserving rewards and security against punishment. Whoever is deficient in these, then his faith will be proportionately deficient. This is the way in which faith increases through obedience, and by good deeds, and it is diminished through disobedience and evil.

Among their fundamental beliefs is endeavouring and striving in matters that benefit in religion and the world, while seeking Allāh's help. So they aspire to what benefits them, and they seek help from Allāh.

By this they achieve sincerity for Allāh in all of their works, and they follow the Messenger of Allāh, being sincere to the one they worship, sincere in adherence to the Message, and giving sincere advice to the believers following their path.

They testify that Muḥammad is His worshipper and His Messenger, sent by Allāh with guidance and the true religion to guide the entire creation, and that he is more worthy of the believers than they themselves are. He is the last of the Prophets, sent to humans and *jinns*, warning and bringing good news, inviting to Allāh by His permission with an illuminating torch, sent by Him to restore the religion, as well as the world, and so that the creatures could abide in worshipping Allāh, seeking His help from what He provided for that.

They know that he (ﷺ) is the most knowledgeable of creatures, the most truthful of them, the most worthy of giving advice about them, and the greatest of them in explaining matters. They love him and honour him, loving him more than they love any other creature, and following him in the foundations and branches of their religion. They rank his sayings and guidance above that of any other person.

They believe that Allāh embodied in him virtues, special traits, and a completeness that was not embodied in any other. So he holds the highest of positions among all creatures, he is the most dignified among them, and he is the most perfect of them in every virtue. He (ﷺ) did not leave behind any good without telling his *ummah* about it, nor any evil without warning them against it.

Similarly, they believe in all of the Books that Allāh revealed, and all of the Messengers that Allāh sent, not making a distinction in this regard between any of the Messengers.

They believe in all of the elements of the Divine Will. That all of the worshipper's actions, whether good or bad, are surrounded by Allāh's knowledge, aforementioned by His pen, permeated by His will, and are all based upon His wisdom. And that He created a will and intent for His worshippers, by which their sayings and actions occur in accordance with His plan for them, they are not forced by it, but they are the choosers. This is particularly so for the believers, because He loves faith for them and decorated their hearts with it, and He hates disbelief, immorality and disobedience for them due to His justice and wisdom.

Among the foundations of *Ahl Sunnah* is that they practice their religion upon *naṣīhah* (sincerety) to Allāh, to His Book, to His Messenger, to the *imāms* and to the body of Muslims. They command the good and forbid the evil in accordance with the obligations of the *sharī'ah*. They command righteousness and maintaining the ties of the womb, kindness to neighbours, to rulers, to average people, honouring the right of any who has a right, and a kindness to all creatures.

They invite to the best and most noble conduct, and they prohibit vile and evil manners. They believe that the most complete among the believers in faith and certainty, is the best among them in deeds and manners, the most truthful among them in speech, the most prone to every good and virtue, the one most remote from every type of vulgarity.

They command maintaining the rites of their religion, according to whatever comes from their Prophet about them, and about their descriptions and regulations. And they warn against that which would cause harm to them and decrease their value.

They believe that *jihād* in the cause of Allāh continues to be valid with every leader of theirs, both righteous and sinner. And that it is the highest limb of the religion. A *jihād* of knowledge and proofs, as well as *jihād* with the sword. And that it is obligatory upon every Muslim to defend the religion with all that he is able to and capable of.

Among their fundamental beliefs is the importance of uniting the Muslims, and struggling to draw their hearts together and bring love between them. They warn from separation, enmity, and hatred between each other, and against all that draws them closer to this.

Among their fundamental beliefs is that they prohibit wronging anyone, be it in their blood, their wealth, their honour, or any of their rights. They command justice and fairness, and they encourage beneficence and good virtue in all of their dealings.

They believe that the best of nations is the nation of Muḥammad (ﷺ), and the best of them are the companions of Allāh's Messenger (ﷺ), particularly the rightly guided *khalīfahs*, the ten who were promised Paradise, the warriors at Badr, those who gave the pledge of *Riḍwān*, the earlier of those who migrated, and the *Anṣār*. So they love the companions as an expression of their faith in Allāh. They teach about the best of them and they refrain from any of the bad that may be said about any of them.

They express their faith in Allāh by honouring the guiding scholars, the just *imāms*, and anyone who holds a noteworthy position of religion or virtue among all of the Muslims. They ask Allāh that He protect them from doubt, from *shirk*, from harshness, from hypocrisy, and from evil conduct. They ask Allāh to strengthen them upon their Prophet's religion until their death.

In all of these fundamentals they have faith, and in them all they believe, and it is to them that they invite.

In the Name of Allāh, the Beneficent, the Merciful. All praise is due to Allāh, may He mention Muḥammad, and his family, and grant him greetings of peace.

Kitāb al-Tawḥīd

Chapter 1

وقول الله تعالى: وما خلقت الجن والإنس إلا ليعبدون

Allāh (ﷻ) said; "I have not created *jinn* and man except to worship Me"

وقول الله تعالى: (وما خلقت الجن والإنس إلا ليعبدون) وقوله: (ولقد بعثنا في كل أمة رسولاً أن أعبدوا الله واجتنبوا الطاغوت) الآية. وقوله: (وقضى ربك ألا تعبدوا إلا إياه وبالوالدين إحسنا) الآية. وقوله: (واعبدوا الله ولا تشركوا به شيئا) الآية. وقوله: (قل تعالوا أتل ما حرم ربكم عليكم ألا تشركوا به شيئا) الآيات.

Allāh (ﷻ) said; "I have not created *jinn* and man except to worship Me" (*al-Dhāriyāt* 51:56) And; "We sent a messenger to every nation [saying]; 'Worship Allāh and shun the *ṭāghūt*.'"(*al-Naḥl* 16:60) And; "Your Lord has ordered that you worship none but He, and that you behave kindly to your parents." (*al-Isrā'* 17:23) And; "Worship Allāh, and do not associate anything with Him." (*al-Nisā'*:36) And; "Say: 'Come! I will recite what your Lord has prohibited for you: That you do not associate anything with Him..." (*al-An'ām* 6:151)

قال ابن مسعود رضي الله عنه: من أراد أن ينظر إلى وصية محمد صلى الله عليه وسلم التي عليها خاتمه فليقرأ قوله تعالى: (قل تعالوا أتل ما حرم ربكم عليكم) - إلى قوله - (وأن هذا صراطي مستقيماً..) الآية.

Ibn Mas'ūd said, "Whoever wants to have a look at the will that Muḥammad (ﷺ) placed his seal upon, then let him recite the Most High's saying; 'Say: "Come! I will recite what your Lord has prohibited for you: That you do not associate anything with Him... and surely this is my Straight Path."' (*al-An'ām* 6: 151-153)[2]

وعن معاذ بن جبل رضي الله عنه قال: كنت رديف النبي صلى الله عليه وسلم على حمار فقال لي: «يا معاذ أتدري ما حق الله على العباد، وما حق العباد على الله؟» فقلت: الله ورسوله أعلم. قال: «حق الله على العباد أن يعبدوه ولا يشركوا به شيئاً، وحق العباد على الله أن لا يعذب من لا يشرك به شيئاً» فقلت: يا رسول الله أفلا أبشر الناس؟ قال: «لا تبشرهم فيتكلوا» أخرجاه في الصحيحين.

Mu'ādh bin Jabal, may Allāh be pleased with him, said; "While I was riding upon a donkey with the Prophet (ﷺ), he said to me; 'O Mu'ādh! Do you know what Allāh's right is upon His worshippers, and what the worshipper's right upon Allāh is?' I replied, 'Allāh and His Messenger know better.' He said, 'Allāh's right upon His worshipper is that they worship Him without associating anything with Him. The worshipper's right upon Allāh is that He does not punish anyone who does not associate anything with Him.' I said, 'Shall I tell this to the people?' He (ﷺ) said, 'Do not inform them since they may depend [solely] on it.'" This was recorded in the two *Ṣaḥīḥs*.

---

[2] The famous commentator on *Kitāb al-Tawḥīd*, Shaykh Sulaymān bin 'Abdullāh bin Muḥammad 'Abd al-Wahhāb (*Taysīr al-'Azīz fī Sharḥ Kitāb al-Tawḥīd*) says, "This report is recorded by al-Tirmidhī who graded it *ḥasan*, Ibn al-Mundhir, Ibn Abī Ḥātim, al-Ṭabarānī similarly, and Abū 'Ubayd and 'Abd bin Ḥumayd reported similarly from al-Rabī'a bin Khuthaym." Al-Arnā'ūṭ said, "Recorded by al-Tirmidhī no. 3072 in *al-Tafsīr*, under *Surāt al-An'ām*, and he graded it *ḥasan*, and it is as he said." (*Fatḥ al-Majīd bi Sharḥ Kitāb al-Tawḥīd* with additional ḥadīth references and grading by 'Abd al-Qādir al-Arnā'ūṭ (Third Edition Damascus-Beirut 1414).) The following points should be mentioned: 1. Al-Tirmidhī's grade was *ḥasan gharīb* 2. The wording with al-Tirmidhī differs; "Whoever takes pleasure in looking at the page which has the seal of Muḥammad (ﷺ) on it, then let these people recite the *āyāt*..." and the rest is the same. So it does not contain the word "will", although it is interpreted to mean that due to the meaning of the *āyāt* in question. See *Tuḥfat al-Aḥwadhī* by al-Mubārakpurī. 3. Al-Ṭabarānī has the same wording from Ibn Mas'ūd as Al-Tirmidhī according to Al-Ḥaythamī's *Majma' al-Bahrayn*. 4. Shaykh Muḥammad Nasir al-Dīn Al-Albānī comments after the text with Al-Tirmidhī, "Weak *isnād*". (*Ḍa'īf Sunan Al-Tirmidhī*)

Perhaps Shaykh Muḥammad Ibn 'Abd al-Wahhāb copied the wording utilised in *Kitāb al-Tawḥīd* from Ibn Kathīr, since it appears that way in his *Tafsīr*, and the part of the chain of narrators that Ibn Kathīr quotes is the same as that with Al-Tirmidhī. Or it could be that he copied it with this wording from one of the other routes that Shaykh Sulaymān mentioned. Allāh knows best.

فيه مسائل:

الأولى: الحكمة في خلق الجن والإنس.

الثانية: أن العبادة هي التوحيد؛ لأن الخصومة فيه.

الثالثة: أن من لم يأت به لم يعبد الله، ففيه معنى قوله(ولا أنتم عابدون ما أعبد).

الرابعة: الحكمة في إرسال الرسل.

الخامسة: أن الرسالة عمّت كل أمة.

السادسة: أن دين الأنبياء واحد.

السابعة: المسألة الكبيرة أن عبادة الله لا تحصل إلا بالكفر بالطاغوت؛ ففيه معنى قوله: (فمن يكفر بالطاغوت ويؤمن بالله) الآية.

الثامنة: أن الطاغوت عام في كل ما عُبِد من دون الله.

التاسعة: عظم شأن ثلاث الآيات المحكمات في سورة الأنعام عند السلف. وفيها عشر مسائل، أولها النهي عن الشرك.

العاشرة: الآيات المحكمات في سورة الإسراء، وفيها ثماني عشرة مسألة، بدأها الله بقوله: (لا تجعل مع الله إلهاً آخر فتقعد مذموماً مخذولاً)؛ وختمها بقوله: (ولا تجعل مع الله إلهاً آخر فتلقى في جهنم ملوماً مدحوراً)، ونبهنا الله سبحانه على عظم شأن هذه المسائل بقوله: (ذلك مما أوحى إليك ربك من الحكمة) .

الحادية عشرة: آية سورة النساء التي تسمى آية الحقوق العشرة، بدأها الله تعالى بقوله: (واعبدوا الله ولا تشركوا به شيئاً) .

الثانية عشرة:التنبيه على وصية رسول الله صلى الله عليه وسلم عند موته.

الثالثة عشرة: معرفة حق الله تعالى علينا.

الرابعة عشرة: معرفة حق العباد عليه إذا أدوا حقه.

الخامسة عشرة: أن هذه المسألة لا يعرفها أكثر الصحابة.

السادسة عشرة: جواز كتمان العلم للمصلحة.

السابعة عشرة: استحباب بشارة المسلم بما يسره.

الثامنة عشرة: الخوف من الاتكال على سعة رحمة الله.

التاسعة عشرة: قول المسؤول عما لا يعلم: الله ورسوله أعلم.

العشرون: جواز تخصيص بعض الناس بالعلم دون بعض.

الحادية والعشرون: تواضعه صلى الله عليه وسلم لركوب الحمار مع الإرداف عليه.

الثانية والعشرون: جواز الإرداف على الدابة.

الثالثة والعشرون: فضيلة معاذ بن جبل.

الرابعة والعشرون: عظم شأن هذه المسألة.

Important Points

1. The wisdom behind the creation of *jinns* and humans.
2. That *al-ʿibādah* refers [in particular] to *tawḥīd*, since it is the subject of the argument [above].
3. Whoever does not come with this, then he has not worshipped Allāh. In this vain is the meaning of His saying; "And you will not worship what I worship." (*al-Kāfirūn* 109:3)
4. The wisdom behind sending the messengers.
5. That the Message [i.e. *tawḥīd*] has been delivered to all nations.
6. That the prophets' religion is one and the same.
7. An issue of major importance here is that the worship of Allāh is not realized without rejecting the *ṭāghūt*. In this vain is the meaning of His (ﷻ) saying; "And whoever rejects the *ṭāghūt* and believes in Allāh, he has grasped the firm handle that will not break..."(*al-Baqarah* 2:256)

8. That the term *ṭāghūt* applies generally to anything that is worshipped other than Allāh.

9. The *salaf* held the three *muḥkamāt āyāt* of *Sūrah al-Anʿām* to be of tremendous importance. These *āyāt* contain ten issues, the first of them being the prohibition of *shirk*.

10. The *muḥkamāt āyāt* of *Sūrah al-Isrā'* - they contain eighteen issues, and Allāh begins them with His saying; "Do not make a god with Allāh, lest you sit disgraced, abandoned." (*al-Isrā'* 17:22) And He ends them by saying; "Do not make a god with Allāh, lest you be thrown condemned and vanquished into *Jahannam*." (*al-Isrā'* 17: 39) Allāh, (ﷻ) has pointed out the tremendous importance of these issues for us by saying; "This is some of the wisdom that your Lord revealed to you." (*al-Isrā'* 17:39)

11. The *ayah* of *Sūrah al-Nisā'* hich has been called the *ayah* of the ten obligations - Allāh begins them by saying; "Worship Allāh, and do not associate anything with Him." (*al-Nisā'* :36)

12. The clarification of the will of Allāh's Messenger upon his death.

13. The knowledge of Allāh's right upon us.

14. The knowledge of the right of the worshippers upon Him if they fulfil His right.

15. That most of the companions were not aware of this issue.

16. The permissibility of withholding knowledge when it is more beneficial to do so.

17. The favourability of informing the Muslim of what facilitates him.

18. The fear of depending solely upon the ampleness of Allāh's mercy.

19. The saying of the one questioned when he does not know the answer, "Allāh and His Messenger know better."

20. The permissibility of departing some knowledge specifically to some people rather than others.

21. The humbleness of the Prophet (ﷺ), in that he rode a donkey with a companion rider.

22. The permissibility of sharing a ride on a riding animal.

23. The virtue of Mu'ādh bin Jabal, may Allāh be pleased with him.
24. The tremendous importance of this matter.

Commentary by 'Allāmah al-Sa'dī

Kitāb al-Tawḥīd

This preface guides the theme of this book from its beginning to its end. Hence the absence of additional introduction since this book only elaborates upon *tawḥīd al-ilāhiyah* and *al-'ibādah* (singling out Allāh in all acts of worship) by mentioning its rulings, boundaries and conditions, its virtues, its evidences, its foundations and divisions, its means of realization and its fruits, its prerequisites, what intensifies it and makes it stronger, or what weakens and enfeebles it, as well as what is achieved or perfected by it.

Know that in the absolute sense *tawḥīd* refers to the knowledge and recognition that the Lord solely possesses the most perfect attributes, acknowledging Him to be the sole possessor of the greatest and most majestic attributes, and singling Him out alone for worship.

The Three Categories

1. *Tawḥīd al-Asmā' wa l-Ṣifāt*

It is the belief that the Lord alone - magnificent is His majesty - is the sole possessor of ultimate perfection in every sense, by the magnificent, majestic, and beautiful characteristics, which none shares with Him in any way whatsoever.

This belief is accomplished by affirming what Allāh affirmed for Himself, or what was affirmed about Him by His Messenger (ﷺ), regarding every name and attribute, those mentioned in the Book and the *Sunnah* befitting His majesty and greatness - without negating anything from them nor denying them, distorting them, or likening them to the characteristics of the creation. One must also negate what He negated from Himself, or whatever His Messenger (ﷺ) negated of deficiencies and faults and all that would negate His perfection.

2. *Tawḥīd al-Rubūbiyah*

The worshipper is to believe that Allāh is the sole Lord of creating, providing, originating, the One who nurtures all creation with its bounty, and nurtures some of His creation - they being the prophets and their followers - with correct creed, beautiful morals, knowledge that provides benefit, and righteous deeds. This is the nurturing that gives benefit to the hearts and souls, producing endless bliss.

3. *Tawḥīd al-Ulūhiyah*, also called *Tawḥīd al-ʿIbādah*

It is the knowledge and recognition that Allāh is the lone possessor of *ulūhiyah* and *ʿubūdiyah* over all of His creatures, singling Him out solely for all worship, making the religion for Allāh alone.

This last type is required and implied by the first two, since al-*ulūhiyah* is a characteristic indicative of the attributes of perfection and it is derived from the attributes of *rubūbiyah* and magnificence, then it is more deserving an attribute of the one worshipped since He is the one described with characteristics of greatness and majesty, and since He is the one who gives His creatures benefit and blessings. Then singling Him (ﷻ) out with the perfect attributes and considering Him alone worthy of *rubūbiyah* necessitates that none deserves worship other than Him. And the objective of the call of the messengers, from the first of them to the last, is the call to this *tawḥīd*.

So in this preface, the author mentions some texts proving that Allāh created the creation for the sake of worshipping Him, for sincere faith in Him, and that this right of His is the most obligatory duty upon them. This is the message of all of the revealed books.

All of the messengers called to this *tawḥīd*, and they forbade contradicting it by *shirk* and rivalry to Allāh, particularly Muḥammad (ﷺ), and particularly the Noble *Qur'ān*. By it He commanded, obligated, and established the greatest of resolutions, He gave the greatest clarification, and He made it known that there is no salvation, success, nor happiness, except by this *tawḥīd*, and that all arguments - those of reason, revelation, wisdom or psychology - all provide proof and evidence to command and require this *tawḥīd*.

So *tawḥīd* is the right of Allāh most obligatory upon His worshippers, it is the greatest of religious commands, the most basic of all fundamentals, and the firmest basis for deeds.

Chapter 2

فضل التوحيد وما يكفر من الذنوب

The virtues of *tawḥīd* and the sins it removes

وقول الله تعالى: (الذين آمنوا و لم يلبسوا إيمانهم بظلم) الآية.

Allāh (ﷻ) said; "Those who believe and do not mix their faith with *ẓulm*...." (*al-An'ām* 6:82)

عن عبادة بن الصامت رضي الله عنه قال: قال رسول الله صلى الله عليه وسلم: (من شهد أن لا إله إلا الله وحده لا شريك له، وأن محمداً عبده ورسوله، وأن عيسى عبد الله ورسوله وكلمته ألقاها إلى مريم وروح منه، والجنة حق، والنار حق أدخله الله الجنة على ما كان من العمل). أخرجاه.

'Ubādah bin al-Ṣāmit said, "Allāh's Messenger (ﷺ) said; 'Whoever testifies that there is no god but Allāh, alone without partners, and that Muḥammad is His worshipper and Messenger, and that 'Isā is a worshipper of Allāh, His Messenger, His word delivered to Maryam, and a soul from Him, and that Paradise is true, and that the Fire is true, Allāh will admit him to Paradise whatever his deeds may be.[3]" (al-Bukhārī and Muslim)

---

[3] It is translated in accordance with the correct interpretation of its meaning, that is, by virtue of this, yet he may be righteous or corrupt, if he is sincere in this it will save him from eternal damnation and grant him Paradise in the end. See *Fatḥ al-Majīd bi Sharḥ Kitāb al-Tawḥīd*. As for the term "word" it means that 'Īsā was created by Allāh's command, "Be", and "soul from Him" means a soul from the souls that Allāh created. See previous reference.

ولهما في حديث عتبان: (فإن الله حرم على النار من قال: لا إله إلا الله يبتغي بذلك وجه الله).

And they also recorded the ḥadīth of ʿItbān: "Surely Allāh prohibited the Fire from whoever said *Lā ilāha illa Allāh* (no one deserves to be worshipped but Allāh), seeking His Face by it."

وعن أبي سعيد الخدري رضي الله عنه عن رسول الله صلى الله عليه وسلم قال: (قال موسى: يا رب، علمني شيئاً أذكرك وأدعوك به. قال: يا موسى: قل لا إله إلا الله. قال: يا رب كل عبادك يقولون هذا. قال: يا موسى، لو أن السموات السبع وعامرهن غيري، والأرضين السبع في كفة، ولا إله إلا الله في كفة، مالت بهن لا إله إلا الله) [رواه ابن حبان، والحاكم وصححه].

Abū Saʿīd al-Khudrī, may Allāh be pleased with him, reported that Allāh's Messenger (ﷺ) said; "Mūsā (*ʿalayhī al-salām*) said; 'O Lord! Teach me something I can remember you and call upon you with!' He (ﷻ) said, 'O Mūsā! Say: "*Lā ilāha illa Allāh*" (none has the right to be worshipped except Allāh).' He said, 'But all of your worshippers say this.' He (ﷻ) said, 'O Mūsā! If the seven heavens and what is in them other than Me, and the seven earths were in a pan (of the Scale) and *Lā ilāha illa Allāh* was in another pan, then *Lā ilāha illa Allāh* would outweigh them.'" Recorded by Ibn Ḥibbān and al-Ḥākim who graded it *ṣaḥīḥ*.[4]

---

[4] This ḥadīth was recorded by Ibn Ḥibbān, al-Ḥākim, al-Nasāʾī in *al-Yawm wal-Laylah*, al-Ṭabarānī in *al-Duʿā* and Al-Bayhaqī in *al-Asmāʾ wa l-Ṣifāt*. Al-Ḥākim graded it *ṣaḥīḥ*, and al-Dhahabī was silent about it, usually indicating his approval. Similarly Ibn Ḥajar graded it *ṣaḥīḥ* in *Fatḥ al-Bārī* 11:208, it has a slightly different chain of narrators with al-Ṭabarānī and Abū Yaʿla about which Al-Ḥaythamī said (*al-Majmaʿ*) "It is recorded by Abū Yaʿla and its men are trustworthy, but among them there is some weakness." Commenting on the chain of Ibn Ḥibbān, ʿAlūsh (*Tashnīf al-Adhān* no. 927) says,"Its chain is weak, Darāj Abū Sumah is weak in his reports from Abū al-Haytham." Ibn al-Mundhir listed Darāj Abū Sumah among the narrators who the ḥadīth scholars differ over saying, "Abū Ḥātim declared him weak, as did al-Dāraquṭnī and others, Aḥmad said, 'His ḥadīths are rejected' al-Nasāʾī said, 'Rejected'" Yet others considered him trustworthy like Yaḥyā bin Maʿīn (it seems that quotes from him are what al-Ḥākim depended upon according to Al-Mundhirī's comments in *al-Targhīb*) and ʿAlī bin al-Madīnī - and particularly al-Tirmidhī in case he reports from Abū al-Haytham (as in this case!). Likewise he was quoted for support by Ibn Khuzaymah. Al-Albānī calls him the possessor and author of *manāḳīr* (rejected ḥadīths) see *al-Ḍaʿīfah* 1:294 & 254. Al-Albānī graded it weak in Ḍaʿīf Mawārid al-Ẓamān no. 295, as did Muqbil bin Hādī in al-Mustadrak no.1988.
There is however a more agreed upon authentic ḥadīth with different wording that gives much of the desired meaning for the context of this point. ʿAbdullāh bin ʿAmr bin al-ʿĀs narrated that the Prophet (ﷺ) said; "When death visited Allāh's Prophet Nūḥ (ﷺ), he

وللترمذي وحسنه عن أنس رضي الله عنه: سمعت رسول الله صلى الله عليه وسلم يقول: (قال الله تعالى: يا ابن آدم؛ لو أتيتني بقراب الأرض خطايا، ثم لقيتني لا تشرك بي شيئاً لأتيتك بقرابها مغفرة).

The ḥadīth of Anas - recorded by Al-Tirmidhī who graded it *ḥasan,* "I heard Allāh's Messenger (ﷺ) saying, 'Allāh (ﷻ) said; "....O son of Ādam! If you came to Me with mistakes filling the bags of the earth, yet you met Me without associating anything with Me, I would come to you with those bags full of forgiveness."'"[5]

فيه مسائل:

الأولى: سعة فضل الله.

الثانية: كثرة ثواب التوحيد عند الله.

الثالثة: تكفيره مع ذلك للذنوب.

الرابعة: تفسير الآية التي في سورة الأنعام.

الخامسة: تأمل الخمس اللواتي في حديث عبادة.

السادسة: أنك إذا جمعت بينه وبين حديث عتبان وما بعده تبين لك معنى قول: (لا إله إلا الله) وتبين لك خطأ المغرورين.

السابعة: التنبيه للشرط الذي في حديث عتبان.

الثامنة: كون الأنبياء يحتاجون للتنبيه على فضل لا إله إلا الله.

---

said to his son; 'I shall narrate to you the will. I command you with two things and I forbid you from two things: I command you with *Lā ilāha illa Allāh*. Surely if the seven heavens and the seven earths were placed on a pan of a scale, and *Lā ilāha illa Allāh* was placed on the other pan of the scale, they would give in to *Lā ilāha illa Allāh*...'" This ḥadīth was recorded by al-Bukhārī in *al-Adab al-Mufrad*, Aḥmad, Al-Bayhaqi in *al-Asmā'*, and also Al-Ṭabarānī according to Al-Ḥaythamī who said, "This *isnād* is *ṣaḥīḥ*." Al-Albānī included it in *al-Ṣaḥīḥah* no. 134, and Shaykh Muqbil bin Hādī included Aḥmad's ḥadīth in *Ṣaḥīḥ al-Musnad manma Laysa fī al-Ṣaḥīḥayn* v.1 p. 544 and he said, "This ḥadīth is *ṣaḥīḥ*."

5 The chain quoted by al-Tirmidhī is weak, but the ḥadīth was graded *ḥasan* by Al-Albānī in *Ṣaḥīḥ al-Jāmi' al-Ṣaghīr* no. 4338, as well as *al-Ṣaḥīḥah* no. 127. There is a stronger narration with Aḥmad, Muslim and others from Abū al-Dharr. Although its wording is different it contains the same information about the bags of sins and forgiveness.

التاسعة: التنبيه لرجحانها بجميع المخلوقات، مع أن كثيراً ممن يقولها يخف ميزانه.

العاشرة: النص على أن الأرضين سبع كالسموات.

الحادية عشرة: أن لهن عماراً.

الثانية عشرة: إثبات الصفات، خلافاً للأشعرية.

الثالثة عشرة: أنك إذا عرفت حديث أنس، عرفت أن قوله في حديث عتبان: (فإن الله حرم على النار من قال لا إله إلا الله، يبتغي بذلك وجه الله) أنه ترك الشرك، ليس قولها باللسان.

الرابعة عشرة: تأمل الجمع بين كون عيسى ومحمد عبدي الله ورسوليه.

الخامسة عشرة: معرفة اختصاص عيسى بكونه كلمة الله.

السادسة عشرة: معرفة كونه روحاً منه.

السابعة عشرة: معرفة فضل الإيمان بالجنة والنار.

الثامنة عشرة: معرفة قوله: (على ما كان من العمل).

التاسعة عشرة: معرفة أن الميزان له كفتان.

العشرون: معرفة ذكر الوجه.

Important Points

1. The extent of Allāh's favours.
2. The numerous rewards Allāh grants for *tawḥīd*.
3. By virtue of this it removes sins.
4. The explanation of the *ayah* in *Sūrah al-An'ām*.
5. The five points posed in the ḥadīth of 'Ubādah.
6. That when you unite these points, the ḥadīth of 'Itbān, and what

follows it, then the meaning of the statement *Lā ilāha illa Allāh* becomes clearer for you, as does the misconception of those who are confused about it.

7. Noting the condition mentioned in the ḥadīth of ʿItbān.
8. The prophets were in need of having the virtues of *Lā ilāha illa Allāh* pointed out to them.
9. Explaining how it is important for all creatures to say it even though many who say it do so in a way that diminishes its value.
10. The text proving that there are seven earths as there are seven heavens.
11. That they have inhabitants.
12. Confirming the attributes, contrary to the *Ashʿarīyah*.
13. That when you are aware of the ḥadīth of Anas, then you know about the saying in the ḥadīth of ʿItbān "Surely Allāh prohibited the Fire from whoever said *Lā ilāha illa Allāh* (none deserves to be worshipped but Allāh), seeking His Face by it" that it is by avoiding *shirk*, not simply saying it with the tongue.
14. Noting the application of "worshipper of Allāh and His Messenger" to both ʿIsā and Muḥammad.
15. Knowing that ʿIsā was particularized as "Allāh's word."
16. That he is a soul from Him.
17. Knowing the virtue of faith in Paradise and the Fire.
18. Being aware of his saying, "whatever his deeds may be."
19. The awareness that the Scale has two pans.
20. The usage of the term "Face".

Commentary by ʿ*Allāmah* al-Saʿdī

The Virtues of *Tawḥīd* and the Sins it Removes

Since the necessity of *tawḥīd* was mentioned previously in the preface, and the fact that it is the most important obligation upon all servants, so here its virtues, its praiseworthy results, and its wonderful rewards are mentioned. There is nothing that produces such good results nor holds such a variety of virtues like *tawḥīd*, for *tawḥīd* with its virtues is the best produce in this world and the Hereafter.

So the author, may Allāh have mercy upon him, said; "And the sins that it removes" for the sake of pointing out the specific along with the general idea, since the forgiveness of sins and their removal is among the general virtues and results of *tawḥīd* that this section bears witness to.

And among its virtues is that it is the greatest means of removing the sorrows of this world and the Hereafter, and warding off punishment in both worlds. It is because of its virtues that one is forbidden from eternity in the Fire - provided that his heart contains a mustard seed's equivalent amount of it - and if it is complete in his heart, then it will prevent him from ever entering the Fire at all.

Among its virtues is that it grants guidance and perfection to its practitioner, complete safety in this world and the Hereafter.

Another of its virtues is that it is the exclusive reason for being granted Allāh's pleasure and rewards, and the luckiest of people - who are granted Muḥammad's (ﷺ) intercession - are those who said *Lā ilāha illa Allāh* with sincerity in their hearts.

Among its most important virtues is that all deeds and sayings, both inner and outer, are dependent upon *tawḥīd* for their acceptability, their completeness, and for the rewards given for them. So all of this is empowered only with the presence of *tawḥīd* and sincerity for Allāh, then these matters can be perfect and complete.

And among its virtues is that it facilitates the accomplishment of good deeds for the servant as well as avoiding evil, and it delivers him from affliction. So when one's faith and *tawḥīd* for Allāh are sincere, any burden he feels to act obediently is lifted, since he hopes for the rewards of His Lord and His pleasure. Avoiding the desires of the soul becomes easier for him, since he fears His displeasure and punishment.

Among its virtues is that when *tawḥīd* is complete in the heart of its bearer, Allāh endears him with faith and adorns his heart with it. He would hate *kufr*, *fisq* and sin, and it places him among the ranks of the guided.

It lightens the worshipper's mishaps and weakens his pain. It is based on the completeness of the worshipper's *tawḥīd* and faith, that his heart is comfortable with his mishaps and misfortunes, and his soul is content, submitting and accepting that Allāh has decreed such trials for him.

Among its greatest virtues is that it frees the worshipper from slavery to created beings, from depending upon them, fearing them, hoping in them, and doing deeds for their sake, and this wins him true honour and respect. By this he will have truly deified Allāh and rendered his worship to him, not hoping in other than Him, nor fearing except Him, not repenting to any but Him. By this he will have realized his success and grant himself a happy end.

Among its virtues - which nothing besides *tawḥīd* can achieve - is that if it is complete and perfected in the heart, and it is realized with certain conviction and total sincerity, then it makes even insignificant deeds increase, multiplying the worth of his deeds and sayings beyond limit or enumeration, and the worshippers' *kalimāt al-ikhlāṣ* the statement "*Lā ilāha illa Allāh*" will tip the Scale such that the heavens, the earths, and all of Allāh's creatures that inhabit them could not come near its weight. As in the ḥadīth of Abū Sa'īd which was mentioned in the discussion, and the ḥadīth mentioning the card containing the statement "*Lā ilāha illa Allāh*" which outweighs ninety-nine scrolls full of sins - each scroll reaching as far as the eyes can see.[6] All of this is granted from saying it with

[6] The author, may Allāh have mercy upon him, is referring to a ḥadīth recorded by Aḥmad, al-Tirmidhī and others (see *al-Ṣaḥīḥah* no. 135), from 'Abdullāh bin 'Amr bin al-'Āṣ that Allāh's Messenger (ﷺ) said; "On the Day of Resurrection, Allāh will distinguish a man from my *ummah* before all creation. Ninety-nine scroll will be unrolled before him, each scroll reaching as far as can be seen. Then it will be said, 'Do you deny any of this? Have My recorders wronged you?' He will reply, 'No my Lord!' So he will be asked, 'Do you have any excuse?' He replies, 'No my Lord!' Then He says, 'There is for you a good deed with Us, you will certainly not be wronged today.' Then a card will be brought out in it is "*Ashhadu anlā ilāha illā Allāh, wa ashhadu anna Muḥammadan 'Abduhū wa rasulūh*," (I bear witness that none deserves to be worshipped except Allāh, and I bear witness that Muḥammad is his servant and Messenger). So He says, 'Bring your scale.' The man says, 'What is this card compared to these scrolls?' He will say, 'You will not be wronged.' So the scrolls will be placed in one pan of the scale, and the card in the other, so the scrolls become light and the card becomes heavy. Nothing outweighs the name of Allāh."

complete sincerity. And how many who say it have not reached this degree because their hearts do not contain *tawḥīd* and sincerity like that present in the heart of this worshipper, nor even close to it.

Among the virtues of *tawḥīd* is that Allāh has granted its people victory, honour, respect, and aid in this life. He grants them guidance and makes things easier for them, setting their affairs right, and strengthening their sayings and actions.

Allāh protects the people of *tawḥīd* and faith from the evils of this world and the Hereafter, and he grants them a good tranquil life and solace in His remembrance. Testimony for this is well known and can be seen often in the Book and the *Sunnah*. And Allāh knows best.

Chapter 3

من حقق التوحيد دخل الجنة بغير حساب

The one who fulfils *tawḥīd* enters paradise without a reckoning

وقول الله تعالى: (إن إبراهيم كان أمة قانتاً لله حنيفا و لم يك من المشركين) . وقال: (والذين هم بربهم لا يشركون) .

Allāh (ﷻ) said; "Ibrāhīm was indeed an *ummah*, purely devout in obedience to Allāh, he was not one of the *mushrikīn* (polytheists)." (*al-Naḥl* 16:120) And; "...and those who do not associate partners with their Lord." (*al-Mu'minūn* 23: 59)

عن حصين بن عبد الرحمن قال: كنت عند سعيد بن جبير فقال: أيكم رأى الكوكب الذي انقض البارحة؟ فقلت: أنا، ثم قلت: أما إني لم أكن في صلاة، ولكني لُدِغت، قال: فما صنعت؟ قلت: ارتقيت قال: فما حملك على ذلك؟ قلت: حديث حدثناه الشعبي، قال وما حدثكم؟ قلت: حدثنا عن بريدة بن الحصيب أنه قال: لا رقية إلا من عين أو حمة. قال: قد أحسن من انتهى إلى ما سمع. ولكن حدثنا ابن عباس عن النبي صلى الله عليه وسلم أنه قال: (عرضت علي الأمم، فرأيت النبي ومعه الرهط، والنبي ومعه الرجل والرجلان، والنبي وليس معه أحد، إذ رفع لي سواد عظيم، فظننت أنهم أمتي، فقيل لي: هذا موسى وقومه، فنظرت فإذا سواد عظيم، فقيل لي: هذه أمتك ومعهم سبعون ألفاً يدخلون الجنة بغير حساب ولا عذاب، ثم نهض فدخل منزله. فخاض الناس في أولئك، فقال بعضهم: فلعلهم الذين صحبوا رسول الله صلى الله عليه وسلم. وقال بعضهم: فلعلهم الذين ولدوا في الإسلام فلم يشركوا بالله شيئاً، وذكروا أشياء، فخرج عليهم رسول الله صلى الله عليه فأخبروه، فقال: (هم الذين لا يسترقون ولا يكتوون ولا يتطيرون وعلى ربهم يتوكلون) فقام عكاشة بن محصن فقال: ادع الله أن يجعلني منهم. قال: (أنت منهم) ثم قام رجل آخر فقال: ادع الله أن يجعلني منهم. فقال: (سبقك بها عكاشة).

Ḥuṣayn bin ʿAbdul-Raḥmān said, "I was once with Saʿīd bin Jubayr when he said, 'Did any of you see the shooting star last night?' I said, 'I did.' Then I said, 'I would have been at the prayer, but I was stung.' He said, 'So what did you do?' I replied, 'I was treated with *ruqyā*'.' He asked, 'What made you do that?' I said, 'A ḥadīth that al-Shaʿbī related to us.' He said, 'What ḥadīth?' I said, 'He reported to us from Buraydah bin al-Ḥuṣayb that he (the Prophet (ﷺ)) said; "*Ruqyā'* is not but for the evil eye or for the poisonous sting."[7]

He responded, 'He does well, who acts upon what he heard. But Ibn ʿAbbās reported to us from the Prophet (ﷺ) that he said; "The nations were displayed before me. I saw a prophet, and with him there was a small group of people, and a prophet with whom there was only one or two persons, and a prophet with no one at all. Then a great mass appeared before me, I thought that it was my *ummah*. It was said to me, 'This is Mūsā and his people.' So I looked, there was another great mass. It was said to me, 'This is your *ummah*, and seventy thousand of them will enter Paradise without reckoning or punishment.'"

Then he stood to enter his house. The people began wondering who they might be, some said, "Maybe they are the companions of Allāh's Messenger (ﷺ)," some said, "Maybe those born in *Islām* who never associated anything with Allāh." And still others were suggested.

Then Allāh's Messenger (ﷺ) appeared before them to tell them, he said, "They are those who do not seek *ruqyā'*, not follow omens, nor get themselves cauterized, and upon their Lord do they trust." Then ʿUkāshah bin Miḥṣan stood and said, "Ask Allāh to make me among them."

He said, "You are one of them." Then another man stood saying, "Ask Allāh to make me among them," he said "ʿUkāshah has beaten you to it."[8]

فيه مسائل:

الأولى: معرفة مراتب الناس في التوحيد.

الثانية: ما معنى تحقيقه.

---

[7] Since it may not be clear from the text, this is an authentic ḥadīth recorded here by Muslim, as well as others. The meaning of *ruqyā'*: recitation over an ailment as a means of treatment. The type condoned by the *Sunnah* utilises *āyāt* from the Qur'ān, the last two *sūrah's* for example.

[8] This ḥadīth is recorded by Muslim. Similar is recorded by al-Bukhārī and others.

الثالثة: ثناؤه سبحانه على إبراهيم بكونه لم يكن من المشركين.

الرابعة: ثناؤه على سادات الأولياء بسلامتهم من الشرك.

الخامسة: كون ترك الرقية والكي من تحقيق التوحيد.

السادسة: كون الجامع لتلك الخصال هو التوكل.

السابعة: عمق علم الصحابة لمعرفتهم أنهم لم ينالوا ذلك إلا بعمل.

الثامنة: حرصهم على الخير.

التاسعة: فضيلة هذه الأمة بالكمية والكيفية.

العاشرة: فضيلة أصحاب موسى.

الحادية عشرة: عرض الأمم عليه، عليه الصلاة والسلام.

الثانية عشرة: أن كل أمة تحشر وحدها مع نبيها.

الثالثة عشرة: قلة من استجاب للأنبياء.

الرابعة عشرة: أن من لم يجبه أحد يأتي وحده.

الخامسة عشرة: ثمرة هذا العلم، وهو عدم الاغترار بالكثرة، وعدم الزهد في القلة.

السادسة عشرة: الرخصة في الرقية من العين والحمة.

السابعة عشرة: عمق علم السلف لقوله: قد أحسن من انتهى إلى ما سمع، ولكن كذا وكذا. فعلم أن الحديث الأول لا يخالف الثاني.

الثامنة عشرة: بعد السلف عن مدح الإنسان بما ليس فيه.

التاسعة عشرة: قوله: (أنت منهم) علم من أعلام النبوة.

العشرون: فضيلة عكاشة.

الحادية والعشرون: استعمال المعاريض.

الثانية والعشرون: حسن خلقه صلى الله عليه وسلم.

Important Points

1. Knowing that people vary in levels of *tawḥīd*.
2. The meaning of fulfilling it.
3. Allāh praised Ibrāhīm by describing him as "not one of the *mushrikīn*."
4. His (ﷻ) praise of the foremost among the *awliyā'* for their escape from *shirk*.
5. That avoiding *ruqyā'* and cauterization is among the traits of *tawḥīd*.
6. That *tawakkul* (dependence upon Allāh) includes these traits.
7. The depth of the companions' knowledge in that they knew they would not achieve this state without deeds.
8. Their desire for whatever is good.
9. The virtue of this *ummah* in both its quantity and quality.
10. The great number of Mūsā's companions.
11. That the nations were displayed for him (ﷺ).
12. That each *ummah* is gathered individually with its prophet.
13. The scarcity of those who respond to the prophets.
14. That a prophet who no one followed will come alone.
15. The fruit of this knowledge; that one should not be mislead by quantity nor give up due to scarcity.
16. The permission for *ruqyā'* in case of the evil eye or poisonous sting.
17. The deep understanding of the *salaf* as seen by the saying, "He has done well who acts upon what he heard, but ..." So know that the first ḥadīth does not contradict the second.

18. The *salaf's* refraining from unnecessarily praising people.
19. His (ﷺ) saying, "You are one of them" is among the indications of prophethood.
20. The virtue of ʿUkāshah.
21. The usage of indirect speech.
22. The model behaviour of the Prophet (ﷺ).

Commentary by ʿ*Allāmah* al-Saʿdī

The one who fulfils *tawḥīd* enters paradise without a reckoning

This chapter follows up and completes the previous chapter. For the fulfilment of *tawḥīd* removes and cleanses one from major and minor *shirk*, from innovated sayings and belief, innovated customs and deeds, and from disobedience. This is achieved by complete sincerity for Allāh in sayings, actions and intent, and by escaping major *shirk*, the nullifier of *tawḥīd*, and minor *shirk*, the negator of its completeness, and by escaping innovation, and the disobedience which tarnishes *tawḥīd*, prevents its completion and hinders its results.

Among the results of ones *tawḥīd* is that his heart is encouraged by faith, *tawḥīd*, and sincerity. He does his deeds out of sincere faith, because he is guided by the commands of Allāh, obeying, repenting, and seeking refuge in Allāh, not damaging that by insisting on disobedient matters. This is the one that enters Paradise without a reckoning, he is among those forerunners who enter it to inhabit its dwellings.

Among the clearest signs of *tawḥīd's* complete fulfilment is devotion to Allāh and firm dependence upon Allāh. Such that in his heart, he is not looking towards creatures for any of his needs nor elevating them, nor asking them with the tongue in any circumstance. Rather he behaves, both outwardly and inwardly, when speaking and acting, loving and hating, in every case - in every situation, he is intending Allāh's Face alone, following Allāh's Messenger.

People vary in degrees in relation to this great position,

"And for all is a level according to what they have done." (*al-An'ām* 6:132 & *al-Aḥqāf* 46:19)

Tawḥīd is not achieved by simple desire or prayer without a true sense of meaning, nor by contentment without works, but it depends on the heart's firmness in the elements of faith, the realization of *iḥsān*, and its true acceptance of the beautiful manners and beautiful righteous deeds.

So by fulfilling *tawḥīd* in this manner, then all of the virtues expounded upon in the previous chapter will result in their entirety.

Chapter 4

الخوف من الشرك

The fear of *shirk*

وقول الله عز وجل: (إن الله لا يغفر أن يشرك به ويغفر ما دون ذلك لمن يشاء) وقال الخليل عليه السلام: (واجنبني وبني أن نعبد الأصنام)

Allāh (ﷻ) said; "Indeed Allāh does not forgive associating partners with Him, and He forgives other than that as He wills," (*al-Nisā'* 4:48 & 116). And *al-Khalīl* (Prophet Ibrāhīm) said, "And prevent me and my descendants from worshipping the idols," (*Ibrāhīm* 14:35).

وفي الحديث: (أخوف ما أخاف عليكم الشرك الأصغر)، فسئل عنه فقال: (الرياء)

And in the ḥadīth; "The thing I fear most for you is the minor *shirk*." He (ﷺ) was asked what that was, he replied, "*Riyā'* (show)."[9]

وعن ابن مسعود رضي الله عنه أن رسول الله صلى الله عليه وسلم قال: (من مات وهو يدعو من دون الله نداً دخل النار) [رواه البخاري].

Ibn Mas'ūd, may Allāh be pleased with him, reported that Allāh's Messenger (ﷺ) said; "Whoever dies and he is calling upon others along with Allāh, he will enter the Fire." Recorded by al-Bukhārī.

ولمسلم عن جابر رضي الله عنه، أن رسول الله صلى الله عليه وسلم قال: (من لقي الله لا يشرك به شيئاً دخل الجنة، ومن لقيه يشرك به شيئاً دخل النار).

---

[9] Al-Mundhirī said, "Recorded by Aḥmad with a good chain, also by Ibn Abū al-Dunyā and Al-Bayhaqī in *Al-Zuhd*, and others..." Shaykh Al-Albānī graded the ḥadīth *ṣaḥīḥ* in *Ṣaḥīḥ al-Targhīb wa l-Tarhīb*, no. 29 (Riyāḍ edition 1409).

Muslim records from Jābir that Allāh's Messenger (ﷺ) said, "Whoever meets Allāh without having associated anything with Him will enter Paradise, and whoever meets Him having associated something with Him will enter the Fire."

فيه مسائل:

الأولى: الخوف من الشرك.

الثانية: أن الرياء من الشرك.

الثالثة: أنه من الشرك الأصغر.

الرابعة: أنه أخوف ما يخاف منه على الصالحين.

الخامسة: قرب الجنة والنار.

السادسة: الجمع بين قربهما في حديث واحد.

السابعة: أنه من لقيه لا يشرك به شيئاً دخل الجنة. ومن لقيه يشرك به شيئاً دخل النار ولو كان من أعبد الناس.

الثامنة: المسألة العظيمة: سؤال الخليل له ولبنيه وقاية عبادة الأصنام.

التاسعة: اعتباره بحال الأكثر، لقوله: (رب إنهن أضللن كثيراً من الناس) .

العاشرة: فيه تفسير (لا إله إلا الله) كما ذكره البخاري.

الحادية عشرة: فضيلة من سلم من الشرك.

Important Points

1. The fear of *shirk*.
2. That *riyā'* is a form of *shirk*.
3. That it is a kind of minor *shirk*.
4. That it is the most dangerous thing for the righteous.
5. The nearness of Paradise and the Fire.

6. Mentioning their nearness in the same ḥadīth.
7. That he who meets Him, without associating anything with Him, enters Paradise; and he who meets Him, while having associated something with Him enters the Fire, even though he may have been the person most prone to worship.
8. The tremendous importance of this issue, such that *al-Khalīl* (Ibrāhīm) asked that he and his offspring be protected from worshipping idols.
9. His concern for the condition of most people when he said, "Lord! Indeed they (the idols) have misguided many of the people." (*Ibrāhīm,* 14:36)
10. The interpretation of *Lā ilāha illa Allāh*, as mentioned by al-Bukhārī.
11. The virtue of the one who is free of *shirk*.

Commentary by *ʿAllāmah* al-Saʿdī

The Fear of *Shirk*

Every instance of *shirk* in *tawḥīd al-ilāhiyah* and *al-ʿibādah* negates *tawḥīd*. And this *shirk* is of two types: The blatant major *shirk*, and the subtle minor *shirk*.

Major *Shirk*

It is to make a rival to Allāh that is called upon as Allāh is called upon, or to fear him, or hope in him, or love him, as Allāh is loved, or to render a type of worship to him. This is the *shirk* which does not leave its practitioner with any *tawḥīd* at all, this is the *mushrik* that Allāh has forbidden from Paradise, and his abode is the Fire.

It doesn't matter whether the worship rendered to other than Allāh is called worship or *tawassul* (seeking a means of nearness to Allāh), or even if it is given a name other than these. All of that is major *shirk*, because what is important is the reality of the thing and its implication, not the word or expression used to describe it.

Minor *Shirk*

This is every saying or action which leads to *shirk*, like aggrandizing creatures in a way that does not quite reach the level of worship. Like, for example, making an oath by other than Allāh, or behaving for show, etc.

Since *shirk* negates *tawḥīd* and necessitates eternal damnation in the Fire, and when it is the major type it makes Paradise unlawful, and since bliss cannot be achieved except by escaping from it, then it is necessary for the worshipper to duly fear it, to hurry in escape from it - its every path, means and cause - and to ask Allāh to protect him from it as was the habit of the prophets, the purified, and the best of the creatures.

The worshipper must struggle to increase and strengthen the sincerity in his heart, and this is done by completely devoting oneself to Allāh - being subjugated, repentant, fearful, hopeful, obedient, seeking His satisfaction and rewards in all that he does without neglecting this in any matter, open or hidden. True sincerity inherently repels both major and minor *shirk*, but whenever a type of *shirk* is present it will weaken one's sincerity.

Chapter 5

الدعاء إلى شهادة أن لا إله الله

The invitation to testify to *Lā ilāha illa Allāh*

وقوله الله تعالى: (قل هذه سبيلي أدعوا إلى الله على بصيرة) الآية.

Allāh (ﷻ) said; "Say: 'This is my way, I invite to my Lord with clarity (*baṣīrah*)[10]." (*Yūsuf* 12:108)

عن ابن عباس رضي الله عنهما، أن رسول الله صلى الله عليه وسلم، لما بعث معاذاً إلى اليمن قال له: (إنك تأتي قوماً من أهل الكتاب فليكن أول ما تدعوهم إليه شهادة أن لا إله إلا الله — وفي رواية: إلى أن يوحدوا الله — فإن هم أطاعوك لذلك، فأعلمهم أن الله افترض عليهم خمس صلوات في كل يوم وليلة، فإن هم أطاعوك لذلك: فأعلمهم أن الله افترض عليهم صدقة تؤخذ من أغنيائهم فترد على فقرائهم، فإن هم أطاعوك لذلك فإياك وكرائم أموالهم، واتق دعوة المظلوم، فإنه ليس بينها وبين الله حجاب) أخرجاه.

Ibn 'Abbās, may Allāh be pleased with him, said; "When Allāh's Messenger (ﷺ) sent Mu'ādh to Yemen he said; 'You are going to a people from the People of the Book, so let the first thing you invite them to be to testify to *Lā ilāha illa Allāh*.' And in one report; 'Let the first thing you invite them to be; "That you single out Allāh..." 'If they obey you in that, then teach them that Allāh has obligated five prayers upon them for every day and night. If they obey you in that then teach them that Allāh has obligated that *ṣadaqah* (charity) be taken from their wealth to be distributed among their poor. If they obey you in that, then beware of taking their prized possessions, and protect yourself from the supplication

[10] *Al-Baṣīrah* means certainty, knowledge and clear insight regarding the matter.

of the oppressed, for there is no screen between it and Allāh.'" Al-Bukhārī and Muslim have recorded it.[11]

ولهما عن سهل بن سعد رضي الله عنه، أن رسول الله صلى الله عليه وسلم قال يوم خيبر: (لأعطين الراية غداً رجلاً يحب الله ورسوله، ويحبه الله ورسوله، يفتح الله على يديه. فبات الناس يدوكون ليلتهم أيهم يعطاها. فلما أصبحوا غدوا على رسول الله صلى الله عليه وسلم كلهم يرجو أن يعطاها. فقال: (أين علي بن أبي طالب؟) فقيل: هو يشتكي عينيه، فأرسلوا إليه، فأتى به فبصق في عينيه، ودعا له، فبرأ كأن لم يكن به وجع، فأعطاه الراية فقال: (انفذ على رسلك حتى تنزل بساحتهم، ثم ادعهم إلى الإسلام وأخبرهم بما يجب عليهم من حق الله تعالى فيه، فوالله لأن يهدي الله بك رجلاً واحداً، خير لك من حمر النعم). يدوكون: يخوضون.

They also recorded from Sahl bin Sa'd, may Allāh be pleased with him, that; "On the Day of Khaybar, Allāh's Messenger (ﷺ) said, 'Tomorrow I will give the flag to a man who loves Allāh and His Messenger, and who is loved by Allāh and His Messenger. Allāh will bring victory by his hands.'

The people spent the entire night wondering who it would be given to. They appeared before Allāh's Messenger the following morning, each of them hoping that he would be the one it was given to. The Prophet (ﷺ) said; 'Where is 'Alī bin Abī Ṭālib?' They said, 'He is suffering from an ailment in his eyes.[12]'

He came after they sent word for him. Then the Prophet (ﷺ) blew in his eyes[13] and he said a *du'ā* for him and he was cured as if he had not suffered at all. He (ﷺ) handed him the flag and said; 'Proceed slowly until you reach outside the enemy encampment. Then invite them to Islām, inform them of what rights of Allāh it [Islām] makes obligatory for them. By Allāh! If Allāh guides one man by you, it is better for you then red camels[14].'"

---

[11] The addition is from *Kitāb al-Tawḥīd* in al-Bukhārī's *Ṣaḥīḥ*. It should be noted that many of the narrations of this ḥadīth include, "...and that Muḥammad is Allāh's Messenger" mentioning both parts of the *shahādatayn* as the first thing to be invited to.

[12] According to a version recorded by Muslim, it was *ramad* - Eng; ophthalmia - an inflammation of the eyes.

[13] That is, he blew a mist of his blessed saliva in his eyes.

[14] A red camel was among the most valued possession to the Arabs of the time.

فيه مسائل:

الأولى: أن الدعوة إلى الله طريق من اتبعه صلى الله عليه وسلم.

الثانية: التنبيه على الإخلاص، لأن كثيراً لو دعا إلى الحق فهو يدعو إلى نفسه.

الثالثة: أن البصيرة من الفرائض.

الرابعة: من دلائل حسن التوحيد: كونه تنزيهاً لله تعالى عن المسبة.

الخامسة: أن من قبح الشرك كونه مسبة لله.

السادسة: وهي من أهمها – إبعاد المسلم عن المشركين لئلا يصير منهم ولو لم يشرك.

السابعة: كون التوحيد أول واجب.

الثامنة: أن يبدأ به قبل كل شيء، حتى الصلاة.

التاسعة: أن معنى: (أن يوحدوا الله)، معنى شهادة: أن لا إله إلا الله.

العاشرة: أن الإنسان قد يكون من أهل الكتاب، وهو لا يعرفها، أو يعرفها ولا يعمل بها.

الحادية عشرة: التنبيه على التعليم بالتدريج.

الثانية عشرة: البداءة بالأهم فالأهم.

الثالثة عشرة: مصرف الزكاة.

الرابعة عشرة: كشف العالم الشبهة عن المتعلم.

الخامسة عشرة: النهي عن كرائم الأموال.

السادسة عشرة: اتقاء دعوة المظلوم.

السابعة عشرة: الإخبار بأنها لا تحجب.

الثامنة عشرة: من أدلة التوحيد ما جرى على سيد المرسلين وسادات الأولياء من المشقة والجوع والوباء.

التاسعة عشرة: قوله: (لأعطين الراية) إلخ. علم من أعلام النبوة.

العشرون: تفله في عينيه علم من أعلامها أيضاً.

الحادية والعشرون: فضيلة علي رضي الله عنه.

الثانية والعشرون: فضل الصحابة في دوكهم تلك الليلة وشغلهم عن بشارة الفتح.

الثالثة والعشرون: الإيمان بالقدر، لحصولها لمن لم يسع لها ومنعها عمن سعى.

الرابعة والعشرون: الأدب في قوله: (على رسلك).

الخامسة والعشرون: الدعوة إلى الإسلام قبل القتال.

السادسة والعشرون: أنه مشروع لمن دعوا قبل ذلك وقوتلوا.

السابعة والعشرون: الدعوة بالحكمة، لقوله: (أخبرهم بما يجب عليهم).

الثامنة والعشرون: المعرفة بحق الله تعالى في الإسلام.

التاسعة والعشرون: ثواب من اهتدى على يديه رجل واحد.

الثلاثون: الحلف على الفتيا.

Important Points

1. That the invitation to Allāh is among the ways of following Allāh's Messenger (ﷺ).
2. The emphasis on sincerity, since most of the people who invite to the truth actually are only inviting to themselves.
3. That "*baṣīrah*" (clarity) is among the obligations.
4. Keeping ones thoughts about Allāh free of blasphemy is among the

signs of healthy *tawḥīd*.

5. Blasphemy against Allāh is a disgusting trait of *shirk*.
6. Among the most important points is the Muslims' distancing himself from the *mushrikīn*, not being in their midst even though he does not commit *shirk* while with them.
7. That *tawḥīd* is the first obligation.
8. That it precedes everything including prayer.
9. That the meaning of "That you single out Allāh" is the same as the meaning of testifying to *Lā ilāha illa Allāh*.
10. That although a person is one of the People of the Book, yet he does not know the meaning of this, or he may be aware of it, but he does not act upon it.
11. The emphasis on teaching in stages.
12. Beginning with the most important things then following with the next most important.
13. The distribution of *al-Zakāh*.
14. The knowledgeable removing doubts from the one seeking knowledge.
15. The prohibition of taking ones most prized possessions.
16. Guarding oneself against the supplication of the oppressed.
17. The information that it (the supplication of the oppressed) is not hindered.
18. Among the evidences of *tawḥīd* is that the master of the messengers and the foremost among the *awliyā'* suffered from hardships, hunger, and infections.
19. His saying, "I will give the flag..." is a sign of prophethood.
20. His blowing in the eyes is also a sign of prophethood.
21. The virtue of 'Alī, may Allāh be pleased with him.
22. The virtue of the companions, that they spent the night wondering about one thing, and they were not concerned with news of the victory.
23. A reminder about faith in the *qadr*; since it (i.e., the flag) was given to one who did not seek it, yet it was not given to those who did.

24. The conduct encompassed by his saying, "Proceed slowly..."
25. The invitation to *Islām* before fighting.
26. That it is permissible to fight those who have already been invited.
27. Inviting with wisdom as he (ﷺ) said, "Inform them what it makes obligatory on them..."
28. Being aware of the rights of Allāh that come with *Islām*.
29. The rewards given to someone when even one person is guided by their hands.
30. Swearing by Allāh in conjunction with issuance of a religious decree.

Commentary by *ʿAllāmah* al-Saʿdī

The Invitation to Testify to *Lā ilāha illa Allāh*

The author's arrangement of these chapters is most appropriate. In the preceding chapters he mentioned the obligation of *tawḥīd* and its virtues, its importance and the importance of its perfection, what fulfils it both outwardly and inwardly, then the fear of what would ruin it. All of this deals with the servant's perfection of *tawḥīd* in himself.

Then in this chapter he mentions the servant's perfecting *tawḥīd* for others by inviting to the testimony of *Lā ilāha illa Allāh*. For the worshipper's *tawḥīd* is not complete until he has perfected every necessary element of it himself, then rushed to bring fulfilment to others with it, and this is the way of all of the prophets. The first thing they invited their people to was the worship of Allāh alone without any partners, and this is the way of the master and *imām* of the prophets (ﷺ). He was the greatest enforcer of this invitation, he invited to the way of his Lord with wisdom, good preaching and arguing with what was best, he was unwavering, he did not give in until Allāh established the religion by him, and guided to the greatest behaviour by him. He (ﷺ) spread His religion to the east and west of the earth by his (ﷺ) blessed invitation. As he (ﷺ) himself invited, he commanded his envoys, and his followers to invite to Allāh and to *tawḥīd* of Him before everything else, because all deeds depend, in both their correctness and acceptability, upon *tawḥīd*.

Therefore, just as it is necessary for the worshipper to practice *tawḥīd* of Allāh, then it is also necessary for him to invite others to Allāh with what is best, and for everyone who is guided by his hands he will be given rewards equivalent to theirs without diminishing any of their rewards at all.

And since the invitation to Allāh, to the testimony of *Lā ilāha illa Allāh*, is obligatory upon everyone, then everyone is responsible for it based upon his ability. So it is necessary for the one who has such knowledge to explain it, to invite, show the way, and give the best guidance to anyone else who does not possess such knowledge. It is more of a duty for the one who is able, either by his body, his hand, his wealth, his prestige, or his impressive speech, than for the one who does not possess any of these abilities. Allāh (ﷻ) said;

فَاتَّقُوا اللَّهَ مَا اسْتَطَعْتُمْ

"Have *taqwa* of Allāh, as much as you are able." (*al-Taghābun* 64:16)

May Allāh have mercy upon he who makes the religion known, even if by half of a word, and destruction in this matter only befalls the servant who forsakes what he is capable of in inviting to this religion.

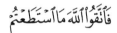

Chapter 6

تفسير التوحيد وشهادة أن لا إله إلا الله
Explaining *tawḥīd* and the testimony *Lā ilāha illā Allāh*

وقول الله تعالى: (أولئك الذين يدعون يبتغون إلى ربهم الوسيلة أيهم أقرب) الآيه وقوله: (وإذ قال إبراهيم لأبيه وقومه إنني برآءٌ مما تعبدون * إلا الذي فطرني) الآية. وقوله: (اتخذوا أحبارهم ورهبانهم أرباباً من دون الله) الآية. وقوله: (ومن الناس من يتخذ من دون الله أنداداً يحبونهم كحب الله) الآية.

Allāh (ﷻ) said; "Those whom they call upon themselves seek a means of becoming nearer to their Lord." (*al-Isrā'* 17:57) And; "When Ibrāhīm said to his father and his people, 'Surely I am innocent of what you worship, except the one who created me.'" (*al-Zukhruf* 43:26-27) And: "They have taken their rabbis and monks as Lords besides Allāh." (*al-Tawbah* 9:31) And; "Among people are those who have taken others as rivals to Allāh, whom they love as they love Allāh." (*al-Baqarah* 2:165)

وفي (الصحيح) عن النبي صلى الله عليه وسلم أنه قال: (من قال: لا إله إلا الله وكفر بما يعبد من دون الله، حرم ماله ودمه، وحسابه على الله عز وجل).

In the *Ṣaḥīḥ*, the Prophet (ﷺ) said; "Whoever says *Lā ilāha illa Allāh,* and disbelieves in what is worshipped other than Allāh, his wealth and blood is unlawful, and his reckoning is with Allāh (ﷻ)."[15]

وشرح هذا الترجمة: ما بعدها من الأبواب.

فيه أكبر المسائل وأهمها: وهي تفسير التوحيد، وتفسير الشهادة، وبيَّنَها بأمور واضحة.

[15] Muslim.

This topic, containing the greatest and most important of issues - that is the explanation of *tawḥīd* and the explanation of the *shahādah* - is detailed further with clear examples in subsequent chapters.

منها: آية الإسراء، بيَّن فيها الرد على المشركين الذين يدعون الصالحين، ففيها بيان أن هذا هو الشرك الأكبر.

Among such examples;

-The *āyah* of *al-Isrā'*, containing a clear refutation of the *mushrikīn* who call upon the righteous, in this is the proof that such behaviour is major *shirk*.

ومنها: آية براءة، بيَّن فيها أن أهل الكتاب اتخذوا أحبارهم ورهبانهم أرباباً من دون الله، وبين أنهم لم يؤمروا إلا بأن يعبدوا إلهاً واحداً، مع أن تفسيرها الذي لا إشكال فيه: طاعة العلماء والعباد في المعصية، لادعائهم إياهم.

-The *āyah* of *Bara'ah* (*al-Tawbah*) explaining that the People of the Book took their rabbis and monks as lords other than Allāh. And it explains that they were commanded to only worship one God, so it clearly refers, with no doubts, to obeying their learned and pious in sin, it does not refer to their calling upon them.

ومنها قول الخليل (عليه السلام) للكفار: (إنني برآء مما تعبدون * إلا الذي فطرني) فاستثنى من المعبودين ربه، وذكر سبحانه أن هذه البراءة وهذه الموالاة: هي تفسير شهادة أن لا إله إلا الله. فقال: (وجعلها كلمة باقية في عقبه لعلهم يرجعون) .

- By al-Khalīl's (ﷺ) saying to the disbelievers; "Surely I am innocent of what you worship, except for the one who created me."

He made an exception for his Lord among those who are worshipped.

And Allāh (ﷻ) mentioned this disavowal and this allegiance as the meaning of the testimony to *Lā ilāha illa Allāh*, He (ﷻ) said; "And he made it a commandment remaining among his offspring that perhaps they may return to." (*al-Zukhruf* 43:28)

ومنها: آية البقرة: في الكفار الذين قال الله فيهم: (وما هم بخارجين من النار) ذكر أنهم يحبون أندادهم كحب الله، فدل على أنهم يحبون الله حباً عظيماً، و لم يدخلهم في الإسلام، فكيف بمن أحب الند أكبر من حب الله؟! فكيف لمن لم يحب إلا الند وحده، و لم يحب الله؟!.

-The *āyah* of *al-Baqarah* where Allāh said about the disbelievers; "And they will not come out of the Fire." (*al-Baqarah* 2:167)

He (ﷻ) mentioned that they loved the rivals as they loved Allāh, showing that they had a great love for Allāh, yet they did not enter into *Islām*, so what about one who loves the rival more than he loves Allāh? And how about the one who loves the rivals but not Allāh?

ومنها قوله صلى الله عليه وسلم: (من قال: لا إله إلا الله وكفر بما يعبد من دون الله حرم ماله ودمه، وحسابه على الله) وهذا من أعظم ما يبيّن معنى (لا إله إلا الله) فإنه لم يجعل التلفظ بها عاصماً للدم والمال، بل ولا معرفة معناها مع لفظها، بل ولا الإقرار بذلك، بل ولا كونه لا يدعو إلا الله وحده لا شريك له، بل لا يحرم ماله ودمه حتى يضيف إلى ذلك الكفر بما يعبد من دون الله، فإن شك أو توقف لم يحرم ماله ودمه. فيالها من مسألة ما أعظمها وأجلها، وياله من بيان ما أوضحه، وحجة ما أقطعها للمنازع.

-The saying of the Prophet (ﷺ); "Whoever says *Lā ilāha illa Allāh*, and disbelieves in what is worshipped other than Allāh, his wealth and blood is unlawful, and his reckoning is with Allāh (ﷻ)."

This is among the greatest explanations of the meaning of *Lā ilāha illa Allāh*. For he did not make the mere utterance of it shelter for one's blood and wealth, not even knowing its meaning and its utterance, nor its acknowledgment, nor even that he does not call upon any but Allāh alone without partners. No, but he did not declare his wealth and his blood unlawful until he attached to that the disbelief in what is worshipped other than Allāh. So if he doubts this or hesitates, his blood and wealth are not unlawful. So what a tremendously important issue it is, and what a clear explanation and proof it is, such that it ends all debate.

Commentary by *ʿAllāmah* al-Saʿdī

Explaining *Tawḥīd* and the Testimony of *Lā ilāha illa Allāh*

These both have the same meaning, so here only their synonymous nature is clarified. And this issue is the greatest and most important of issues as the author said, may Allāh have mercy upon him. The true meaning of *tawḥīd* is the knowledge and awareness that the Lord is alone in all of His perfect attributes and to render worship sincerely to Him alone. This depends upon two matters;

1. Negating all divinity from other than Allāh, such that it is known and believed that neither divinity, nor any element of worship is due to any creature, nor a prophet who was sent, nor a angel holding an honoured station, nor anyone else, and believing that not one part or parcel of this is due to any creature.

2. Confirming divinity to Allāh the most High alone, without any partners, singling Him out with all implications of divinity, including all the perfect attributes. This belief alone is not sufficient until the servant accompanies it by sincerely rendering religion to Allāh, abiding in *Islām*, faith and *iḥsān*, maintaining the rights of Allāh and the rights of the creatures with the sole intent of Allāh's Face, seeking His reward and acceptance.

This teaches that the disavowal of worshipping other than Allāh completes the expression and fulfilment of *tawḥīd*. That taking rivals that are loved as Allāh is loved or obeyed as Allāh is obeyed, or when deeds are done for them as they are done for Allāh, then this is the severest negation of the meaning of *Lā ilāha illā Allāh*.

The author, may Allāh have mercy upon him, explains that one of the greatest clarifications of the meaning of *Lā ilāha illā Allāh* is the Prophet's (ﷺ) saying,

"Whoever says *Lā ilāha illa Allāh*, and disbelieves in what is worshipped other than Allāh, his wealth and blood is unlawful, and his reckoning is with Allāh (ﷻ)."

He (ﷺ) did not make the mere statement a shelter for his blood and wealth, not even knowing its meaning and its utterance, nor its acknowledgment, nor even that he does not call upon any but Allāh alone without partners. No, but he did not declare his wealth and his blood unlawful until he attached to that the disbelief in what is worshipped other than Allāh. So if he doubts this or hesitates, his blood and wealth are not unlawful.

So this necessitates believing that it is obligatory to worship Allāh alone without partners, and to accept that with both creed and utterance, and to worship Allāh alone in obedience and submission to Him, and to disavow whatever belief, saying, or action negates that. Yet this is not complete except with the love of those who uphold *tawḥīd* of Allāh and allegiance and assistance for them, and by hating the people of disbelief, and *shirk*, and having enmity for them. Mere utterance of an expression or slogans without real meaning are not enough for this. Rather it is essential that this includes knowledge, creed, sayings and actions. So these things are interdependent, such that if one of them is contradicted then the rest of them are contradicted. And Allāh knows best.

Chapter 7

من الشرك لبس الحلقة والخيط ونحوهما لرفع البلاء أو دفعه

Wearing bracelets and cords etc., to remove afflictions or to seek protection is a form of *shirk*

وقول الله تعالى: (قل أفرأيتم ما تدعون من دون الله إن أرادنيَ الله بضر هل هن كاشفات ضره) الآية.

Allāh (ﷻ) said; "Say: 'Have you seen those that they call on besides Allāh? If Allāh decreed harm for me, would they be able to prevent the harm'" (*al-Zumar* 39:38)

عن عمران بن حصين رضي الله عنه، أن النبي صلى الله عليه وسلم رأى رجلاً في يده حلقة من صفر، فقال: (ما هذه)؟ قال: من الواهنة. فقال: (انزعها فإنها لا تزيدك إلا وهناً، فإنك لو مت وهي عليك، ما أفلحت أبداً) رواه أحمد بسند لا بأس به.

ʿImrān bin Ḥuṣayn, may Allāh be pleased with him, reported that; "The Prophet (ﷺ) saw a man with a brass bracelet on his [upper] arm. He said; 'What is this.' He said, 'It is for [protection] against *wāhinah*[16].'' He said, 'Take it off, it will only increase your weakness, for if you died while it was on you, you would

[16] "It is a disease that afflicts the shoulders or the entire arm, *ruqyā'* is used against it. And they say that it is an illness that afflicts the biceps. Sometimes something like pearls are worn around it ... it afflicts men but not women ...." *Al-Nihāyah* by Ibn al-Athir. See *Taysīr al-ʿAzīz*.

never have success.'" This was recorded by Aḥmad whose chain of narrators is without a problem.[17]

وله عن عقبة بن عامر رضي الله عنه مرفوعاً: (من تعلق تميمة فلا أتم الله له، ومن تعلق ودعة فلا ودع الله له) وفي رواية: (من تعلق تميمة فقد أشرك).

And he also has a *marfū'* report from 'Uqbah bin 'Āmir; "Whoever wears a charm[18], may Allāh not protect him, and whoever wears a shell, may Allāh not protect him."[19]

And in one narration; "Whoever wears a charm, he has committed *shirk*."[20]

ولابن أبي حاتم عن حذيفة أنه رأى رجلاً في يده خيط من الحمى فقطعه، وتلا قوله: (وما يؤمن أكثرهم بالله إلا وهم مشركون) .

Ibn Abū Ḥātim records that Ḥudhayfah; "Saw a man with a cord for [protection against] fever on his arm, so he cut it up and recited Allāh's (ﷻ) saying; 'And most of them do not believe in Allāh without committing *shirk*.'" (*Yūsuf* 12: 106)[21]

فيه مسائل:

الأولى: التغليظ في لبس الحلقة والخيط ونحوهما لمثل ذلك.

الثانية: أن الصحابي لو مات وهي عليه ما أفلح. فيه شاهد لكلام الصحابة: أن الشرك الأصغر أكبر من الكبائر.

[17] Similar is recorded by Ibn Ḥibbān, Ibn Mājah, and Al-Ṭabarānī, etc. Al-Arnā'ūṭ labeled it *ṣaḥīḥ*. Al-Albānī graded it weak due to two defects in its transmission. See *al-Ḍa'īfah* no. 1029 and *Ghāyāt al-Marām* no.296.

[18] *Tamīmah*, Abū al-Sa'ādāt (Ibn al-Athīr; *al-Nihāyah*) said, "... beads that the Arabs attached to their children believing that they would protect them from the evil eye...." See *Fatḥ al-Majīd*.

[19] Recorded by Aḥmad, Abū Ya'la, al-Ṭaḥāwī, Al-Ṭabarānī, al-Ḥākim and others. Al-Ḥākim graded it *ṣaḥīḥ*, and al-Dhahabī agreed. Al-Albānī graded it as weak in *Al-Ḍa'īfah* no. 1266, *Ḍa'īf al-Jāmi' al-Ṣaghīr* no. 5703, due to one of its narrators. However, in *al-Ṣaḥīḥah* no. 492 he brings it after the following wording that mentions *shirk*, also narrated from '*Uqbah*. So it seems that the second wording quoted is the more correct.

[20] Recorded by Aḥmad and al-Ḥākim. Al-Ḥaythamī said that the reporters in Aḥmad's chain are trustworthy, and al-Ḥākim and Al-Albānī graded it *ṣaḥīḥ*. See *al-Ṣaḥīḥah* no. 492.

[21] It seems from the chain quoted by Ibn Kathīr that this report is *ḥasan*.

الثالثة: أنه لم يعذر بالجهالة.

الرابعة: أنها لا تنفع في العاجلة بل تضر، لقوله: (لا تزيدك إلا وهناً).

الخامسة: الإنكار بالتغليظ على من فعل مثل ذلك.

السادسة: التصريح بأن من تعلق شيئاً وكل إليه.

السابعة : التصريح بأن من تعلق تميمة فقد أشرك.

الثامنة : أن تعليق الخيط من الحمى من ذلك.

التاسعة: تلاوة حذيفة الآية دليل على أن الصحابة يستدلون بالآيات التي في الشرك الأكبر على الأصغر، كما ذكر بن عباس في آية البقرة.

العاشرة: أن تعليق الودع عن العين من ذلك.

الحادية عشرة: الدعاء على من تعلق تميمة، أن الله لا يتم له، ومن تعلق ودعة، فلا ودع الله له، أي لا ترك الله له.

Important Points

1. The danger of wearing bracelets and cords and similar items.
2. That if the wearer dies with it on he will not succeed. This supports the statement of the companions, that minor *shirk* is worse than major sins.
3. That ignorance is not an excuse for this.
4. That it will not bring any benefit in this life, only harm, since he (ﷺ) said, "It will only increase your weakness."
5. The harsh rebuke of whoever does something like this.
6. It explains that when someone wears one of these things he becomes entrusted to it.
7. The explanation that someone who wears a charm has committed *shirk*.
8. The explanation that wearing a cord for fever is the same.

9. Ḥudhayfah's recitation of the *āyah* proves that the companions used to quote *āyāt* about major *shirk* as proof against minor *shirk*, as Ibn 'Abbās did with the *āyah* of *al-Baqarah*.
10. That wearing a shell for protection against the evil eye falls into the same category.
11. Supplicating against the one who wears a charm, that Allāh does not give him protection, and for the one who wears a shell, "may Allāh not protect him", this means "may Allāh abandon him."

Commentary by *'Allāmah* al-Sa'dī

Wearing Bracelets and Cords etc., to Remove Afflictions or to Seek Protection is a form of *Shirk*

The understanding of this chapter depends upon awareness of the rules for understanding means [i.e., antidotes or treatments etc]. In order to clarify this point, it is necessary for the worshipper to be aware of three regulations regarding means;

1. That he does not assign abilities to them except those confirmed legislatively or those that they are potentially capable of.

2. That the worshipper does not depend upon them, rather he depends upon the one who gives them their abilities and makes them work, using only the lawful types of means with the objective of benefiting from them.

3. That he knows that no matter what the strengths or abilities of the means are, they still depend upon Allāh's decree and His will, there is no escape for them from that.

So Allāh (ﷻ) makes them effective as He wills. If He wills, He sustains their effectiveness so the worshippers can use them. By this, they are aware of the completeness of His wisdom since it is He that regulates the cause and the effects, and they known that if He wills otherwise then it will be as He wills. So the worshippers have not depended upon the means, since they are aware of His complete control, and that the unrestricted right of disposal and the unrestricted right of effectiveness is solely Allāh's. This is what is obligatory upon the worshipper in his thinking and behaviour regarding every type of means.

When this is known, then it is realised that if someone wears a bracelet or a cord or anything else with the aim of removing afflictions after they occur, or as a defence against them, then he has committed *shirk*. If he thinks that this is the thing that defends and the thing that relieves, then this is major *shirk*. And if he believes that it has some share with Allāh in creating and originating, then it is *shirk* in *rubūbiyah*. And it is *shirk* in *ʿubūdiyah* as much as he submits himself to that and his heart depends upon it, hoping and expecting it to bring him benefit. If he believes that Allāh alone is the reliever and protector, but that the means does possess the ability to protect against ailments, then he has given it abilities beyond the abilities that legislation permits, or those that are possible for it. In this case what he has done is unlawful and delusional from the perspective of the *sharīʿah*, as well as the perspective of possibility.

As for the *sharīʿah*, it has in fact issued a severe prohibition against these things, and that which it prohibits cannot be beneficial.

As for possibility, then these things are not among those conventional means, nor the non conventional means, that lead to the result intended. Nor are they among the permissible beneficial antidotes.

It is for this reason that it falls into the category of a means leading to *shirk*, especially if the heart relies upon it for such results. Such reliance is a type of *shirk* and a road leading to it.

So when these things are not among the means of the *sharīʿah* that have been legislated upon the tongue of His Prophet which earn Allāh's pleasure and rewards, nor among those potential means - those that are known or considered to give some benefit - then because the heart has such dependence upon it, hoping for its benefit, then it is necessary for the believer to avoid them to complete his faith and *tawḥīd*. When his *tawḥīd* is complete, his heart will not depend upon it to give him benefit. This also contradicts reason since he would have relied upon something that was not worthy of dependence nor capable of providing any benefit whatsoever, rather it only causes harm.

The *sharīʿah* is built upon perfecting the religion of the creatures by eliminating the idols and dependence upon creatures, and upon perfecting their reason by eliminating fallacies and superstitions, and endeavouring in matters that promote healthy reason, to purify the souls, strengthening them on all fronts, whether in their religion or in their worldly life. And Allāh knows best.

Chapter 8

ما جاء في الرقي والتمائم

What is said about *ruqyā* and charms

في (الصحيح) عن أبي بشير الأنصاري رضي الله عنه أنه كان مع رسول الله صلى الله عليه وسلم في بعض أسفاره، فأرسل رسولاً أن لا يبقين في رقبة بعير قلادة من وتر أو قلادة إلا قطعت.

It is reported in the *Ṣaḥīḥ*, from Abū Bashīr al-Anṣārī, may Allāh be pleased with him; "That he was with Allāh's Messenger (ﷺ) during some of his travels. So he dispatched someone with the directive that he should not leave any camel's neck with a charmed necklace - or - any necklace, without breaking it."[22]

وعن ابن مسعود رضي الله عنه قال: سمعت رسول الله صلى الله عليه وسلم يقول: (إن الرقى والتمائم والتولة شرك) [رواه أحمد وأبو داود].

Ibn Masʿūd, may Allāh be pleased with him said; "I heard Allāh's Messenger (ﷺ) saying, '*Ruqyā*, charms, and *tiwalah* are *shirk*.'" Recorded by Aḥmad and Abū Dāwūd.[23]

وعن عبد الله بن عكيم مرفوعاً: (من تعلق شيئاً وكل إليه). [رواه أحمد والترمذي].

And from ʿAbdullāh bin ʿUkaym is the *marfūʿ* report, "Whoever depends upon something, he is entrusted to it." Recorded by Aḥmad and Al-Tirmidhī.[24]

---

[22] Al-Bukhārī, Muslim and others.

[23] It is also recorded by Ibn Mājah, Ibn Ḥibbān and al-Ḥākim who graded it *ṣaḥīḥ* and al-Dhahabī agreed. See *al-Ṣaḥīḥah* no. 331.

[24] Recorded also by al-Ḥākim. There is some discussion about its authenticity. Al-Albānī graded it *ḥasan* in *Ghāyat al-Marām* no. 297 due to a *ṣaḥīḥ mursal* report from al-Ḥasan, as well as a weak *marfūʿ* report via al-Ḥasan through Abū Hurayrah.

(التمائم): شيء يعلق على الأولاد من العين، لكن إذا كـــان المعلـــق من القرآن، فرخص فيه بعض السلف، وبعضهم لم يرخص فيه، ويجعله من المنهي عنه، منهم ابن مسعود رضي الله عنه.

Tamā'im (charms) are things that were put on children to ward off the evil eye. Some of the *salaf* made an exception for it if it contained something from the *Qur'ān*, while others did not, they still considered it among the prohibited, among the latter was Ibn Mas'ūd, may Allāh be pleased with him.

و(الرقى): هي التي تسمى العزائم، وخص منه الدليل ما خلا من الشرك، فقد رخص فيه رسول الله صلى الله عليه وسلم من العين والحمة.

Ruqyā is that which is known as *'azā'im* [incantation], if it is proven to be free of *shirk*, then Allāh's Messenger (ﷺ) permitted it in the case of the evil eye and for poisonous stings.

و(التولة): شيء يصنعونه يزعمون أنه يحبب المرأة إلى زوجها، والرجل إلى امرأته.

Tiwalah is something that they did with the claim that it makes a woman more loved by her husband, or vice-versa.

وروى أحمد عن رويفع قال: قال لي رسول الله صلى الله عليه وسلم: (يا رويفع! لعل الحياة تطول بك، فأخبر الناس أن من عقد لحيته، أو تقلد وتراً، أو استنجى برجيع دابة أو عظم، فإن محمداً بريء منه).

Aḥmad reported from Ruwayfi'; "Allāh's Messenger (ﷺ) said to me; 'O Ruwayfi'! Perhaps you will live a long life. So tell the people; Whoever ties his beard, or wears a necklace, or cleans himself with the droppings of animals, or bones, then surely Muḥammad is innocent of him.'"[25]

وعن سعيد بن جبير رضي الله عنه، قال: (من قطع تميمة من إنسان كان كعدل رقبة) [رواه وكيع]. وله عن إبراهيم قال: كانوا يكرهون التمائم كلها، من القرآن وغير القرآن.

[25] Also recorded by Abū Dāwūd, about whose chain Shaykh Sulaymān bin 'Abdullāh bin Muḥammad bin 'Abd al-Wahhāb said, "This chain is good", as well as al-Nasā'ī, whose chain was labeled *ḥasan* by al-Nawawī and *ṣaḥīḥ* by others including al-Albānī in *Ṣaḥīḥ al-Jāmi'* no. 7910.

Sa'īd bin Jubayr said; "Whoever destroys people's charms, he is like one who has freed a slave." Recorded by Waki'.[26]

And with him from Ibrāhīm who said; "They objected to all types of charms, whether they contained the Qur'ān or not"[27]

فيه مسائل:

الأولى: تفسير الرقي والتمائم.

الثانية: تفسير التولة.

الثالثة: أن هذه الثلاثة كلها من الشرك من غير استثناء.

الرابعة: أن الرقية بالكلام الحق من العين والحمة ليس من ذلك.

الخامسة: أن التميمة إذا كانت من القرآن فقد اختلف العلماء هل هي من ذلك أم لا؟.

السادسة: أن تعليق الأوتار على الدواب عن العين، من ذلك.

السابعة: الوعيد الشديد على من تعلق وتراً.

الثامنة: فضل ثواب من قطع تميمة من إنسان.

التاسعة: أن كلام إبراهيم لا يخالف ما تقدم من الاختلاف، لأن مراده أصحاب عبد الله بن مسعود.

Important Points

1. The explanation of *ruqyā* and *tamā'im*.
2. The explanation of *tiwalah*.

---

[26] "Waki' is Ibn al-Jarrāḥ bin Waki' al-Kufi, a trustworthy *imām* and author of among others *al-Jāmi'*. Imām Aḥmad and others from his time reported from him. He died in the year 197 H." (*Taysīr al-'Azīz*)

[27] The narrator is Ibrāhīm al-Nakha'ī. He is speaking about the companions of Ibn Mas'ūd like *'Alqamah* and others. Ibid.

3. That these three, without exception are *shirk*.
4. That *ruqyā* with the True Words for the evil eye and poisonous sting is not *shirk*.
5. That when charms consist of the *Qur'ān* then the scholars have differed over it; is it from this category or not?
6. That putting necklaces on animals for the evil eye is *shirk*.
7. The severe warning for anyone who wears these types of necklaces.
8. The virtuous rewards for the one who destroys people's charms.
9. That the statement of Ibrāhīm does not contradict the previous mentioned difference of opinion, because he was talking about the companions of ʿAbdullāh [Ibn Masʿūd].

Commentary by ʿ*Allāmah* al-Saʿdī

What is said about *Ruqyā* and Charms

Charms are necklaces relied upon by the hearts of the people who wear them. The discussion about them is the same as was with bracelets and cords as preceded.

Among them is that which constitutes major *shirk*, like that which includes statements that seek help from the *shayāṭīn* or other creatures. Seeking help from other than Allāh- when none but Allāh has the power to help- is *shirk* as is discussed later, if Allāh wills.

Among them is that which is unlawful like whatever contains words whose meanings are not comprehensible, this is because it may lead to *shirk*.

As for the signets which contain *Qur'ān* or Prophetic ḥadīths, or recommended sacred supplications, then it is preferred to avoid them due to the absence of mention about them by the *sharīʿah*. Additionally, they may cause one to commit other unlawful acts. Especially since most people who wear them do not honour their sacredness, and they enter filthy places with them on.

The details of *ruqyā'* are as follows;

If it is done with the *Qur'ān* or *sunnah* or good words, then it is recommended for the one administering it because it falls into the category of doing good for someone, because of the benefits that it contains. Then, for the one it is administered to, it is simply allowed, as long as he does not seek it to be done. For part of the worshipper's reliance upon Allāh and strengthening his certainty in Him is that he does not ask help from any creature, not for *ruqyā*, nor otherwise. Rather if he asks someone to supplicate for him he must keep in mind that the one supplicating is performing worship that he himself benefits from, and its results may also benefit the one he supplicates for. This is one of the most fascinating implications and most marvellous realities of *tawḥīd* that is not understood or acted upon except by the most complete of worshippers.

If the *ruqyā* includes supplicating to other than Allāh and seeking cures from other than Him, then this is major *shirk*, because he is calling upon and asking for help from other than Allāh.

So take heed to this point, and beware that the rulings for the causes and effects of *ruqyā'* are the same as the rulings in that regard mentioned earlier.

Chapter 9

من تبرك بشجرة أو حجر ونحوهما

On seeking the blessings of trees, stones and other things

وقول الله تعالى: ﴿أفرأيتم اللّات والعزى﴾ الآيات.

Allāh (ﷻ) said; Have you not seen al-Lāt and al-ʿUzzā..." (*al-Najm* 53: 19-20)

عن أبي واقد الليثي، قال: خرجنا مع رسول الله صلى الله عليه وسلم إلى حنين ونحن حدثاء عهد بكفر، وللمشركين سدرة يعكفون عندها وينوطون بها أسلحتهم، يقال لها: ذات أنواط، فمررنا بسدرة فقلنا: يا رسول الله أجعل لنا ذات أنواط كما لهم ذات أنواط فقال رسول الله صلى الله عليه وسلم: (الله أكبر! إنها السنن، قلتم — والذي نفسي بيده — كما قالت بنو إسرائيل لموسى: ﴿اجعل لنا إلهاً كما لهم آلهة قال إنكم قوم تجهلون﴾ (لتركبن سنن من كان قبلكم). [رواه الترمذي وصححه].

Abū Wāqid al-Laythī said "We went with Allāh's Messenger to Ḥunayn while we had just recently left disbelief. The *mushrikīn* had a lote tree which they used to frequent and hang their swords upon. They called it *dhāt al-anwāṭ* (possessor of the medals of honour). We said, 'O Messenger of Allāh, can you make a *dhāt al-anwāṭ* for us like their *dhāt al-anwāṭ*?'

Allāh's Messenger (ﷺ) said, '*Allāhu akbar*! This way that you have mentioned, by the One in whose Hand my soul is, is just like what the children of Isrā'īl asked Mūsā; "'Make a god for us like their god.' He said, 'Surely you are an ignorant people. (*al-Aʿrāf* 7:138) You will follow the way of those before you.'" Recorded by Al-Tirmidhī who declared it *ṣaḥīḥ*.[28]

[28] Al-Tirmidhī graded it *ḥasan ṣaḥīḥ*. It is also recorded by others. Al-Albānī graded it *ṣaḥīḥ* in *Ṣaḥīḥ al-Jāmiʿ* no. 3601.

فيه مسائل:

الأولى: تفسير آية النجم.

الثانية: معرفة صورة الأمر الذي طلبوا.

الثالثة: كونهم لم يفعلوا.

الرابعة: كونهم قصدوا التقرب إلى الله بذلك، لظنهم أنه يحبه.

الخامسة: أنهم إذا جهلوا هذا فغيرهم أولى بالجهل.

السادسة: أن لهم من الحسنات والوعد بالمغفرة ما ليس لغيرهم.

السابعة: أن النبي صلى الله عليه وسلم لم يعذرهم، بل رد عليهم بقوله: (الله أكبر إنها السنن، لتتبعن سنن من كان قبلكم) فغلظ الأمر بهذه الثلاث.

الثامنة: الأمر الكبير، وهو المقصود: أنه أخبر أن طلبتهم كطلبة بني إسرائيل لما قالوا لموسى: (اجعل لنا إلهاً) .

التاسعة: أن نفي هذا معنى (لا إله إلا الله)، مع دقته وخفائه على أولئك.

العاشرة: أنه حلف على الفتيا، وهو لا يحلف إلا لمصلحة.

الحادية عشرة: أن الشرك فيه أكبر وأصغر، لأنهم لم يرتدوا بهذا.

الثانية عشرة: قولهم: (ونحن حدثاء عهد بكفر) فيه أن غيرهم لا يجهل ذلك.

الثالثة عشرة: التكبير عند التعجب، خلافاً لمن كرهه.

الرابعة عشرة: سد الذرائع.

الخامسة عشرة: النهي عن التشبه بأهل الجاهلية.

السادسة عشرة: الغضب عند التعليم.

السابعة عشرة: القاعدة الكلية، لقوله (إنها السنن).

الثامنة عشرة: أن هذا عَلم من أعلام النبوة، لكونه وقع كما أخبر.

التاسعة عشرة: أن كل ما ذم الله به اليهود والنصارى في القرآن أنه لنا.

العشرون: أنه متقرر عندهم أن العبادات مبناها على الأمـــر، فصـــار فيه التنبيه على مسائل القبر. أما (من ربك)؟ فواضح، وأما (من نبيك)؟ فمن إخباره بأنباء الغيب، وأما (ما دينك)؟ فمن قولهم: (اجعل لنا إلهاً) إلخ.

الحادية والعشرون: أن سنة أهل الكتاب مذمومة كسنة المشركين.

الثانية والعشرون: أن المنتقل من الباطل الذي اعتاده قلبه لا يُؤمن أن يكون في قلبه بقية من تلك العادة لقولهم: ونحن حدثاء عهد بكفر.

Important Points

1. The explanation of the *āyah* in *Sūrah al-Najm*.
2. Being aware of the gist of the matter that they sought.
3. What they requested was not provided.
4. They sought nearness to Allāh by such request, thinking that He would like that.
5. That if they were ignorant of this point, then others would be more ignorant about it.
6. That they had of good [rewards] and had the promise of forgiveness, what others do not have of this.
7. That the Prophet (ﷺ) did not excuse them for this, rather he rebuked them by saying, "*Allāhu akbar*! This way... This is the way followed by those before you." So by these three statements, he (ﷺ) emphasized the gravity of the matter.
8. The most important matter, and it is the point here; that he (ﷺ) told them that they were seeking what the children of Isrā'īl sought when they asked Mūsā, "Make a god for us."
9. That such request is negated by the meaning of *Lā ilāha illa Allāh*, yet it was overlooked by them.
10. Swearing when stating a ruling, and he (ﷺ) did not swear except

for good reason.

11. That *shirk* can be of the minor as well as major type; they were not apostates because of this.

12. Their saying, "We had just recently left disbelief..." implies that others among them were not ignorant of that.

13. Saying the *takbīr* when astonished, contrary to those who object to this.

14. Closing the means.

15. The prohibition from imitating the people of ignorance.

16. Teaching while angry.

17. The encompassing principle implied by his saying, "This is the way [*sunan*]..."

18. That this is a sign of Prophethood, because it has occurred as he informed it would.

19. That what Allāh censured the Jews and the Christians for in the *Qur'ān*, is with us too.

20. That according to them, acts of worship were built upon commands, to the point that when questioned in the grave, "Who is you Lord ." that would be clear, as for "Who is your prophet." That is whoever brought them the revelation of the unseen, but as far as "What is your religion?" then it is as they said, "Make for us..." to the end.

21. That the blameworthy *sunnah* of the People of the Book is the same as the *sunnah* of the *mushrikīn*.

22. That when one leaves falsehoods that he believes in his heart, there is no guarantee that his heart does not still hold some of those ideas. This is due to their saying, "While we had just recently left disbelief."

Commentary by ʿ*Allāmah* al-Saʿdī

On Seeking Blessings from Trees, Stones and other things

Meaning that this is *shirk*, and the behaviour of the *mushrikīn*. The scholars agree that the *sharīʿah* has not assigned any blessings to be derived from trees or stones or spots or tombs. For this type of seeking blessings becomes excessive until the thing becomes supplicated to and worshipped. And this is major *shirk* according to the guidelines that were discussed before. This generally applies to everything, even the Station of Ibrāhīm, the tomb of the Prophet (ﷺ), and the rock at Bayt al-Maqdis or any other virtuous place.

As for touching the Black stone and facing it, and touching the southern corner of the honoured Kaʿbah, then this is prescribed worship of Allāh, exalting Allāh, and subjection to His majesty, He is the one that is worshipped by doing that. So this is honouring the Creator and service to Him, and that is honouring the creatures and deifying them. The difference between the two is like the difference between the supplication which is done out of sincerity and *tawḥīd* to Allāh, and the supplication to the creatures which is *shirk* and making equals to Him.

Chapter 10

ما جاء في الذبح لغير الله

What is said about slaughtering for other than Allāh

وقول الله تعالى: (قل إن صلاتي ونسكي ومحياي ومماتي لله رب العالمين * لا شر يك له) الآية، وقوله: (فصل لر بك وأنحر) .

Allāh (ﷻ) said; "Say: 'Surely my prayer, my sacrificing, my living and dying are for Allāh the Lord of the worlds, there is no partner for Him.'" (*al-An'ām* 6:162-163) And; "So pray to your Lord and sacrifice [to Him]." (*al-Kawthār* 108:2)

عن علي رضي الله عنه قال: حدثني رسول الله صلى الله عليه وسلم بأربع كلمات: (لعن الله من ذبح لغير الله، لعن الله من لعن والديه. لعن الله من آوى محدثاً، لعن الله من غير منار الأرض) [رواه مسلم].

'Alī, may Allāh be pleased with him, said; "Allāh's Messenger (ﷺ) narrated four statements to me: 'Allāh's curse be upon the one who sacrifices to other than Allāh, Allāh's curse be upon the one who curses his parents, Allāh's curse be upon the one who shelters an innovator, Allāh's curse be upon one who alters the borders of the land.'" Recorded by Muslim.

وعن طارق بن شهاب، أن رسول الله صلى الله عليه وسلم قال: (دخل الجنة رجل في ذباب، ودخل النار رجل في ذباب) قالوا: وكيف ذلك يا رسول الله؟! قال: (مر رجلان على قوم لهم صنم لا يجوزه أحد حتى يقرب له شيئاً، فقالوا لأحدهما قرب قال: ليس عندي شيء أُقرِّب قالوا له: قرب ولو ذباباً، فقرب ذباباً، فخلوا سبيله، فدخل النار، وقالوا للآخر: قرب، فقال: ما كنت لأقرب لأحد شيئاً دون الله عز وجل، فضربوا عنقه فدخل الجنة) [رواه أحمد].

Ṭāriq bin Shihāb said, that Allāh's Messenger (ﷺ) said; "A man entered Paradise because of flies, and a man entered the Fire because of flies." They [the companions] asked; "How is that O Messenger of Allāh?" He said, "Two men entered upon some people who had an idol. They would not allow anyone to pass through until they offered it something. So they said to one of them, 'Make your offer.' He said, 'I do not have anything with me to offer.' They said, 'Offer something, even if it is just some flies.' So he offered some flies, then they let him go about his way. So he entered the Fire. They told the other one, 'Make an offer.' He said, 'I will not offer anything to anyone other than Allāh (ﷻ).' So they slashed his neck, and he entered Paradise.'" Recorded by Aḥmad.[29]

فيه مسائل:

الأولى: تفسير (إن صلاتي ونسكي).

الثانية: تفسير (فصل لربك وأنحر).

الثالثة: البداءة بلعنة من ذبح لغير الله.

الرابعة: لعن من لعن والديه، ومنه أن تلعن والدي الرجل فيلعن والديك.

الخامسة: لعن من آوى محدثاً وهو الرجل يحدث شيئاً يجب فيه حق لله فيلتجيء إلى من يجيره من ذلك.

السادسة: لعن من غير منار الأرض، وهي المراسيم التي تفرق بين حقك في الأرض وحق جارك، فتغيرها بتقديم أو تأخير.

السابعة: الفرق بين لعن المعيّن، ولعن أهل المعاصي على سبيل العموم.

الثامنة: هذه القصة العظيمة، وهي قصة الذباب.

التاسعة: كونه دخل النار بسبب ذلك الذباب الذي لم يقصده، بل فعله تخلصاً من شرهم.

[29] According to al-Arnā'ūṭ, this was recorded by Aḥmad in *Al-Zuhd* as a *ṣaḥīḥ mawqūf* report to Salmān al-Farsi (رضي الله عنه). It is not in Aḥmad's *Musnad* as noted by Shaykh Sulaymān in *Taysīr al-ʿAzīz*.

العاشرة: معرفة قدر الشرك في قلوب المؤمنين، كيف صبر ذلك على القتل، و لم يوافقهم على طلبتهم، مع كونهم لم يطلبوا منه إلا العمل الظاهر.

الحادية عشرة: أن الذي دخل النار مسلم، لأنه لو كان كافراً لم يقل: (دخل النار في ذباب).

الثانية عشرة: فيه شاهد للحديث الصحيح (الجنة أقرب إلى أحدكم من شراك نعله، والنار مثل ذلك).

الثالثة عشرة: معرفة أن عمل القلب هو المقصود الأعظم حتى عند عبدة الأوثان.

Important Points

1. The explanation of "Surely my prayer, my sacrifice..."
2. The explanation of "So pray to your Lord and make sacrifice [to Him]."
3. Instituting a curse on the one who sacrifices to other than Allāh.
4. Cursing the one who curses his parents, this includes when you curse a persons parents so he returns the curse upon your parents.
5. Cursing the one who shelters an innovator. That is a person who innovates something that Allāh alone has the right over, so he seeks refuge of one who will help him in that.
6. Cursing the one who alters the land's borders, that is the boundaries which distinguish between your property and your neighbours, so he alters it by increasing or decreasing it.
7. Distinguishing between the curse and the one who is cursed, cursing the people of disobedience is a general application.
8. The story of the flies and its significance.
9. A man entered the Fire on account of the flies which he had no intention of offering, but he did it simply out of escaping the harm of those people.
10. Knowing the effect of *shirk* in the hearts of the believers. The one had patience even until he was killed. He did not give in to what they sought from him, even though they were only asking him to do a physical deed.

11. That the one who entered the fire was a Muslim, for if he was a disbeliever, then he (ﷺ) would not have said, "entered the Fire because of flies."
12. It testifies to the authentic ḥadīth, "Paradise is nearer to one of you than the straps of his sandals, as to the Fire."
13. Knowing that the heart will make the best intention, even when worshipping idols.

Commentary by ʿ*Allāmah* al-Saʿdī

What is said about Sacrificing to Other than Allāh

Meaning that it is *shirk*. For indeed the texts of the Book and the *Sunnah* are clear in the command to sacrifice to Allāh, and doing that sincerely for His Face. Just as they are clear in that regard with the case of prayer. Allāh has accompanied sacrifice with prayer in a number of places in His Book.

So when it is confirmed that sacrifice is for Allāh, for the sake of worship and out of the greatest obedience, then sacrifice to other than Allāh is among the greatest *shirk*, removing one from the sanctity of *Islām*.

Major *shirk* has a simple rule or a definition which encompasses both its categories and its elements. It is when the worshipper devotes a category or element of worship to other than Allāh. So every belief, saying or action, which is confirmed to be ordered by the *sharīʿah*, then it is devoted solely to Allāh, with faith, *tawḥīd* and sincerity, and devoting it to other than Him is *shirk* and *kufr*. So you must adhere to this principle of major *shirk* which will not leave any doubt.

Similarly minor *shirk* has a simple rule; it is defined as everything that is not considered worship, which is a means, a path, or a way to major *shirk* - be it in intentions, sayings, or actions.

So you must adhere to these two guidelines regarding major and minor *shirk*. By doing this you will be able to understand the chapters that preceded, and those that follow in this book, and by which you will be able to distinguish between the matters which many are confused over. And Allāh is the One whom we seek from.

Chapter 11

لا يذبح لله بمكان يذبح فيه لغير الله

No sacrificing in a place where sacrifices are offered to other than Allāh

وقول الله تعالى: (لا تَـقُم فيه أبداً) الآية.

Allāh (ﷻ) said; "Do not ever stand in it, " (*al-Tawbah* 9:108)

عن ثابت بن الضحاك رضي الله عنه، قال: نذر رجل أن ينحر إبلاً ببوانة، فسأله النبي صلى الله عليه وسلم فقال: (هل كان فيها وثن من أوثان الجاهلية يعبد)؟ قالوا: لا. قال: (فهل كان فيها عيد من أعيادهم)؟ قالوا: لا. فقال رسول الله صلى الله عليه وسلم: (أوف بنذرك، فإنه لا وفاء لنذر في معصية الله، ولا فيما لا يملك ابن آدم) [رواه أبو داود، وإسنادها على شرطهما].

Thābit bin al-Ḍaḥḥāk, may Allāh be pleased with him, said; "A man vowed to sacrifice a camel at Buwānah. So he asked the Prophet (ﷺ) about it. The Prophet (ﷺ) said, 'Are there now, or were there before idols like those of *jāhilīyyah* in it?' He said, 'No.'He said, 'Are any of their celebrations held there?' He said, 'No.' Allāh's Messenger (ﷺ) said; 'Fulfil your vow, but there is to be no fulfilling a vow for disobedience to Allāh, nor for what the son of Ādam is incapable of.'" Recorded by Abū Dāwūd, and its chain meets their criteria i.e. the criteria of [al-Bukhārī and Muslim][30]

---

[30] Shaykh Muqbil bin Hādī al-Wādi'ī has agreed with this grading of the chain in *al-Ṣaḥīḥ al-Musnad manmā laysa fī al-Ṣaḥīḥayn*.

فيه مسائل:

الأولى: تفسير قوله: (لا تَـقُم فيه أبداً) .

الثانية: أن المعصية قد تؤثر في الأرض، وكذلك الطاعة.

الثالثة: رد المسألة المشكلة إلى المسألة البيّنة ليزول الإشكال.

الرابعة: استفصال المفتي إذا احتاج إلى ذلك.

الخامسة: أن تخصيص البقعة بالنذر لا بأس به إذا خلا من الموانع.

السادسة: المنع منه إذا كان فيه وثن من أوثان الجاهلية ولو بعد زواله.

السابعة: المنع منه إذا كان فيه عيد من أعيادهم ولو بعد زواله.

الثامنة: أنه لا يجوز الوفاء بما نذر في تلك البقعة، لأنه نذر معصية.

التاسعة: الحذر من مشابهة المشركين في أعيادهم ولو لم يقصده.

العاشرة: لا نذر في معصية.

الحادية عشرة: لا نذر لابن آدم فيما لا يملك.

Important Points

1. The explanation of the His (ﷺ) saying, "Do not ever stand in it."
2. That disobedience has a lasting effect in the world, as does obedience.
3. Referring a vague question to a clear one, to eliminate the ambiguity.
4. The *mufti* asking about details when their is a need to do that.
5. That there is no harm in specifying a particular place when making a vow, provided that it is free of other preventive factors.

6. It is prohibited when there are idols of *jāhilīyyah* present, or if there were such idols, although they no longer remain.[31]
7. The prohibition of vows at a place where celebrations of the *mushrikīn* are held even if they are not celebrated at that place any more.
8. That it is not allowed to fulfil a vow at such place because such a vow involves disobedience.
9. The warning against resembling the *mushrikīn* in their celebrations, even unintentionally.
10. No vows containing disobedience.
11. No vows for the son of Ādam containing what he is incapable of.

Commentary by *ʿAllāmah* al-Saʿdī

No Sacrificing in a Place where Sacrifices are Offered to other than Allāh

What is better than following the previous chapter with this one! Whereas the earlier deals with what is intended, this deals with what leads to such intentions. That being a category of major *shirk*, and this, a means to *shirk*.

If it is a place in which the *mushrikūn* performed sacrifices to become nearer to their gods, and associating partners with Allāh, then this is a place of the rituals of *shirk*. So if a Muslim slaughters an animal at that place, even if he only intends Allāh by it, then he has resembled the *mushrikīn* in their *shirk* at that shrine. Outward consent invites to inner consent and draws one to it. It is for this reason that the *sharīʿah* prohibits imitating the *kuffār* in their rituals, celebrations, manners, and their dress, and it gathers the

[31] For this and the following point, the reader may speculate about holy places such as the Kaʿbah, where the *mushrikīn* of the past performed acts of *shirk*. The principle which governs this topic, i.e., whatever Allāh legislated through His Prophet (ﷺ) is part of the correct religion, regardless of whether it was practiced by anyone else before him (ﷺ), may be reviewed in Ibn Taymiyah's *Iqtiḍā' al-Ṣirāt al-Mustaqīm*. A revised translation of it is available, entitled, "*The Right Way*" (Pub: *Maktabah Darussalam*).

things that are particular to them, distancing the Muslims from conforming to them on the outside which is a means leading to inclination and dependence upon them. Such that it is prohibited to offer optional prayers at a time when the *mushrikīn* prostrate to other than Allāh, out of the fear of appearing to do that which was warned against.

Chapter 12

من الشرك النذر لغير الله

Vows to other than Allāh are acts of *shirk*

وقول الله تعالى: (يوفون بالنذر) وقوله: (وما أنفقتم من نفقة أو نذرتم من نذر فإن الله يعلمه)

Allāh (ﷻ) said; "They fulfil their vows and fear a day whose distress abounds." (*al-Insān* 76:7) And; "And whatever spending you do, or vows you make, surely Allāh knows it." (*al-Baqarah* 2:270)

وفي (الصحيح) عن عائشة رضي الله عنها، أن رسول الله صلى الله عليه وسلم قال: (من نذر أن يطيع الله فليطعه، ومن نذر أن يعصي الله فلا يعصه).

In the *Ṣaḥīḥ*, it is recorded that ʿĀ'ishah, may Allāh be pleased with, her said; "Whoever vows to obey Allāh, let him obey Him. Whoever vows to disobey Allāh, he must not disobey Him."[32]

فيه مسائل:

الأولى: وجوب الوفاء بالنذر.

الثانية: إذا ثبت كونه عبادة لله فصرفه إلى غيره شرك.

الثالثة: أن نذر المعصية لا يجوز الوفاء به.

[32] Al-Bukhārī.

Important Points

1. The fulfilment of vows is obligatory.
2. If it is confirmed that a thing is worship of Allāh, than rendering it to other than Him is *shirk*.
3. That it is not allowed to fulfil the vow involving disobedience.

ʿAllāmah Saʿdī made no comments here

Chapter 13

من الشرك الاستعاذة بغير الله

Seeking refuge in other than Allāh is *shirk*

وقول الله تعالى: (وأنه كان رجال من الإنس يعوذون برجال من الجن فزادوهم رهقاً) .

Allāh (ﷻ) said; "There were some people among the humans who sought refuge with some people among the *jinn*. So they increased their misguidance." (*al-Jinn* 72:6)

وعن خولة بنت حكيم رضي الله عنها قالت: سمعت رسول الله صلى الله عليه وسلم يقول: (من نزل منزلاً فقال: أعوذ بكلمات الله التامات من شر ما خلق، لم يضره شيء حتى يرحل من منزله ذلك) [رواه مسلم].

Khawlah bint Ḥakīm said; "I heard Allāh's Messenger (ﷺ) saying; 'Whoever enters his home and says, "I seek refuge in the complete words of Allāh from the evil of what He created." Nothing will harm him until he leaves from his home." Recorded by Muslim.

فيه مسائل:

الأولى: تفسير آية الجن.

الثانية: كونه من الشرك.

الثالثة: الاستدلال على ذلك بالحديث، لأن العلماء استدلوا به على أن كلمات الله غير مخلوقة، قالوا: لأن الاستعاذة بالمخلوق شرك.

الرابعة: فضيلة هذا الدعاء مع اختصاره.

الخامسة: أن كون الشيء يحصل به مصلحة دنيوية من كف شر أو جلب نفع - لا يدل على أنه ليس من شرك.

Important Points

1. The explanation of the *āyah* in *Sūrah al-Jinn*.
2. Seeking refuge in other than Allāh is *shirk*.
3. This is supported by the ḥadīth, because the scholars use it to prove that Allāh's words are not created, they say, 'Because seeking refuge in creatures is *shirk*."
4. The merit of this supplication even though it is brief.
5. Despite the fact that a thing may lead to some worldly benefit, by hindering evil or obtaining benefit, that does not prove that it is not *shirk*.

ʿAllāmah Saʿdī made no comments here

Chapter 14

من الشرك أن يستغيث بغير الله أو يدعو غيره

Seeking refuge in other than Allāh, or calling other than Him is a type of *shirk*.

وقوله تعالى: (ولا تدع من دون الله ما لا ينفعك ولا يضرك فإن فعلت فإنك إذاً من الظالمين وإن يمسسك الله بضر فلا كاشف له إلا هو) الآية. وقوله: (فابتغوا عند الله الرزق واعبدوه) الآية. وقوله: (ومن أضل ممن يدعوا من دون الله من لا يستجيب له إلى يوم القيامة) الآيتان. وقوله: (أمن يجيب المضطر إذا دعاه ويكشف السوء) .

Allāh (ﷻ) said; "Do not call upon other than Allāh, that which cannot bring you benefit, nor cause you any harm. If you do so, then you will be among the great wrongdoers. If Allāh afflicts you with harm, none can remove it except for Him." (*Yūnus* 10:106-107) And He (ﷻ) said; "So seek sustenance from Allāh, and worship Him, and be thankful to Him, to Him is the return." (*al-ʿAnkabūt* 17:29) "And who is more deviant than the one who calls upon other than Allāh who will not answer him until the Day of resurrection." (*al-Aḥqāf* 46:5-6) And; "Who is it that answers the suffering when he calls Him, and removes the pain?!" (*al-Nahl* 27:62)

وروي الطبراني بإسناده أنه كان في زمن النبي صلى الله عليه وسلم منافق يؤذي المؤمنين، فقال بعضهم: قوموا بنا نستغيث برسول الله صلى الله عليه وسلم من هذا المنافق. فقال النبي صلى الله عليه وسلم: (إنه لا يستغاث بي، وإنما يستغاث بالله عز وجل).

Al-Ṭabarānī reports a chain of narration that; "During the time of the Prophet (ﷺ) there was a hypocrite troubling the believers. Someone said; 'Come with us to seek help from Allāh's Messenger (ﷺ) against this hypocrite.' So the Prophet (ﷺ) said; 'There is no seeking help from me, only seeking help from Allāh.'"[33]

---

[33] Similar is recorded by Aḥmad. It is a weak narration due to the presence of Ibn Lahiyʿah.

فيه مسائل:

الأولى: أن عطف الدعاء على الاستغاثة من عطف العام على الخاص.

الثانية: تفسير قوله: (ولا تدع من دون الله ما لا ينفعك ولا يضرك)

الثالثة: أن هذا هو الشرك الأكبر.

الرابعة: أن أصلح الناس لو يفعله إرضاء لغيره صار من الظالمين.

الخامسة: تفسير الآية التي بعدها.

السادسة: كون ذلك لا ينفع في الدنيا مع كونه كفراً.

السابعة: تفسير الآية الثالثة.

الثامنة: أن طلب الرزق لا ينبغي إلا من الله، كما أن الجنة لا تطلب إلا منه.

التاسعة: تفسير الآية الرابعة.

العاشرة: أنه لا أضل ممن دعا غير الله.

الحادية عشرة: أنه غافل عن دعاء الداعي لا يدري عنه.

الثانية عشرة: أن تلك الدعوة سبب لبغض المدعو للداعي وعداوته له.

الثالثة عشرة: تسمية تلك الدعوة عبادة للمدعو.

الرابعة عشرة: كفر المدعو بتلك العبادة.

الخامسة عشرة: أن هذه الأمور سبب كونه أضل الناس.

السادسة عشرة: تفسير الآية الخامسة.

السابعة عشرة: الأمر العجيب وهو إقرار عبدة الأوثان أنه لا يجيب المضطر إلا الله، ولأجل هذا يدعونه في الشدائد مخلصين له الدين.

الثامنة عشرة: حماية المصطفى صلى الله عليه وسلم حمى التوحيد والتأدب مع الله عز وجل.

Important Points

1. The relationship between "calling upon" (*du'ā*) and "seeking help" (*istaghāthah*) is as simple as the relationship between a general thing and a specific one.[34]
2. The explanation of the saying, "Do not call upon others such that will not bring you any benefit nor harm."
3. That this is major *shirk*.
4. That in the case of the most righteous person, if he intentionally does this with other than Allāh, then he becomes one of the great wrongdoers.
5. The explanation of the *āyah* afterwards.
6. This will bring no benefit in this world since it is *kufr*.
7. The explanation of the third *āyah*.
8. That one is not to seek his sustenance except from Allāh, just as Paradise is not to be sought except from Him.
9. The explanation of the fourth *āyah*.
10. That none is more deviant than the one who calls upon other than Allāh.
11. That the one being called upon is heedless of the caller's call, he is not aware of it at all.
12. That this is a type of insult from the one calling to the one being called, causing enmity between them.
13. That call to the one being called upon is named, "worship."
14. The disbelief of the one who calls because of that worship.
15. It is for these reasons that he is the most deviant of people.
16. The explanation of the fifth *āyah*.
17. The wonder of accepting the worship of idols, when none but Allāh is able to answer the one suffering, and because of this fact

[34] That is, seeking help is a type of *du'ā*. This point was mentioned because many defend asking the dead for help with the claim that doing so is not the same as the "calling upon" forbidden by the *āyāt* that the author mentioned.

they call upon Him, making the entire religion sincerely for Him, when they are in severe distress.

18. The Chosen one's (ﷺ) defence of *tawḥīd*, and the manners with Allāh.

Commentary by *Allāmah* al-Sa'dī

Seeking Refuge in other than Allāh, or Calling other than Him is a type of *Shirk*.

When the preceding guideline for the rule of *shirk* is understood, that is - one who renders any act of worship to other than Allāh is committing *shirk* - then these three chapters, which the author cites to clarify this point, will be clearly understood.

An oath is an act of worship that Allāh praised those who fulfil, and the Prophet (ﷺ) commanded fulfilling the oaths that involve obedience. Certainly every matter that the *shārī'ah* praised, or every matter that praise is mentioned for the one who fulfils it, or every matter that the *shārī'ah* commands, is worship.

And since worship is a name that encompasses everything that Allāh loves and is pleased with, being deeds, or statements, whether apparent or internal, then oaths certainly fall into this category.

Similarly, Allāh commanded seeking protection against all evil from Him alone, and He commanded seeking assistance for every kind of trouble and mishap from Him alone. So sincerity for Allāh in these acts is a form of faith and *tawḥīd*, and rendering them to other than Allāh is a form of *shirk* and making equals to Him.

The difference between *du'ā* [calling or supplicating] and *istaghāthah* [seeking aid or succor], is that the *du'ā* is more general, applying to all circumstances, where *istaghāthah* is the *du'ā* to Allāh in dire circumstances. So in both cases it is necessary to render it sincerely to Allāh alone. He (ﷻ) is the answerer of the *du'ā* of the supplicant, He is the reliever of the distress of those in dismay. Whoever calls upon other than Him, be it a prophet, an angel, a *walī* etc., or whoever seeks the aid of other than Allāh in a matter that none has the power over but Allāh - then he is a disbelieving *mushrik*. Just as he has left the religion, so too has he defied his own reason. For not one of the creatures is solely capable of the slightest speck of benefit or defence for himself or anyone else, but all are in need of Allāh in every troubling circumstance that effects them.

Chapter 15

قول الله تعالى: أيشركون مالا يخلق شيئاً

The Saying of Allāh (ﷻ); "Do they make partners with that which has not created anything"

قول الله تعالى: (أيشركون مالا يخلق شيئاً وهم يخلقون * ولا يستطيعون لهم نصراً) الآية.
وقوله: (والذين تدعون من دونه ما يملكون من قطمير) الآية.

The Saying of Allāh (ﷻ); "Do they make partners with that which has not created anything, and they are themselves created, and they are unable to aid them?" (*al-A'rāf* 7:191-192). And His (ﷻ) saying; "And those whom you call upon other than Allāh, they have not the least bit of power." (*Fāṭir* 35:13)

وفي (الصحيح) عن أنس قال: شُجَّ النبي صلى الله عليه وسلم يوم أحد وكسرت رباعيته، فقال: (كيف يفلح قوم شَجُّوا نبيهم)؟ فنزلت: (ليس لك من الأمر شيء)

In the *Ṣaḥīḥ*, it is reported from Anas; "On the day of *Uḥud*, the Prophet (ﷺ) suffered a wound that broke one of his molars. He said, 'How can a people who wound their prophet succeed?'" So the *āyah* was revealed; "It is not for you to control things." (*Āl 'Imrān* 3:128)

وفيه عن ابن عمر رضي الله عنهما أنه سمع رسول الله صلى الله عليه وسلم يقول إذا رفع رأسه من الركوع في الركعة الأخيرة من الفجر: (اللهم العن فلاناً وفلاناً) بعدما يقول: (سمع الله لمن حمده، ربنا ولك الحمـــــد) فأنزل الله تعالى: (ليس لك من الأمر شيء) الآية

And similarly from Ibn 'Umar, may Allāh be pleased with them, that he heard Allāh's Messenger (ﷺ) saying when raising his head from *rukū* in the last *raka'ah* of *fajr*, after saying "Allāh listens to those who praise Him"; "O Allāh! Curse so and so..." So Allāh revealed the *āyah*; "It is not for you to control things." (*Āl 'Imrān* 3:128)[35]

وفي رواية: يدعو على صفوان بن أمية، وسهيل بن عمرو والحارث بن هشام، فنزلت (ليس لك من الأمر شيء)

And in one report; "He supplicated against Ṣafwān bin 'Umayyah and Suhayl bin 'Amr, and al-Ḥārith bin Hishām, so it was revealed; "It is not for you to control things." (*Āl 'Imrān* 3:128)"[36]

وفيه عن أبي هريرة رضي الله عنه قال: قام رسول الله صلى الله عليه وسلم حين أنزل عليه: (وأنذر عشيرتك الأقربين) قال: (يا معشر قريش ــ أو كلمة نحوها ــ اشتروا أنفسكم، لا أغني عنكم من الله شيئاً، يا عباس بن عبد المطلب لا أغني عنك من الله شيئاً، يا صفية عمة رسول الله صلى الله عليه وسلم لا أغني عنك من الله شيئاً، ويا فاطمة بنت محمد سليني من مالي ما شئت لا أغني عنك من الله شيئاً).

Similarly from Abū Hurayrah, may Allāh be pleased with him, who said; "Allāh's Messenger (ﷺ) was standing with us when the *āyah* was revealed; 'And warn your family and your relatives' (*Al-Sha'rā'* 26:214)

So he said, 'O people of Quraysh' - or something similar - 'Purchase yourselves, I cannot guarantee you anything with Allāh! O 'Abbās bin 'Abd al-Muṭṭālib! I cannot guarantee anything for you with Allāh! O Ṣafiyah, aunt of Allāh's Messenger (ﷺ)! I cannot guarantee you anything with Allāh! And O Fāṭimah daughter of Muḥammad! Ask me of my wealth as you wish, but I cannot guarantee you anything from Allāh!'"[37]

فيه مسائل:

الأولى: تفسير الآيتين.

الثانية: قصة أحد.

الثالثة: قنوت سيد المرسلين وخلفه سادات الأولياء يؤمنون في الصلاة.

---

[35] Al-Bukhārī and al-Nasā'ī.

[36] Al-Bukhārī.

[37] Al-Bukhārī.

الرابعة: أن المدعو عليهم كفار.

الخامسة: أنهم فعلوا أشياء ما فعلها غالب الكفار. منها: شجهم نبيهم وحرصهم على قتله، ومنها: التمثيل بالقتلى مع أنهم بنو عمهم.

السادسة: أنزل الله عليه في ذلك (ليس لك من الأمر شيء)

السابعة: قوله: (أو يتوب عليهم أو يعذبهم فإنهم ظالمون) فتاب عليهم فآمنوا.

الثامنة: القنوت في النوازل.

التاسعة: تسمية المدعو عليهم في الصلاة بأسمائهم وأسماء آبائهم.

العاشرة: لعنه المعين في القنوت.

الحادية عشرة: قصته صلى الله عليه وسلم لما أنزل عليه: (وأنذر عشيرتك الأقربين).

الثانية عشرة: جدّه صلى الله عليه وسلم في هذا الأمر، بحيث فعل ما نسب بسببه إلى الجنون، وكذلك لو يفعله مسلم الآن.

الثالثة عشرة: قوله للأبعد والأقرب: (لا أغني عنك من الله شيئاً) حتى قال: (يا فاطمة بنت محمد لا أغني عنك من الله شيئاً) فإذا صرح صلى الله عليه وسلم وهو سيد المرسلين بأنه لا يغني شيئاً عن سيدة نساء العالمين، وآمن الإنسان أنه صلى الله عليه وسلم لا يقول إلا الحق، ثم نظر فيما وقع في قلوب خواص الناس الآن ـــ تبين له التوحيد وغربة الدين.

Important Points

1. The explanation of the two *āyāt*.
2. The narration of *Uḥud*.
3. The *qunūt* of the master of the Messengers, and behind him the foremost among the *awliyā'* saying *āmīn* during the prayer.
4. That those being supplicated against were disbelievers.
5. They were doing things that most of the disbelievers did not do;

they assaulted their prophet and attempted to kill him, and they were killing and mutilating, even though their victims were their relatives.

6. Allāh revealed to him (ﷺ) about that, "It is not for you to control things."
7. His saying, "Or He changes them or He punishes them." So He changed them so that they believed.
8. The *qunūt* during catastrophes.
9. Naming those supplicated against in prayer by their names and their fathers names.
10. Invoking the curse during the *qunūt*.
11. That when the revelation occurred; "And warn your family and relatives." He did that.
12. His (ﷺ) seriousness in this matter, to the extent that he would do something for which he would be insulted with the claim that he was crazy. As would happen if a Muslim were to do this today.
13. He (ﷺ) said to both his near and distant relatives; "I cannot guarantee you anything with Allāh." Even saying, "O Fāṭimah daughter of Muḥammad, I cannot guarantee you anything from Allāh."

So when it is clear that he is the master of the Messengers and that he cannot guarantee anything for the leader of women of the worlds - and the people believe that he (ﷺ) does not say except for what is true - then look at what has occurred in people's hearts, especially these days. This makes the meaning of *tawḥīd*, and the rareness of religion clear.

Commentary by ʿ*Allāmah* al-Saʿdī

Allāh's (ﷻ) saying; "Do they make partners with that which has not created anything..."

This begins the demonstration of the arguments and evidences for *tawḥīd*. The arguments for *tawḥīd*, both those textually reported, and those of reason, are unequalled.

Earlier it was mentioned that the two types of *tawḥīd - tawḥīd al-Rubūbiyah*, and *tawḥīd al-Asmā' wa al-Ṣifāt* have the greatest and most abundant evidences, proving that the one who is alone in creating and originating, the one who is considered absolutely perfect among all existence, is the only one who deserves worship.

Similarly, knowing the creatures attributes is among the proofs of *tawḥīd*, as well as knowing the attributes of those worshipped besides Allāh. So all of those who are worshipped besides Allāh - be they angels, humans, trees, stones or otherwise - they all are in need of Allāh. They are all incapable, holding not in their hands even the benefit equal to a grain, they have not created anything, they are themselves created, having no control over harm, benefit, death, life, or resurrection. Allāh (ﷻ) is the creator of every creature, and He is the provider of all things provided, the initiator of all matters, the harming, the benefiting, the giving, the withholding, the one in whose Hand is the authority over everything, to Him everything returns, He is the final goal, the final end, and the one everything is subjected to.

What is a greater proof than this one, the one that Allāh repeated and declared in many places of His Book and upon the tongue of His Messenger. It proves instinctually, as well as by reason, just as it proves by revealed texts that *tawḥīd* of Allāh is the truth and a necessity. In the same way it proves the falsehood of *shirk*.

If the most noble of all creatures (ﷺ) does not have any power to help the nearest related creatures to him, nor to bring them mercy, than what about others besides him? It is clear that whoever makes *shirk* with Allāh and equates with Him any of the creatures, then he has spoiled his ability to reason, aside from having spoiled his religion.

So the attributes of Allāh (ﷻ), His magnificent qualities and His uniqueness in absolute perfection, these are among the greatest proofs that there is none who deserves worship except for Him.

Similarly the attribute of the entire creation, that it is in need and dependant upon its Lord in its every matter, and that there is nothing perfect in it except for the greatest of evidences that its Lord gave it, falsifying the divinity of anything in it.

So whoever knows Allāh and knows the creation, then such knowledge requires him to worship Allāh alone, practising his religion sincerely for Him. He depends upon Him, praises Him, and thanks Him, with his tongue, his heart and his limbs. He forsakes entrusting his fear, hope and obedience to creatures. And Allāh knows best.

Chapter 16

قول الله تعالى: حتى إذا فُزِّع عن قلوبهم

Allāh (ﷻ) said; "Until when terror leaves their hearts"

قول الله تعالى: (حتى إذا فُزّع عن قلوبهم قالوا ماذا قال ربكم قالوا الحق وهو العلي الكبير)

Allāh (ﷻ) said; "Until when terror leaves their hearts, and they are asked; 'What did your Lord say?' They respond, 'The truth! And He is the most High, the most Great.'" (*Sabā'* 34:23)

وفي (الصحيح) عن أبي هريرة رضي الله عنه عن النبي صلى الله عليه وسلم قال: (إذا قضى الله الأمر في السماء ضربت الملائكة بأجنحتها خضعاناً لقوله، كأنه سلسلة على صفوان ينفذهم ذلك. حتى إذا فُزِّع عن قلوبهم قالوا: ماذا قال ربكم؟ قالوا: الحق وهو العلي الكبير فيسمعها مسترق السمع ــ ومسترق السمع هكذا بعضه فوق بعض ــ وصفه سفيان بكفه فحرفها وبدد بين أصابعه ــ فيسمع الكلمة فيلقيها إلى من تحته، ثم يلقيها الآخر إلى من تحته، حتى يلقيها عن لسان الساحر أو الكاهن فربما أدركه الشهاب قبل أن يلقيها، وربما ألقاها قبل أن يدركه، فيكذب معها مائة كذبة فيقال: أليس قد قال لنا يوم كذا وكذا: كذا وكذا فيصدق بتلك الكلمة التي سمعت من السماء).

In the *Ṣaḥīḥ* from Abū Hurayrah, may Allāh be pleased with him, that the Prophet (ﷺ) said, "When Allāh decrees a matter in the heavens, the angels beat their wings in humility to His saying, as if it were a chain striking a stone, it effects them like that. When the terror leaves their hearts, it is said, 'What has your Lord said?' They say, 'The truth! And He is the most High the most

Great.' So this is heard by those who try to steal a listen, they try to steal a listen like this, one on top of another" - so Sufyān demonstrated this with his hand, he held up his hand, and separated its fingers "he hears the word, then he conveys it to the one below him, then the other one conveys it to the one below him until it is conveyed upon the tongue of the magician or the fortuneteller. Sometimes it is struck by a shooting star before it reaches them, and sometimes it reaches them without being struck. Then they add a hundred lies to it. So it is said, 'Didn't he say such and such would happen to us today?' In this way they believe him because of the word that was heard from the heavens.'"[38]

وعن النواس بن سمعان رضي الله عنه قال: قال رسول الله صلى الله عليه وسلم: (إذا أراد الله تعالى أن يوحي بالأمر تكلم بالوحي أخذت السماوات منه رجفة — أو قال رعدة — شديدة خوفاً من الله عز وجل. فإذا سمع ذلك أهل السماوات صعقوا وخرّوا سجداً. فيكون أول من يرفع رأسه جبريل، فيكلمه الله من وحيه بما أراد، ثم يمر جبريل على الملائكة، كلما مر بسماء سأله ملائكتها: ماذا قال ربنا يا جبريل؟ فيقول جبريل: قال الحق وهو العلي الكبير فيقولون كلهم مثل ما قال جبريل. فينتهي جبريل بالوحي إلى حيث أمره الله عز وجل).

Al-Nawās bin Sama'ān, may Allāh be pleased with him, said that the Prophet (ﷺ) said; "When Allāh (ﷻ) intends to reveal a matter, He speaks the revelation. When He has spoken, the heavens are struck with severe trembling - or he said - severe thundering, out of fear of Allāh (ﷻ). So when the inhabitants of the heavens hear that, they are stunned and fall down prostrating to Allāh. The first to raise his head is Jibrīl. Allāh tells him the revelation that He has willed, then Jibrīl passes by the angels through each heaven with the angels asking him, 'O Jibrīl! What has our Lord said?' Jibrīl says, 'The truth, and He is the most High the most Great.' Then all of them say as Jibrīl said. Then Jibrīl delivers the revelation where Allāh (ﷻ) commanded him to...." [39]

فيه مسائل:

الأولى: تفسير الآية.

الثانية: ما فيها من الحجة على إبطال الشرك، خصوصاً من تعلق على الصالحين، وهي الآية التي قيل: إنها تقطع عروق شجرة الشرك من القلب.

الثالثة: تفسير قوله: (قالوا الحق وهو العلي الكبير)

[38] Al-Bukhārī.

[39] This ḥadīth is recorded by Ibn Jarīr, Ibn Khuzaymah, Ibn Abū Ḥātim and Al-Ṭabarānī. (See *Taysīr al-'Azīz*)It was graded weak by al-Albānī in his notes on Ibn Abū 'Āṣim's *Al-Sunnah*.

الرابعة: سبب سؤالهم عن ذلك.

الخامسة: أن جبريل هو الذي يجيبهم بعد ذلك بقوله: (قال كذا وكذا).

السادسة: ذكر أن أول من يرفع رأسه جبريل.

السابعة: أن يقول لأهل السماوات كلهم، لأنهم يسألونه.

الثامنة: أن الغشي يعم أهل السماوات كلهم.

التاسعة: ارتجاف السماوات لكلام الله.

العاشرة: أن جبريل هو الذي ينتهي بالوحي إلى حيث أمره الله.

الحادية عشرة: ذكر استراق الشياطين.

الثانية عشرة: صفة ركوب بعضهم بعضاً.

الثالثة عشرة: إرسال الشهب.

الرابعة عشرة: أنه تارة يدركه الشهاب قبل أن يلقيها، وتارة يلقيها في أذن وليه من الإنس قبل أن يدركه.

الخامسة عشرة: كون الكاهن يصدق بعض الأحيان.

السادسة عشرة: كونه يكذب معها مائة كذبة.

السابعة عشرة: أنه لم يصدق كذبه إلا بتلك الكلمة التي سمعت من السماء.

الثامنة عشرة: قبول النفوس للباطل، كيف يتعلقون بواحدة ولا يعتبرون بمائة؟!.
التاسعة عشرة: كونهم يلقي بعضهم إلى بعض تلك الكلمة ويحفظونها ويستدلون بها.

العشرون: إثبات الصفات خلافاً للأشعرية المعطلة.

الحادية والعشرون: التصريح بأن تلك الرجفة والغشي كانا خوفاً من الله عز وجل.

الثانية والعشرون: أنهم يخرون لله سجداً.

Important Points

1. The explanation of the *āyah*.
2. What it contains of proof of the futility of *shirk*. Specifically, depending upon the righteous, and they call this *āyah* the one that rips the roots of *shirk's* tree from the heart.
3. Explanation of the *āyah* "They say, 'The truth! And He is the most High the most Great.'"
4. The reason for their being asked about that.
5. That after that, Jibrīl answers by saying, "He said such and such."
6. Mentioning that the first to raise his head is Jibrīl.
7. That he says this to all of the inhabitants of the heavens because they ask him.
8. That the shock effects all of the inhabitants of the heavens.
9. The heavens shaking from Allāh's words.
10. That Jibrīl is the one who delivers the revelation to where Allāh commands.
11. Mention of the *shayatīn* eavesdropping.
12. Their mounting one above another.
13. Sending the shooting stars.
14. That sometimes the shooting star strikes before it is conveyed, and sometimes it is conveyed to the ear of his friend among humans before it strikes him.
15. That the fortuneteller sometimes tells the truth.
16. That he tells one hundred lies with that.
17. That his lies would never contain any truth without the words he heard from the heavens.
18. The souls' acceptance of false statements. How they will depend upon one, and not consider the other hundred.
19. That they pass the word down from one to the other, each retaining it and augmenting it.
20. Confirmation of the attributes, contrary to the denials of the

Ashʿarīyah.

21. That the thundering and shaking are due to fear of Allāh (ﷻ).
22. That they fall, prostrating to Allāh.

Commentary by *ʿAllāmah* al-Saʿdī

Allāh (ﷻ) said; "Until when terror leaves their hearts, and they are asked; 'What did your Lord say?' They respond, 'The truth! And He is the most High, the most Great.'" (*Sabā'* 34:23)

This is another magnificent proof of the obligation of *tawḥīd* and the futility of *shirk*. It is a reminder of the texts that demonstrate the Lords might and greatness which vanquishes and melts away the honour of the most important creatures, it humiliates the angels and the entire universe both high and low. They are utterly incapable when they hear His words or when He reveals some of His greatness and majesty. The entire creation is subdued by His might, acknowledging His greatness and majesty, practising humility for Him, in awe of Him. So whoever is this impressive, then He is the Lord whom none deserves worship, praise, exaltation, gratitude, honouring, and deification except Him. Any other than Him deserves none of this. Just as absolute perfection, might, greatness, and sheerly majestic attributes and absolute wonder - all of it belongs to Allāh - then it is not possible that other than He be attributed with any of it. So in this way - apparent and inward worship - all of it is His exclusive right, a right that none is partner to in any sense at all.

Chapter 17

الشفاعـــة

Intercession

وقول الله تعالى: (وأنذر به الذين يخافون أن يحشروا إلى ربهم ليس لهم من دونه ولي ولا شفيع) وقوله: (قل لله الشفاعة جميعاً) وقوله: (من ذا الذي يشفع عنده إلا بإذنه) وقوله: (وكم من ملك في السموات لا تغني شفاعتهم شيئاً إلا من بعد أن يأذن الله لمن يشاء ويرضى) وقوله: (قل ادعوا الذين زعمتم من دون الله لا يملكون مثقال ذرة في ا لسموات ولا في الأرض) الآيتين.

Allāh (ﷻ) said; "And warn with it those who fear being gathered before their Lord; there is no guardian or intercessor for them other than He." (*al-An'ām* 6: 51) And; "Say: 'All intercession is Allāh's.'" (*al-Zumar* 39:44) And; "Who is it that intercedes with Him without His permission?" (*al-Baqarah* 2:255) And His (ﷻ) saying; "And how many angels are there in the heavens, nothing guarantees me of their intercession, except whom Allāh gives permission to as He wills, and accepts." (*al-Najm* 53:26) And; "Say: 'Call those other than Allāh whom you claim! They do not have even a grain's worth of authority in the heavens and the Earth." (*al-Sabā'* 34:22-23)

قال أبو العباس: نفى الله عما سواه كل ما يتعلق به المشركون، فنفى أن يكون لغيره ملك أو قسط منه، أو يكون عوناً لله، و لم يبق إلا الشفاعة، فبين أنها لا تنفع إلا لمن أذن له الرب، كما قال تعالى: (ولا يشفعون إلا لمن ارتضى) فهذه الشفاعة التي يظنها المشركون، هي منتفية يوم القيامة كما نفاها القرآن، وأخبر النبي صلى الله عليه وسلم أنه يأتي فيسجد لربه ويحمده، لا يبدأ بالشفاعة أولاً، ثم يقال له: ارفع رأسك، وقل يسمع، وسل تُعط، واشفع تُشفع.

Abū al-'Abbās [Ibn Taymiyyah] said; "Allāh negated everything other than Him that the *mushrikīn* relied upon. He negated authority and power from other than Him, nor are there any assistants to Allāh. Only the possibility of their intercession remains. Then He clarified that it would not be of any benefit except for whom the Lord permitted it. As He said; "And none intercedes except for whom He allows." (*al-Anbiyā'* 21:28) The intercession which the *mushrikīn* believed in is the one that is denied on the Day of Resurrection, just as it is negated by the *Qur'ān*. The Prophet (ﷺ) informed that he, '...comes and prostrates to His Lord, and praises Him' - not first beginning with intercession - then it will be said of him, 'Raise your head. Speak and be heard, ask and be given, intercede and it will be granted.'

وقال له أبو هريرة: من أسعد الناس بشفاعتك يا رسول الله؟ قال: (من قال لا إله إلا الله خالصاً من قلبه) فتلك الشفاعة لأهل الإخلاص بإذن الله، ولا تكون لمن أشرك بالله.

And Abū Hurayrah asked him (ﷺ); 'Who is the luckiest person to receive your intercession?' He said, 'Whoever says *Lā ilāha illa Allāh* sincerely in his heart.' This is the intercession for the people of sincerity by Allāh's permission, it is not for the one who associates with Allāh.

وحقيقته: أن الله سبحانه هو الذي يتفضل على أهل الإخلاص فيغفر لهم بواسطة دعاء من أذن له أن يشفع، ليكرمه وينال المقام المحمود.

The reality is that Allāh (ﷻ) is the one who grants forgiveness for the people of sincerity, so He forgives them by means of the supplication of the one who He grants permission to intercede, as an honour to him, and granting him the most praiseworthy status.

فالشفاعة التي نفاها القرآن ما كان فيها شرك، ولهذا أثبت الشفاعة بإذنه في مواضع، وقد بيَّن النبي صلى الله عليه وسلم أنها لا تكون إلا لأهل التوحيد والإخلاص. انتهى كلامه.

So the intercession which the *Qur'ān* negates in some places is that of *shirk*, and similarly it confirmed the intercession with His permission in some places. And the Prophet (ﷺ) explained that this would not be issued except for the people of *tawḥīd* and sincerity."

فيه مسائل:

الأولى: تفسير الآيات.

الثانية: صفة الشفاعة المنفية.

الثالثة: صفة الشفاعة المثبتة.

الرابعة: ذكر الشفاعة الكبرى، وهي المقام المحمود.

الخامسة: صفة ما يفعله صلى الله عليه وسلم، وأنه لا يبدأ بالشفاعة أولاً، بل يسجد، فإذا أذن الله له شفع.

السادسة: من أسعد الناس بها؟.

السابعة: أنها لا تكون لمن أشرك بالله.

الثامنة: بيان حقيقتها.

Important Points

1. The explanation of the *āyāt*.
2. The description of the type of intercession that has been denied.
3. The description of the confirmed type of intercession.
4. Mentioning the great intercession, that is the most praised status (*al-maqām al-maḥmūd*).
5. The description of what he (ﷺ) will do, in that he does not begin simply with interceding, rather he prostrates, then he is permitted to intercede.
6. Who is the luckiest person to receive it?
7. That it is not done for those who associate with Allāh.
8. The explanation of its reality.

Commentary by ʿ*Allāmah* al-Saʿdī

Intercession

The author only mentions intercession among these chapters because the *mushrikīn* defended their *shirk* and their calling upon the angels, prophets and *awliyā'* by saying,

"We know that they are just creatures without authority, but since they are honoured for their sake by Allāh, and granted a high position, we call on them to bring us nearer to Allāh, and so that they will intercede for us with Him. Just like one would do with the advisors of the kings or sultans, requesting them to mediate in order that their needs be taken care of and their problems solved."

This is the greatest of falsehoods. The great King of kings, the one who is feared by everyone, the one whom the entire creation is humiliated before - they have likened Him (ﷻ) to the needy kings, who depend upon their advisors and ministers to maintain their rule and support their power.

Allāh falsified this claim. He explained that all intercession is His, just like all authority is His. None intercedes with Him without His permission, and He does not permit intercession except for him whose saying and actions He is pleased with, and He will not be pleased with anyone unless he practices *tawḥīd*, and performs his deeds sincerely for Him.

He explained that the *mushrik* gets no part or parcel of intercession. He (ﷻ) clarified that the confirmed intercession, which occurs only by His permission - is reserved specifically for intercession on behalf of the people of sincerity, and that all of it comes from Him, from His mercy, as an honour for the intercessor, it is His mercy and pardon for the one interceded for. This is the type of intercession that in reality is praiseworthy, and this is the one which He permits for Muḥammad (ﷺ), thereby honouring him with the most praiseworthy status.

This is what both the Book and the *Sunnah* have explained about the details of intercession. And the author, may Allāh have mercy upon him, mentioned the statement of Shaykh Taqi al-Dīn (Ibn Taymiyyah) for this topic, and it is clear enough.

So the goal of this chapter is to mention the texts proving the futility of every means and cause that the *mushrikīn* depended upon their gods for, and that they in fact have no authority at all, not the least portion, nor share, nor assistance, nor maintenance of it, nor the ability to intercede for anything at all. All of that belongs to Allāh alone, so that necessitates that He alone be the one worshipped.

Chapter 18

قول الله تعالى: إنك لا تهدي من أحببت

Allāh's (ﷻ) saying, "It is not you who guides whom you love..."

قول الله تعالى: (إنك لا تهدي من أحببت) الآية.

Allāh's (ﷻ) saying, "It is not you who guides whom you love..." (*al-Qaṣaṣ* 28: 56)

وفي (الصحيح) عن ابن المسيب عن أبيه قال: (لما حضرت أبا طالب الوفاة جاءه رسول الله صلى الله عليه وسلم وعنده عبد الله بن أبي أمية وأبو جهل، فقال له: (يا عم، قل: لا إله إلا الله، كلمة أحاج لك بها عند الله) فقالا له: أترغب عن ملة عبد المطلب؟ فأعاد عليه النبي صلى الله عليه وسلم، فأعادا فكان آخر ما قال: هو على ملة عبد المطلب وأبى أن يقول: لا إله إلا الله. فقال النبي صلى الله عليه وسلم: (لأستغفرن لك ما لم أنه عنك) فأنزل الله عز وجل(ما كان للنبي والذين آمنوا أن يستغفروا للمشركين) الآية. وأنزل الله في أبي طالب: (إنك لا تهدي من أحببت ولكن الله يهدي من يشاء) .

In the *Ṣaḥīḥ*, it is recorded from Ibn al-Musayyab from his father saying; "When death came to Abū Ṭālib, Allāh's Messenger (ﷺ) came to visit him, and 'Abdullāh bin 'Umayyah and Abū Jahl were present. He (ﷺ) said, 'O Uncle, say *Lā ilāha illa Allāh*, a statement by which I will plead for you before Allāh.' They said, 'Have you left the religion of 'Abd al-Muṭṭalib?' So the Prophet (ﷺ) repeated what he said. The last thing he said was, '"I remain upon the religion of 'Abd al-Muṭṭalib, and I refuse to say *Lā ilāha illa Allāh*.' The Prophet (ﷺ) said, 'Then I will seek forgiveness for you as long as I am not forbidden from doing so.' So Allāh revealed the *āyah*; 'It is not for the Prophet and those who believe to seek forgiveness for the *mushrikīn*, even if they be their closest relatives.'" (*al-Tawbah* 9: 113) And Allāh revealed about Abū Ṭālib; "'It is not for you to guide whom you love, but Allāh guides whom He wills...'"(*al-Qaṣaṣ* 28:56)[40]

فيه مسائل:

الأولى: تفسير قوله: (إنك لا تهدي من أحببت ولكن الله يهدي من يشاء) .

الثانية: تفسير قوله: (ما كان للنبي والذين آمنوا أن يستغفروا للمشركين) الآية.

الثالثة: وهي المسألة الكبرى - تفسير قوله صلى الله عليه وسلم: (قل: لا إله إلا الله) بخلاف ما عليه من يدعي العلم.

الرابعة: أن أبا جهل ومن معه يعرفون مراد النبي صلى الله عليه وسلم إذ قال للرجل: (قل لا إله إلا الله). فقبح الله من أبو جهل أعلم منه بأصل الإسلام.

الخامسة: جدّه صلى الله عليه وسلم ومبالغته في إسلام عمه.

السادسة: الرد على من زعم إسلام عبد المطلب وأسلافه.

السابعة: كونه صلى الله عليه وسلم استغفر له فلم يغفر له، بل نهي عن ذلك.

الثامنة: مضرة أصحاب السوء على الإنسان.

التاسعة: مضرة تعظيم الأسلاف والأكابر.

العاشرة: الشبهة للمبطلين في ذلك، لاستدلال أبي جهل بذلك.

الحادية عشرة: الشاهد لكون الأعمال بالخواتيم، لأنه لو قالها لنفعته.

الثانية عشرة: التأمل في كبر هذه الشبهة في قلوب الضالين، لأن في القصة أنهم لم يجادلوه إلا بها، مع مبالغته صلى الله عليه وسلم وتكريره، فلأجل عظمتها ووضوحها عندهم، اقتصروا عليها.

[40] Al-Bukhārī and Muslim.

Important Points

1. Explanation of the *āyah* "It is not for you to guide whom you love, but Allāh guides whom He wills..."
2. Explanation of His (ﷻ) saying, "It is not for the Prophet and the believers to seek forgiveness for the *mushrikīn* even if they are their closest relatives, after it has become clear to them that they are the inhabitants of the Fire."
3. The great issue of the explanation of his saying, "Say; '*Lā illāha illa Allāh*'" In that it contradicts the claims of some about its knowledge (is that knowing its meaning is enough).
4. That Abū Jahl and those with him were aware of what it meant when the Prophet (ﷺ) said to someone, "Say; '*Lā illaha illā Allāh*'" May Allāh disgrace anyone who is less knowledgeable about the foundation of *Islām* than Abū Jahl.
5. His (ﷺ) seriousness and sense of responsibility to have his uncle submit.
6. The refutation of anyone who claims that 'Abd al-Muṭṭalib and his ancestors were Muslims.
7. That the Prophet (ﷺ) prayed for his (uncle's) forgiveness, but he was not forgiven, and that was forbidden.
8. The harmful effects that the evil ones have over people.
9. The harmful effects of exalting one's ancestors and elders.
10. That the custom of *jāhilīyyah* was to use the way of the ancestors as an argument unto itself.
11. Support for the fact that one's deeds depend upon their endings, because if he had said it, then it would have benefited him.
12. The important role that pride for ancestors in the hearts of the deviant plays in this problem, because the story indicates that this was the only thing they used as their argument, while he (ﷺ) continued coaxing him and repeating it, yet for the sake of their great honour for their ancestors, and their respect for them, they considered it sufficient enough to limit their argument to that.

Commentary by *ʿAllāmah* al-Saʿdī

Allāh's (ﷻ) saying; "It is not for you to guide whom you love, but Allāh guides whom He wills..."

This chapter corresponds to the previous one. Even though he (ﷺ) is as he is; the absolute best creature and the most honoured by Allāh and the nearest to Him, yet he is not able to guide whom he loves to the correct way. But all guidance is in the Hand of Allāh, He is the sole guide for the hearts, just as He is the sole Creator of the creatures, clarifying that He is the true God.

As for his saying; "Surely you (Muḥammad) guide to the straight path." (*Al-Shūra* 52) The meaning of guidance here is clarification, and that he (ﷺ) is the one who conveys the revelation from Allāh which guides the creatures.

Chapter 19

ما جاء أن سبب كفر بني آدم وتركهم دينهم هو الغلو في الصالحين

The cause of *kufr* for the children of Ādam, and their leaving their religion, is exaggerating over the righteous

وقول الله عز وجل: (يا أهل الكتاب لا تغلوا في دينكم) .

Allāh (ﷻ) said; "O people of the book! Do not exaggerate in your religion." (*al-Nisā'* 4: 171)

وفي (الصحيح) عن ابن عباس رضي الله عنهما في قول الله تعالى: (وقالوا لا تذرُنَّ آلهتكم ولا تذرُنَّ وداً ولا سواعاً ولا يغوث ويعوق ونسراً) قال: (هذه أسماء رجال صالحين من قوم نوح، فلما هلكوا أوحى الشيطان إلى قومهم أن انصبوا إلى مجالسهم التي كانوا يجلسون فيها أنصاباً وسموها بأسمائهم، ففعلوا، و لم تعبد، حتى إذا هلك أولئك ونسي العلم، عبدت).

It is reported in the *Ṣaḥīḥ* from Ibn ʿAbbās, may Allāh be pleased with them, regarding the saying of Allāh (ﷻ); "They say: 'Do not forsake your gods! Do not forsake Wadd nor Suwāʿ nor Yaghūth nor Nasr.'" (*Nūḥ* 71:23) He said, "...These are names of some of the righteous among the people of Nūḥ. When they passed away, *shayṭān* inspired their people to erect images of them at the places where they used to sit with them, and to place their names on them. So they did that, but they did not worship them until these people passed away. Then knowledge was lost and people began to worship them."[41]

---

[41] Al-Bukhārī.

وقال ابن القيم: قال غير واحد من السلف: لما ماتوا عكفوا على قبورهم ثم صوروا تماثيلهم، ثم طال عليهم الأمد فعبدوهم.

Ibn al-Qayyim said; "Others among the *salaf* said, 'When they died, they would spend much of their time staying at their grave sites, then they made images of them. After a long period of time passed they began worshipping them."

وعن عمر أن رسول الله صلى الله عليه وسلم قال: (لا تطروني كما أطرت النصارى ابن مريم، إنما أنا عبد، فقولوا: عبد الله ورسوله) [أخرجاه].

ʿUmar said, that Allāh's Messenger (ﷺ) said; "Do not aggrandize me as the Christians did with the son of Maryam. I am only a worshipper, so say, 'Allāh's worshipper and Messenger.'" They (al-Bukhārī and Muslim) recorded it.

وقال: قال رسول الله صلى الله عليه وسلم: (إياكم والغلو، فإنما أهلك من كان قبلكم الغلو).

He (ﷺ) said; "Beware of exaggeration! For it was only exaggeration that destroyed those before you."[42]

ولمسلم عن ابن مسعود أن رسول الله صلى الله عليه وسلم قال: (هلك المتنطعون) قالها ثلاثاً.

And with Muslim from Ibn Masʿūd, that Allāh's Messenger (ﷺ) said; "Those who go to extremes are ruined." He said it three times.

فيه مسائل:

الأولى: أن من فهم هذا الباب وبابين بعده، تبين له غربة الإسلام، ورأى من قدرة الله وتقليبه للقلوب العجب.

الثانية: معرفة أول شرك حدث على وجه الأرض أنه بشبهة الصالحين.

الثالثة: أول شيء غيّر به دين الأنبياء، وما سبب ذلك مع معرفة أن الله أرسلهم.

الرابعة: قبول البدع مع كون الشرائع والفطر تردها.

الخامسة: أن سبب ذلك كله مزج الحق بالباطل، فالأول: محبة الصالحين، والثاني: فعل أناس من أهل العلم والدين شيئاً أرادوا به خيراً، فظن من بعدهم أنهم أرادوا به غيره.

[42] Recorded by Aḥmad, al-Nasāʾī, Ibn Mājah and others via Ibn ʿAbbās (رضي الله عنهما). It was graded *ṣaḥīḥ* in *Ṣaḥīḥ al-Jāmiʿ* no. 2680, and *al-Ṣaḥīḥah* no. 1283.

السادسة: تفسير الآية التي في سورة نوح.

السابعة: جبلة الآدمي في كون الحق ينقص في قلبه، والباطل يزيد.

الثامنة: فيه شاهد لما نقل عن السلف أن البدعة سبب الكفر.

التاسعة: معرفة الشيطان بما تؤول إليه البدعة ولو حسن قصد الفاعل.

العاشرة: معرفة القاعدة الكلية، وهي النهي عن الغلو، ومعرفة ما يؤول إليه.

الحادية عشرة: مضرة العكوف على القبر لأجل عمل صالح.

الثانية عشرة: معرفة النهي عن التماثيل، والحكمة في إزالتها.

الثالثة عشرة: معرفة عظم شأن هذه القصة، وشدة الحاجة إليها مع الغفلة عنها.

الرابعة عشرة: وهي أعجب وأعجب: قراءتهم إياها في كتب التفسير والحديث، ومعرفتهم بمعنى الكلام، وكون الله حال بينهم وبين قلوبهم حتى اعتقدوا أن فعل قوم نوح هو أفضل العبادات، واعتقدوا أن ما نهى الله ورسوله عنه، فهو الكفر المبيح للدم والمال.

الخامسة عشرة: التصريح أنهم لم يريدوا إلا الشفاعة.

السادسة عشرة: ظنهم أن العلماء الذين صوروا الصور أرادوا ذلك.

السابعة عشرة: البيان العظيم في قوله صلى الله عليه وسلم: (لا تطروني كما أطرت النصارى ابن مريم) فصلوات الله وسلامه على من بلغ البلاغ المبين.

الثامنة عشرة: نصيحته إيانا بهلاك المتنطعين.

التاسعة عشرة: التصريح بأنها لم تعبد حتى نسي العلم، ففيها بيان معرفة قدر وجوده ومضرة فقده.

العشرون: أن سبب فقد العلم موت العلماء.

Important Points

1. Whoever understands this chapter, and the two after it, then the uniqueness of *Islām* will become clear to him. He will see some of Allāh's ability, and the amazing way that He changes hearts.
2. Knowing that the first *shirk* to appear on Earth resulted from confusion about the righteous.
3. The first thing to change the religion of the prophets, and what caused it, even though it was known that it was Allāh who sent them.
4. The acceptance of innovation even though legislation and instinct would reject it.
5. That the cause of all of this is mixing the truth with falsehood. The first was love for the righteous, and the second was what some people among the knowledgeable did intending only good by it. But those after them thought they intended something else.
6. The explanation of the *āyah* in *Sūrah Nūḥ*.
7. The nature of man; the truth diminishes in his heart, while falsehood increases.
8. In this is testimony for reports from the *salaf* that innovation is the cause of *kufr*. And that it is more beloved to *Iblīs* than disobedience, because disobedience is repented from, while innovation is not.
9. *Shayṭān's* knowledge of what innovation leads to even when the intention is good.
10. Learning the general principle, and that is the prohibition of exaggeration and knowing what it leads to.
11. The harm of devoting one's time by graves for the sake of righteous deeds.
12. The prohibition of images and the wisdom behind eradicating them.
13. Being aware of the importance of this story, and emphasising the need for it since it is overlooked.
14. It is the most remarkable wonder, they read it in the books of *tafsīr* and ḥadīth, and they understand the meanings of the words, but Allāh has put a screen between this and their hearts. They believe

that what the people of Nūḥ did was the best kind of worship, and they believe that only the type of disbelief that makes blood and wealth lawful was prohibited by Allāh and His Messenger.

15. The clarification that they only intended intercession by their acts.
16. They believed that the people of knowledge who made the images had the same intent.
17. The great clarification of his saying; "Do not aggrandize me as the Christians did with the son of Maryam." So may Allāh mention and grant peace to he who conveyed the message clearly.
18. His warning to us about the destruction of the excessive.
19. The clarification that they did not begin their worship of the images until after knowledge had vanished. This indicates the necessity of an awareness of the importance of its presence, and the harms of its absence.
20. That the cause of knowledge vanishing is the death of the scholars.

Commentary by *ʿAllāmah* al-Saʿdī

The cause of disbelief for the children of Ādam and their leaving their religion is exaggeration over the righteous.

Exaggeration is to exceed the boundaries by rendering some part of a right due to Allāh alone to the righteous. None has any share at all in Allāh's rights, He is the absolutely perfect, the absolutely independent, and the absolute authority in every sense. He is the one who none is worthy of the right of worship or deification other than Him. So whoever exaggerates with any creature, such that he makes an image of it, then he is equating these things to the Lord of the worlds, and that is the most dangerous *shirk*.

Know that rights are of three types:

1. Rights particularly for Allāh, there being no equal with Him in them. Like deifying Him and worshipping Him alone with no partners, longing and turning to Him with fear, hope, and love.

2. Rights particular to His messengers. That is, honouring them, respecting them, and upholding their particular rights.

3. Shared rights, that is faith in Allāh and in His Messenger, obedience to Allāh and to His Messenger, love of Allāh and of His Messenger. Here the right is Allāh's in its foundation, and for His Messenger in accordance with the right of Allāh.

So the people of truth recognize the distinction between these three types of rights, they establish worship of Allāh sincerely making the religion for Him, and they maintain the rights of the His messengers and the *awliyā* based upon their different stations and ranks. And Allāh knows best.

Chapter 20

ما جاء من التغليظ فيمن عبد الله عند قبر رجل صالح فكيف إذا عبده

The detriment of the one who worships Allāh at someone's grave, So how about when he worships its inhabitant?

في (الصحيح) عن عائشة رضي الله عنها أن أم سلمة ذكرت لرسول الله صلى الله عليه وسلم كنيسة رأتها في أرض الحبشة وما فيها من الصور. فقال: (أولئك إذا مات فيهم الرجل الصالح أو العبد الصالح بنوا على قبره مسجداً، وصوروا فيه تلك الصور أولئك شرار الخلق عند الله) فهؤلاء جمعوا بين الفتنتين، فتنة القبور، وفتنة التماثيل.

In the *Ṣaḥīḥ*, it is recorded from ʿĀ'ishah, that Umm Salamah told Allāh's Messenger (ﷺ) about a church she saw in the land of al-Ḥabashah, and about the images that in contained. So he said, "These are the kind of people, that when a righteous man among them died, or - a righteous worshipper - they built a *masjid* over his grave, and they made those images in it. Those are the most evil creatures to Allāh."[43]

[Ibn Taymiyyah comments:] "So these people combined two *fitnahs*, the *fitnah* of the graves, and the *fitnah* of images."[44]

ولهما عنها قالت: (لما نُزل برسول الله صلى الله عليه وسلم طفق يطرح خميصة له على وجهه، فإذا اغتم بها كشفها، فقال ـــ وهو كذلك ـــ : «لعنة الله على اليهود والنصارى، اتخذوا قبور أنبيائهم مساجد» يحذر ما صنعوا، ولولا ذلك أبرز قبره، غير أنه خشي أن يتخذ مسجداً، [أخرجاه].

---

[43] Al-Bukhārī, Muslim and others.

[44] This is a quote from Ibn Taymiyah.

They also recorded that she said, "When [death] came to Allāh's Messenger (ﷺ) he draped part of his *khamīṣah* over his face. When he had trouble breathing he removed it saying: 'Allāh's curse be upon the Jews and the Christians, they took their prophets' graves as *masjids*,' warning against what they did. If not for that, then his grave would be outside. But he feared that it would be taken as a *masjid*." Recorded by al-Bukhari and Muslim.

ولمسلم عن جندب بن عبد الله قال: سمعت النبي صلى الله عليه وسلم قبل أن يموت بخمس وهو يقول: (إني أبرأ إلى الله أن يكون لي منكم خليل، فإن الله قد اتخذني خليلاً، كما اتخذ إبراهيم خليلاً، ولو كنت متخذاً من أمتي خليلاً، لاتخذت أبا بكر خليلاً، ألا وإن من كان قبلكم كانوا يتخذون قبور أنبيائهم مساجد، ألا فلا تتخذوا القبور مساجد، فإني أنهاكم عن ذلك).

Jundab bin 'Abdullāh said, "Five days before he died, I heard the Prophet (ﷺ) saying; 'Surely I am innocent before Allāh of having taken a *khalīl* from among you. For surely Allāh has taken me as His *khalīl*, just as He took Ibrāhīm as His *khalīl*. Yet if I were to have taken a *khalīl* from among my *ummah*, then I would take Abū Bakr as a *khalīl*. Truly those before you would take their prophets graves as *masjids*. So do not take the graves as *masjids*. I have certainly forbidden you from that'" (Muslim).

فقد نهى عنه في آخر حياته، ثم إنه لعن — وهو في السياق — من فعله، والصلاة عندها من ذلك، وإن لم يُبْنَ مسجد، وهو معنى قولها: خشي أن يتخذ مسجداً، فإن الصحابة لم يكونوا ليبنوا حول قبره مسجداً، وكل موضع قصدت الصلاة فيه فقد اتخذ مسجداً، بل كل موضع يصلى فيه يسمى مسجداً، كما قال صلى الله عليه وسلم: (جعلت لي الأرض مسجداً وطهوراً).

He (ﷺ) forbade that on other occasions. Then, he cursed those who do that, as reported. This includes prayer at their sites even if they are not inside *masjids*. This is the meaning of the saying, "He feared that it would be taken as a *masjid*." So the companions would not build a *masjid* over his grave. And every place intended for prayer is a place that is "taken as a *masjid*." Rather, any place prayed in is called a *masjid*. As he (ﷺ) said, "...The Earth has been made a *masjid* for me and a purifier...."[45]

ولأحمد بسند جيد عن ابن مسعود رضي الله عنه مرفوعاً: (إن من شرار الناس من تدركهم الساعة وهم أحياء والذين يتخذون القبور مساجد) [رواه أبو حاتم في صحيحه].

[45] Al-Bukhārī and Muslim.

And with Aḥmad is a good *marfū*ʿ chain from Ibn Masʿūd, (ﷺ); "Of the evilest people are those who meet the [Final] Hour living, and those who take the graves as *masjids*." It is recorded by Abū Ḥātim [i.e. Ibn Ḥibbān] in his *Ṣaḥīḥ*.[46]

فيه مسائل:

الأولى: ما ذكر الرسول صلى الله عليه وسلم فيمن بنى مسجداً يعبد الله فيه عند قبر رجل صالح، ولو صحت نية الفاعل.

الثانية: النهي عن التماثيل، وغلظ الأمر في ذلك.

الثالثة: العبرة في مبالغته صلى الله عليه وسلم في ذلك. كيف بيّن لهم هذا أولاً، ثم قبل موته بخمس قال ما قال، ثم لما كان في السياق لم يكتف بما تقدم.

الرابعة: نهيه عن فعله عند قبره قبل أن يوجد القبر.

الخامسة: أنه من سنن اليهود والنصارى في قبور أنبيائهم.

السادسة: لعنه إياهم على ذلك.

السابعة: أن مراده صلى الله عليه وسلم تحذيره إيانا عن قبره.

الثامنة: العلة في عدم إبراز قبره.

التاسعة: في معنى اتخاذها مسجداً.

العاشرة: أنه قرن بين من اتخذها مسجداً وبين من تقوم عليهم الساعة، فذكر الذريعة إلى الشرك قبل وقوعه مع خاتمته.

الحادية عشرة: ذكره في خطبته قبل موته بخمس: الرد على الطائفتين اللتين هما أشرّ أهل البدع، بل أخرجهم بعض السلف من الثنتين والسبعين فرقة، وهم الرافضة والجهمية. وبسبب الرافضة حدث الشرك وعبادة القبور، وهم أول من

[46] This ḥadīth's chain is *ḥasan*. It was also recorded by Ibn Khuzaymah, Aḥmad and others. Al-Bukhārī has quoted a *muʿallaq* form of the first half of it in the Book of *Fitn* of his *Ṣaḥīḥ*. See *Ṣaḥīḥ Ibn Khuzaymah* (no. 789 notes by al-ʿAẓami with Al-Albānī consulting), and *Tashnīf al-Adhān* no. 1085.

بنى عليها المساجد.

الثانية عشرة: ما بلي به صلى الله عليه وسلم من شدة النزع.

الثالثة عشرة: ما أكرم به من الخلّة.

الرابعة عشرة: التصريح بأنها أعلى من المحبة.

الخامسة عشرة: التصريح بأن الصديق أفضل الصحابة.

السادسة عشرة: الإشارة إلى خلافته.

Important Points

1. The Messenger's (ﷺ) warning about the construction of *masjids* to worship Allāh at the graves of righteous people, even if the one doing so has a good intention.
2. The prohibition of images, and the intensity of the command in that regard.
3. His (ﷺ) elucidation when conveying this, in that he first explained it to them, then five days before he died he said as he did. Then later, he was still not content that what he had said earlier was sufficient.
4. He forbade from doing such at his grave, before he had a grave.
5. That this is among the *sunan* of the Jews and Christians regarding their prophets graves.
6. He cursed them because of that.
7. His intentional warning for us about his grave.
8. The reason for his grave not being in the open.
9. The meaning of "taking as a *masjid*."
10. That those who take them as such, and those who meet the Hour were mentioned together. So he mentioned the means of *shirk* before its occurrence, while he was dying.
11. He mentioned this five days before his death. In this is a refutation of two parties whom amount to the most evil of the people of innovation. Rather some scholars have even considered them to be

removed from the seventy-two sects. These are the *Rāfiḍah*, and the *Jahimiyyah*. Because it was the *Rāfiḍah* that began the *shirk* of worshipping at the graves. And they were the first who built *masjids* upon them.

12. What he was tried with during the pain of death.
13. That he was distinguished with the status of *khullah*. (i.e., being Allāh's *khalīl*)
14. The clarification that this is an honour greater than love.
15. The clarification that *al-Ṣiddīq* was the most virtuous of the Companions.
16. Indicating his *khilāfah*.

For *ʿAllāmah* al-Saʿdi's Commentary See Next Chapter

Chapter 21

ما جاء أن الغلو في قبور الصالحين يصيرها أوثاناً تعبد من دون الله

Exaggeration at the graves of the righteous turns them into idols for worship besides Allāh.

روى مالك في (الموطأ): أن رسول الله صلى الله عليه وسلم قال: (اللهم لا تجعل قبري وثناً يعبد، اشتد غضب الله على قوم اتخذوا قبور أنبيائهم مساجد)

Mālik records in *al-Muwaṭṭa'* that Allāh's Messenger (ﷺ) said; "O Allāh! Do not let my grave become an idol that is worshipped. Allāh's wrath is intensified upon people taking their prophets graves as *masjids*."[47]

ولابن جرير بسنده عن سفيان عن منصور عن مجاهد: (أفرءيتم اللات والعزى) قال: كان يلت لهم السويق فمات فعكفوا على قبره، وكذلك قال أبو الجوزاء عن ابن عباس: كان يلت السويق للحاج.

From Ibn Jarīr with a chain to Sufyān, from Manṣūr, from Mujāhid, "Have you seen al-Lāt and al-'Uzzā..." (*al-Najm* 53:20) He said; "He used to prepare *sawīq* for them. Then he died. So they devoted their time by his grave."[48] And Abū al-Jawzā' said similarly from Ibn 'Abbās, "He prepared *sawīq* during Hajj."[49]

---

[47] Also recorded by Aḥmad, al-Bazzār and others. Al-Albānī graded it *ṣaḥīḥ* in *Tahdhīr al-Sājid* no.11.

[48] Similar is recorded by Sa'īd bin Manṣūr.

[49] Recorded by al-Bukhārī.

وعن ابن عباس رضي الله عنهما قال: لعن رسول الله صلى الله عليه وسلم زائرات القبور، والمتخذين عليها المساجد والسرج. [رواه أهل السنن].

Ibn ʿAbbās, may Allāh be pleased with them, said, "Allāh's Messenger (ﷺ) cursed the women visitors of the graves, and those who take them as *masjids* and illuminate them." Recorded by the *Sunan* compilers.[50]

فيه مسائل:

الأولى: تفسير الأوثان.

الثانية: تفسير العبادة.

الثالثة: أنه صلى الله عليه وسلم لم يستعذ إلا مما يخاف وقوعه.

الرابعة: قرنه بهذا اتخاذ قبور الأنبياء مساجد.

الخامسة: ذكر شدة الغضب من الله.

السادسة: وهي من أهمها – معرفة صفة عبادة اللات التي هي من أكبر الأوثان.

السابعة: معرفة أنه قبر رجل صالح.

الثامنة: أنه اسم صاحب القبر، وذكر معنى التسمية.

التاسعة: لعنه زَوَّارَات القبور.

العاشرة: لعنه من أسرجها.

---

[50] Recorded by Al-Tirmidhī, Abū Dāwūd, and al-Nasā'ī and others and it is weak with this wording. The first part (expressing the curse upon women who visit graves) is authentic, recorded by Ibn, Mājah, Al-Tirmidhī and others. *Ṣaḥīḥ Sunan Al-Tirmidhī* no. 843, *Ṣaḥīḥ al-Jāmiʿ* no. 5109, *Silsilat al-Ahādīth al-Ḍaʿīfah* no. 225. See *Taysīr al-ʿAzīz al-Ḥamīd*, and *Fatḥ al-Majīd* for important quotes from scholars about the evil of illuminating the buildings over graves. Shaykh al-Albānī has pointed out that although there is no authentic ḥadīth mentioning the curse for it, it remains an innovation nevertheless (*al-Ḍaʿīfah*). As for the curse upon the women who visit the graves, this is to be understood as a curse upon those women who frequently visit the graves, not as a prohibition of them visiting the graves at all. This is the view that rectifies the different ḥadīths, and it is in accordance with the understanding of ʿĀ'ishah (رضي الله عنها). She was questioned in this regard when she visited her brother's grave. She said that the Prophet (ﷺ) "forbade us from visiting the graves, then he commanded it." See *Aḥkām al-Janā'iz* by Al-Albānī for the complete discussion of this matter.

Important Points

1. The explanation of the meaning of word *awthān* (idols)
2. The explanation of the meaning of worship.
3. That he (ﷺ) was warning against what he feared would actually occur.
4. He coupled this with taking the prophets graves as *masjids*.
5. Mentioning the intensity of Allāh's wrath.
6. Of the most important points is learning the origin of Lāt's worship, and that this was one of the most important idols.
7. Knowing that it's origin is the grave of a righteous person.
8. That it is the name of a person in a grave, and mentioning the origin of its name [that is *latta* - to mix].
9. Cursing the women who visit graves.
10. Cursing those who illuminate them.

Commentary by *ʿAllāmah* al-Saʿdī

What is said about the detriment of the one who worships Allāh at someone's grave, so how about when he worships its inhabitant? What is said that exaggeration at the graves of the righteous turns them into idols for worship other than Allāh.

What the author mentions in these two chapters becomes clear with the details of what is done at the graves of the righteous and others. Such behaviour falls into two categories; the allowed and the prohibited.

The allowed is whatever is mentioned as lawful by the *sharīʿah* about visiting graves. This is governed by the rule that one does not take up travelling to do so, and that he is visiting the graves of Muslims who followed the *sunnah*. So by his supplications for these people - his uncles, his relatives, and those whom he knew personally - he is doing some good for them in particular, by supplications that seek pardon for them, forgiveness and mercy. And he accomplishes good for himself by following the *sunnah* and being reminded of the Hereafter and contemplating such matters.

The prohibited type consists of two categories;

1. The prohibited avenues that lead to *shirk* like touching the grave and seeking a means to be closer to Allāh because of the grave's inhabitant. Performing *ṣalāh* at the grave, decorating it and enshrining it with a structure, and any such exaggeration with it or its inhabitant, that does not quite reach the level of worship.

2. Major *shirk*, like supplicating to the inhabitants of the grave, or seeking their help and making some requests from them regarding this life or the Hereafter. This is major *shirk*, and it is this that the worshippers of the idols do with their idols.

There is no difference here whether the one who does that believes that those in the grave are able to bring about the outcome he seeks, or whether they are used as intermediaries with Allāh. It was indeed the *mushrikīn* who said,

> "We do not worship them except to bring us nearer to Allāh." (*al-Zumar* 43: 3)

And;

> "They say, 'These people intercede for us with Allāh.'" (*Yūnus* 10:18)

Whoever claims that one has not committed *kufr* by calling upon the inhabitants of the grave unless and until he thinks that they control the benefit and can protect him from harm- and that (a person has not committed *kufr* if he) believes that Allāh is the one who does this, but that the graves' inhabitants are simply a means between them and Allāh whom they call upon and seek from - then he has also committed *kufr*.

He who makes such a claim has certainly lied against what comes in the Book and the *Sunnah*, and what the *ummah* has agreed upon, which is that whoever calls on other than Allāh then he is a *mushrik* disbeliever in either of the two cases mentioned. Whether he believes that those called upon are in control or simply intermediaries. And this is well known by necessity in the religion of *Islām*.

So it is necessary for you to recognise this categorisation in order to discern the importance of this chapter, to see the harms and *fitnahs* that result from this, and none is saved from its *fitnah* except for the one who is aware of the truth and adheres to it.

Chapter 22

ما جاء في حماية المصطفى صلى الله عليه وسلم جناب التوحيد وسده كل طريق يوصل إلى الشرك

What has been reported about *al-Muṣṭafā's* (ﷺ) protection of *Tawḥīd* and his closing every way that leads to *shirk*

وقول الله تعالى: (لقد جاءكم رسول من أنفسكم) الآية.

Allāh (ﷻ) said; "A Messenger has come to you from among yourselves." (*al-Tawbah* 9:128)

عن أبي هريرة رضي الله عنه قال: قال رسول الله صلى الله عليه وسلم: (لا تجعلوا بيوتكم قبوراً، ولا تجعلوا قبري عيداً، وصلوا عليّ، فإن صلاتكم تبلغني حيث كنتم) رواه أبو داود بإسناد حسن، ورواته ثقات.

Abū Hurayrah (رضي الله عنه) said; "Allāh's Messenger (ﷺ) said; 'Do not make your homes into graves, and do not make my grave a place of celebration. And say send *ṣalāh* upon me, for surely your *ṣalāh* will reach me from wherever you are.'" Recorded by Abū Dāwūd with a *ḥasan* chain, whose narrators are trustworthy.[51]

وعن علي بن الحسين: أنه رأى رجلاً يجيء إلى فرجة كانت عند قبر النبي صلى الله عليه وسلم، فيدخل فيها فيدعو، فنهاه، وقال: ألا أحدثكم حديثاً سمعته من أبي عن جدي عن رسول الله صلى الله عليه وسلم قال: (لا تتخذوا قبري عيداً، ولا بيوتكم قبوراً، وصلوا عليّ فإن تسليمكم يبلغني أين كنتم). [رواه في المختارة].

---

[51] The ḥadīth was graded *ṣaḥīḥ* in *Ṣaḥīḥ al-Jāmiʿ* no. 7226.

From ʿAlī bin al-Ḥuṣayn; "That he saw a man come to the opening at the grave of the Prophet (ﷺ), he entered through it to supplicate. So he stopped him and said, 'Shall I narrate to you a ḥadīth that I heard from my father, from my grandfather, from the Messenger of Allāh (ﷺ), he said, "Do not take my grave as a place of celebration, nor your houses as graves. Say *ṣalāt* upon me, surely your greeting will reach me wherever you are." Recorded in *al-Mukhtārah*.[52]

فيه مسائل:

الأولى: تفسير آية براءة.

الثانية: إبعاده أمته عن هذا الحمى غاية البعد.

الثالثة: ذكر حرصه علينا ورأفته ورحمته.

الرابعة: نهيه عن زيارة قبره على وجه مخصوص، مع أن زيارته من أفضل الأعمال.

الخامسة: نهيه عن الإكثار من الزيارة.

السادسة: حثه على النافلة في البيت.

السابعة: أنه متقرر عندهم أنه لا يصلى في المقبرة.

الثامنة: تعليله ذلك بأن صلاة الرجل وسلامه عليه يبلغه وإن بعد، فلا حاجة إلى ما يتوهمه من أراد القرب.

التاسعة: كونه صلى الله عليه وسلم في البرزخ تعرض أعمال أمته في الصلاة والسلام عليه.

Important Points

1. The explanation of the *āyah* of *Sūrah al-Bara'ah*.
2. His (ﷺ) severe warning for his *ummah* against this.
3. It reminds us of his concern, his kindness, and mercy for us.

---

[52] *Ṣaḥīḥ*. See *Faḍl al-Ṣalāt ʿalāl-Nabī* (ﷺ) nos. 20 &30.

4. His prohibition of visiting his grave under the conditions mentioned, even though visiting it is among the best deeds.
5. His prohibition of visiting it often.
6. His emphasis of performing optional prayers in the home.
7. He emphasized to them not to pray in graveyards.
8. He gave the reason for this, that even if a person is far away, his *ṣalāh* upon him will be conveyed to him. So there is no reason for one to believe he must be close.
9. He (ﷺ) is in *al-Barzakh*, and is presented with whatever his *ummah* says of *ṣalāh* and *salām* upon him.

Commentary by *ʿAllāmah* al-Saʿdī

What has been Reported about *al-Muṣṭafā's* (ﷺ) Protection of *Tawḥīd* and His Closing every Way that Leads to *Shirk*

If one were to look for the texts of the Book and the *Sunnah* regarding this topic, then he would find many texts emphasizing all that strengthens, supports, and nourishes *tawḥīd*. They emphasis turning to Allāh, and strengthening the heart's dependence upon Allāh, hoping and fearing in Him alone. They encourage things that strengthen the aspiration for the virtues and blessings of *tawḥīd*, and the desire to hasten to bring this about. They encourage that which will liberate the worshipper from being enslaved to creatures, freeing him from dependence upon them in any way, without exaggerating over any of them. They teach perfection in both inner and outward deeds, making them complete and sincere, texts urging for the true spirit of *ʿubūdiyah* out of perfect sincerity for Allāh alone.

This is followed by prohibiting sayings and actions of exaggeration for created beings. And the prohibition from imitating the *mushrikīn*, because it leads to preferring them. And prohibiting sayings and actions that it is feared will lead to *shirk*, all of this to protect *tawḥīd*. Prohibiting all means leading to *shirk* is a mercy for the believers, so that they are able to continue in what they were created for, worshipping Allāh outwardly and inwardly, and perfecting this, so that their happiness and success will be complete. There are many well know texts bearing witness to these matters.

Chapter 23

ما جاء أن بعض هذه الأمة يعبد الأوثان

What is said about some of this *ummah* worshipping idols

وقول الله تعالى: (ألم تر إلى الذين أوتوا نصيباً من الكتاب يؤمنون بالجبت والطاغوت) وقوله تعالى: (قل هل أُنبئُكم بشرٍ من ذلك مثوبة عند الله من لعنه الله وغضب عليه وجعل منهم القردة والخنازير وعبد الطاغوت) وقوله تعالى: (قال الذين غلبوا على أمرهم لنتخذن عليهم مسجدًا).

Allāh (ﷻ) said; "Have you not seen those who have been given a portion of the Book, believing in *jibt* and the *ṭāghūt*." (*al-Nisā'* :51) And; "Say: 'Shall I give you of what is worse than that in requital with Allāh? Those who Allāh has cursed and whom His anger is upon, making them into monkeys and pigs, who worshipped the *ṭāghūt*..." (*al-Mā'idah* 5:60) "Those who [came later] said, 'Let us build a *masjid* over them.'" (*al-Kahf* 18:21)

عن أبي سعيد رضي الله عنه، أن رسول الله صلى الله عليه وسلم قال: (لتتبعن سنن من كان قبلكم حذو القذّة بالقذّة، حتى لو دخلوا جحر ضب لدخلتموه) قالوا: يا رسول الله، اليهود والنصارى؟ قال: (فمن)؟ أخرجاه،

Abū Sa'īd al-Khudrī (ؓ) reported that Allāh's Messenger (ﷺ) said, "You will follow the way of those before you precisely, so much so that if they entered the hole of a lizard, then you too would enter it." They said, "O Messenger of Allāh! Is that the Jews and Christians?" He said, "Who else?" Recorded by al-Bukhārī and Muslim.

ولمسلم عن ثوبان رضي الله عنه أن رسول الله صلى الله عليه وسلم قال: (إن الله زوى لي الأرض، فرأيت مشارقها ومغاربها، وإن أمتي سيبلغ ملكها ما زوي لي منها، وأعطيت

الكنزين: الأحمر والأبيض، وإني سألت ربي لأمتي أن لا يهلكها بسنة بعامة، وأن لا يسلط عليهم عدواً من سوى أنفسهم فيستبيح بيضتهم، وإن ربي قال: يا محمد إذا قضيت قضاءً فإنه لا يرد وإني أعطيتك لأمتك ألا أهلكهم بسنة بعامة وألا أسلط عليهم عدواً من سوى أنفسهم فيستبيح بيضتهم، ولو اجتمع عليهم من بأقطارها حتى يكون بعضهم يهلك بعضاً ويسبي بعضهم بعضًا)،

Collected by Muslim, from Thawbān (ﷺ), that Allāh's Messenger (ﷺ) said, "Indeed Allāh gathered the Earth for me so that I saw its east and its west. And surely my *ummah's* authority shall reach to all that was shown to me of it. And He granted the two treasures; the red and the white. I asked my Lord that my *ummah* not be destroyed by drought, and that it not be overcome by enemies outside of them. My Lord said; 'O Muḥammad! When I issue a decree it is not reversed. I have granted for your *ummah* that they will not be destroyed by universal drought. And that they not be overcome by enemies outside themselves even if they gather against them in droves, but some of them will destroy others, and some will capture others."

ورواه البرقاني في صحيحه، وزاد: (وإنما أخاف على أمتي الأئمة المضلين، وإذا وقع عليهم السيف لم يرفع إلى يوم القيامة، ولا تقوم الساعة حتى يلحق حي من أمتي بالمشركين، وحتى تعبد فئة من أمتي الأوثان، وإنه سيكون في أمتي كذّابون ثلاثون، كلهم يزعم أنه نبي، وأنا خاتم النبيين، لا نبي بعدي. ولا تزال طائفة من أمتي على الحق منصورة لا يضرهم من خذلهم حتى يأتي أمر الله تبارك وتعالى).

It is also recorded by al-Barqāni, in his *Ṣaḥīḥ*, with the addition; "...But what I fear for my *ummah* is deviant leaders, and when the sword occurs between them, it will not be removed until the Day of Resurrection. And the Hour will not occur until a tribe from my *ummah* unites with the *mushrikīn'* and until a large group of my *ummah* worships the idols. There will be thirty liars in my *ummah*, each of them claiming that he is a prophet. I am the finality of the prophets, there is no prophet after me. And a party of my *ummah* shall remain victorious upon the truth, they will not be harmed by those who abandon them until Allāh's (ﷻ) decree comes to them."[53]

فيه مسائل:

الأولى: تفسير آية النساء.

الثانية: تفسير آية المائدة.

[53] Recorded by Muslim as noted, and Al-Tirmidhī. The addition is included in versions with Aḥmad, Ibn Mājah, most of the rest of it is with Abū Dāwūd. It was graded *ṣaḥīḥ* in *Ṣaḥīḥ al-Jāmi'* no. 1773, and al-*Ṣaḥīḥah* no. 2.

الثالثة: تفسير آية الكهف.

الرابعة: وهي أهمها: ما معنى الإيمان بالجبت والطاغوت في هذا الموضع؟: هل هو اعتقاد قلب، أو هو موافقة أصحابها مع بغضها ومعرفة بطلانها؟.

الخامسة: قولهم إن الكفار الذين يعرفون كفرهم أهدى سبيلاً من المؤمنين.

السادسة: وهي المقصود بالترجمة - أن هذا لا بد أن يوجد في هذه الأمة، كما تقرر في حديث أبي سعيد.

السابعة: التصريح بوقوعها، أعني عبادة الأوثان في هذه الأمة في جموع كثيرة.

الثامنة: العجب العجاب خروج من يدّعي النبوة، مثل المختار، مع تكلمه بالشهادتين وتصريحه بأنه من هذه الأمة، وأن الرسول حق، وأن القرآن حق وفيه أن محمداً خاتم النبيين، ومع هذا يصدق في هذا كله مع التضاد الواضح. وقد خرج المختار في آخر عصر الصحابة، وتبعه فئام كثيرة.

التاسعة: البشارة بأن الحق لا يزول بالكلية كما زال فيما مضى، بل لا تزال عليه طائفة.

العاشرة: الآية العظمى أنهم مع قلتهم لا يضرهم من خذلهم ولا من خالفهم.

الحادية عشرة: أن ذلك الشرط إلى قيام الساعة.

الثانية عشرة: ما فيه من الآيات العظيمة، منها: إخباره بأن الله زوى له المشارق والمغارب، وأخبر بمعنى ذلك فوقع كما أخبر، بخلاف الجنوب والشمال، وإخباره بأنه أعطي الكنزين، وإخباره بإجابة دعوته لأمته في الاثنتين، وإخباره بأنه منع الثالثة، وإخباره بوقوع السيف، وأنه لا يرفع إذا وقع، وإخباره بإهلاك بعضهم بعضاً وسبي بعضهم بعضاً، وخوفه على أمته من الأئمة المضلين، وإخباره بظهور المتنبئين في هذه الأمة، وإخباره ببقاء الطائفة المنصورة. وكل هذا وقع كما أخبر، مع أن كل واحدة منهما من أبعد ما يكون في العقول.

الثالثة عشرة: حصر الخوف على أمته من الأئمة المضلين.

الرابعة عشرة: التنبيه على معنى عبادة الأوثان.

Important Points

1. The explanation of the *āyah* of *Sūrah al-Nisā'*.
2. The explanation of the *āyah* of *Sūrah al-Mā'idah*.
3. The explanation of the *āyah* of *Sūrah al-Kahf*.
4. Of utmost importance here is the meaning of *imān* in *al-jibt* and *al-ṭāghūt*; is it belief in the heart, or is it the approval of its practitioner while he hates it and is aware of its falsehood?
5. Their saying (i.e., the Jews) that the disbelievers, while aware of their disbelief, are more guided than the believers.[54]
6. The goal of this topic, that this will definitely happen to this *ummah*, as acknowledged by the ḥadīth of Abū Sa'īd.
7. The declaration of its occurrence, that is that many groups of this *ummah* will worship idols.
8. The most amazing point, the appearance of claimants to prophethood - like al-Mukhtār - while he utters the *shahadatayn* and declares that he is a member of this *ummah*, and he declares that the Messenger and the Qur'ān are the truth, and that Muḥammad is the finality of the prophets, and yet clearly contradicting all of this while acknowledging its truthfulness. *Al-Mukhtār* appeared at the end of the companions' time, and he was followed by many groups.

[54] This is in reference to the remainder of the first *āyah* quoted in this chapter; "...They who say about those who disbelieve that they are more guided to the right way than the believers." (*Al-Nisā'*:51-2) It has been narrated from Ibn 'Abbās (ﷺ) that when Ka'b bin Ashraf came to Makkah, the Quraysh said to him, "You are the best of the people of al-Madīnah and their chief." He replied, "Yes." They said, "Haven't you seen this person who is deprived of male off-spring, outcast from his people, claiming that he is better than us. While we are the caretakers of Ḥajj, the custodians of the Ka'bah, those who provide drink for the pilgrims?!" He said, "You are better than him." So the following was revealed; "Surely the one who defames you, he is the one who is cut-off." (*al-Kawthar* 108: 3) And; "...They who say about those who disbelieve that they are more guided to the right way than the believers. It is they whom Allāh has cursed..." (*Al-Nisā'* :51-2) This report was recorded by Aḥmad and al-Ṭabarī. Ibn Kathīr mentioned it, and a similar narration was reported by Ibn Abī Ḥātim and al-Bazzār. Shaykh Muqbil bin Hādī graded it *ṣaḥīḥ* in *Ṣaḥīḥ al-Musnad min Asbāb al-Nuzūl* (pp. 77 & 274). However he classified it as a *mursal* narration, referring the reader to his discussion of that in his notes on Ibn Kathīr's *Tafsīr*.

9. The good news that the truth will not completely vanish as it did in the past, but that there is a party that will never lose it.
10. The magnificent sign that though fought, they will not be harmed by those who abandon or oppose them.
11. That this condition remains until the Hour is established.
12. The magnificent signs that these texts contain;
    - His (ﷺ) informing that Allāh displayed the east and the west and he told of what that means. It occurred as he informed, but on the contrary, not the south and the north.
    - He informed that he would be granted the two treasures.
    - He informed that two of his supplications were answered
    - He informed that the third supplication was withheld.
    - He informed of the coming of the sword, and that there would be no relief from it once it began.
    - He informed of the appearance of claimants to prophethood in this *ummah*.
    - He informed of the survival of the victorious party.

All of this has occurred as he informed, even though each defies reason.

13. Restricting the fear for his *ummah* to misguided leaders.
14. His emphasis of the meaning of worshipping idols.

Commentary by *ʿAllāmah* al-Saʿdī

What is said about Some of this *Ummah* worshipping Idols

The goal of this discussion is to warn of *shirk* and to beware of it, and that it is a matter that will occur in this *ummah* without a doubt, and the refutation of those who claim that whoever says *Lā ilāha illa Allāh,* and is labeled with Islām, then he remains with his Islām, even if he were to do what negates that. Like seeking help from the inhabitants of graves and supplicating to them, referring to such acts as "*tawassul*" rather than worship. This indeed is falsehood.

So "*wathin*" [idol] is a name encompassing all that is worshipped other than Allāh, it makes no difference whether it is a tree a stone or statues, it makes no differences whether those worshipped are prophets, the righteous or the wicked in this matter because this is a form of worship, and worship is a right of Allāh alone. So whoever calls upon other than Allāh or worships other than Him, then he has taken him as an idol, and by doing so he has left the religion, and he does not retain any benefit of the epithet of *Islām*. How many *mushriks*, atheists and disbelieving hypocrites use the term Islām! Of consequence is the spirit of the religion and its fulfilment, not the mere appellation or expressions which do not fulfil it. [55]

[55] The following quotes from Shaykh Muḥammad bin ʿAbd al-Wahhāb, may Allāh have mercy upon him, will benefit the reader for the correct interpretation of the comments of Shaykh al-Saʿdī, may Allāh have mercy upon him; "As for what has been stated about me by my opponents; that I make *takfīr* based on my opinions and allegiances, or that I make *takfīr* of the ignorant one whom the proof has not been established upon, this is simply dangerous slander by which they desire to prevent the people from the religion of Allāh and His Messenger (ﷺ)." And; "We only make *takfīr* of one who makes *shirk* with Allāh in His ʿ*ulūhiyah*, after we have clearly proven the falsehood of his *shirk* to him." *Majmūʿah Muallafāt al-Imām Muḥammad bin ʿAbd al-Wahhāb* (5:25 & 60)

Chapter 24

ما جاء في السحر

What is said about magic

وقول الله تعالى: (ولقد علموا لمن اشتراه ماله في الآخرة من خلاق) وقوله: (يؤمنون بالجبت والطاغوت).

Allāh (ﷻ) said, "They knew that those who bought it would have no share [of good] in the Hereafter." (*al-Baqarah* 2:102) "They believed in the *jibt* and the *ṭāghūt*." (*al-Nisā'* :51)

قال عمر: (الجبت): السحر، (والطاغوت): الشيطان. وقال جابر: الطواغيت كهان كان ينزل عليهم الشيطان في كل حي واحد.

'Umar said, "*Al-Jibt* is magic, and the *ṭāghūt* is the *shayṭān*." [56] Jābir said, "The *tawāghīt* [plural of *ṭāghūt*] are the fortunetellers, every village has one that the *shayṭān* inspires." [57]

---

[56] Ibn Kathīr said, "Abū al-Qāsim al-Baghawī said, 'Abū Rūh al-Baladī informed us, Abū al-Ahwās Salām bin Salīm informed us from Abū Isḥāq, from Ḥasān - that is Ibn Fā'id al-'Abbāsī who said, 'Umar bin al-Khaṭṭāb (ﷺ) said that *jibt* is magic and *ṭāghūt* is *shayṭān*... [and the quote is longer than noted]' And this is reported by Ibn Jarīr, and Ibn Abū Ḥātim via a ḥadīth of al-Thawrī from Abū Isḥāq from Ḥasān..." Ibn Kathīr says afterwards, "And the opinion that the *ṭāghūt* means the *shayṭān* is very strong..." (*Tafsīr al-Qur'ān al-'Aẓīm*; *Sūrah al-Baqarah* 2: 256)

[57] According to Shaykh Sulaymān, this is part of a longer narration from Wahb bin Munnabih who is asking Jābir (ﷺ). It is recorded by Ibn Abū Ḥātim. Ibn Kathīr mentions part of it in his *Tafsīr*.

وعن أبي هريرة رضي الله عنه أن رسول الله صلى الله عليه وسلم قال: (اجتنبوا السبع الموبقات)
قالوا: يا رسول الله: وما هن؟ قال: (الشرك بالله، والسحر، وقتل النفس التي حرم الله إلا بالحق،
وأكل الربا، وأكل مال اليتيم، والتولي يوم الزحف، وقذف المحصنات الغافلات المؤمنات).

Abū Hurayrah (رضي الله عنه) said that Allāh's Messenger (ﷺ) said; "Stay clear of the
seven destroyers." They asked, "O Allāh's Messenger, what are they?" He said,
"*Shirk* with Allāh; magic; taking a life which Allāh has made unlawful except
as is required; consuming interest, consuming the wealth of an orphan, fleeing
from the battlefield, and slandering the innocent believing women."[58]

وعن جندب مرفوعاً: (حد الساحر ضربه بالسيف) رواه الترمذي، وقال: الصحيح أنه
موقوف.

And a *marfū*' report from Jundab, "The punishment for the magician is striking
him with the sword." Recorded by Al-Tirmidhī who said, "That it is *mawqūf* is
what is correct."[59]

وفي (صحيح البخاري) عن بجالة بن عبدة قال: كتب عمر بن الخطاب: أن اقتلوا كل ساحر
وساحرة، قال: فقتلنا ثلاث سواحر.

In *Ṣaḥīḥ al-Bukhārī* from Bajālah bin 'Abdah who said, "'Umar bin al-
Khaṭṭāb wrote, 'Kill every magician and sorceress.' He said, 'So we killed three
magicians."[60]

---

[58] Al-Bukhārī and Muslim.

[59] See *Ḍa'īf Sunan Al-Tirmidhī* no. 1501.

[60] Shaykh Sulaymān says, "This report is recorded by al-Bukhārī as the author mentioned.
But it does not mention killing the magicians in it. It's wording follows; "From Bajālah
bin 'Abdah who said, 'I was a secretary for Juza' bin Mu'āwiyah, al-Aḥnaf's uncle. A letter
came to us from 'Umar bin al-Khaṭṭāb one year before he died. [It said]; "Cancel every
dhul-mahram marriage contracted among the Zoroastrians.' And 'Umar did not take the
jizyah from the Zoroastrians until 'Abdul-Raḥmān bin 'Awf had testified that Allāh's
Messenger (ﷺ) took it from the Zoroastrians of Ḥajar." So the author attributed it to
al-Bukhārī intending only the basis of the saying not its exact wording. It is recorded in
summary by al-Tirmidhī and al-Nasā'ī, and 'Abdul-Razzāq, Aḥmad, Abū Dāwūd, and al-
Bayhaqī recorded the longer version. And al-Qaṭī'ī recorded it in the second volume of his
Fawā'id with the addition. He said [with *isnād* to Bajālah]; "'Umar bin al-Khaṭṭāb wrote
to us: 'Announce to the Zoroastrians near you that they abandon performing marriages
between their mothers, daughters, and brothers, then their food will be as we have been
accustomed with the People of the Book. Then kill every fortuneteller and magician."' I
say, its chain is *ḥasan*." (*Taysīr al-'Azīz*)

وصح عن حفصة رضي الله عنها: أنها أمرت بقتل جارية لها سحرتها، فقتلت، وكذلك صح عن جندب. قال أحمد: عن ثلاثة من أصحاب النبي صلى الله عليه وسلم.

And it is correct from Ḥafṣah (ﷺ) that she ordered the killing of a female servant of hers that was a sorceress. So she was killed.[61] And that is also correct from Jundab.[62]

Aḥmad said, "From three of the companions of the Prophet (ﷺ)." [the three above mentioned]

فيه مسائل:

الأولى: تفسير آية البقرة.

الثانية: تفسير آية النساء.

الثالثة: تفسير الجبت والطاغوت، والفرق بينهما.

الرابعة: أن الطاغوت قد يكون من الجن، وقد يكون من الإنس.

الخامسة: معرفة السبع الموبقات المخصوصات بالنهي.

السادسة: أن الساحر يكفر.

السابعة: أنه يقتل ولا يستتاب.

الثامنة: وجود هذا في المسلمين على عهد عمر، فكيف بعده؟

Important Points

1. The explanation of the *āyah* of *Sūrah al-Baqarah*.
2. The explanation of the *āyah* of *Sūrah al-Nisā'* .

---

[61] Recorded in by Mālik in *al-Muwaṭṭā'*, and its chain is disconnected (al-Arnā'ūṭ).

[62] The Jundab here is Jundab al-Khayr al-Azadī, i.e., Ibn Ka'b bin 'Abdullāh who killed a magician according to Abū Ḥātim. Some say he was the same as Jundab bin Zuhayr, others say contrarily. There is a narration with al-Bukhārī in *al-Tārīkh* mentioning "al-Azadī" killing the magician, as well with as al-Bayhaqī in *al-Dalā'il.* (See *Taysīr al-'Azīz*)

3. The explanation of *jibt* and *ṭāghūt*, and the difference between them.
4. That the *ṭāghūt* can be from the *jinns*, as well as humans.
5. Learning the seven destroyers specifically prohibited.
6. That the magician commits disbelief.
7. That he is killed without seeking his repentance.
8. This existed among the Muslims during the time of ʿUmar, so how about now?

ʿ*Allāmah* Saʿdī made no comments here

Chapter 25

بيان شيء من أنواع السحر

Clarifying some points about the different types of magic

قال أحمد: حدثنا محمد بن جعفر، حدثنا عوف عن حيان بن العلاء، حدثنا قطن بن قبيصة عن أبيه أنه سمع النبي صلى الله عليه وسلم قال: (إن العيافة والطرق والطيرة من الجبت).

Aḥmad said, Muḥammad bin Ja'far reported to us, that 'Awf reported to us, from Ḥayyān bin al-'Alā', that Qaṭan bin Qabīṣah reported to us from his father, that he heard the Prophet (ﷺ) saying, "*'Iyāfah* [augury], *ṭarq*, and omens are from *jibt*."[63]

قال عوف: العيافة: زجر الطير، والطرق: الخط يخط بالأرض والجبت، قال: الحسن: رنة الشيطان. إسناده جيد ولأبي داود والنسائي وابن حبان في صحيحه، المسند منه.

'Awf said, "*'Iyāfah* [augury] is predictions based on birds, and *ṭarq* is the lines etched in the earth.[64]

---

[63] This ḥadīth was also recorded by Abū Dāwūd, Ibn Ḥibbān, and al-Nasā'ī in *al-Sunan al-Kubrā*. Al-Nawawī graded the chain with Abū Dāwūd as *ḥasan*. Through its routes there is confusion over one of its narrators. Some say Ḥayān bin al-'Alā', some Ḥibbān (or Ḥayān) bin Mukhāriq Abū Ya'la, some say Ḥayān bin 'Umayr. If it were Ḥayān bin 'Umayr Abū al-'Alā' al-Baṣrī al-Qaysī, he was considered trustworthy by al-Nasā'ī and Ibn Ḥibbān. But Isḥāq bin Manṣūr reported from Aḥmad and Yaḥyā that the reporter of this ḥadīth is not Ibn 'Umayr. It may be that al-Nawawī (in *Riyāḍ al-Ṣalihīn*) thought that the Ḥayān bin al-'Alā' in Abū Dāwūd's (and Aḥmad's) chain was the trustworthy one, but this was denied by Aḥmad. See *Ghāyat al-Marām*, no. 301 and Ḍa'īf Mawārid al-Ẓamān no. 171 where Al-Albānī labeled the ḥadīth weak.

[64] Stated after the above ḥadīth by Abū Dāwūd. 'Awf is Ibn Abī Jamīlah of al-Baṣrah, better known as 'Awf al-'Arābī. He died in the year 46 or 47 H (*Fatḥ al-Majīd*). The problem of the chain discussed above, is over who he was narrating from, but not over what he said.

Al-Ḥasan said that *jibt* is "the screaming of *shayṭān*" with a good *isnād*. The *musnad* [ḥadīth above] is with Abū Dāwūd, al-Nasā'ī, and Ibn Ḥibbān in his *Ṣaḥīḥ*.[65]

وعن ابن عباس رضي الله عنهما قال: قال رسول الله صلى الله عليه وسلم (من اقتبس شعبة من النجوم، فقد اقتبس شعبة من السحر، زاد ما زاد) [رواه أبو داود] وإسناده صحيح.

Ibn 'Abbās said that Allāh's Messenger (ﷺ) said, "Whoever learns a portion of knowledge about the stars, he has learned a portion of magic: the more of one the more of the other." Recorded by Abū Dāwūd and its chain is *ṣaḥīḥ*.[66]

وللنسائي من حديث أبي هريرة رضي الله عنه: (من عقد عقدة ثم نفث فيها فقد سحر، ومن سحر فقد أشرك، ومن تعلق شيئاً وكل إليه).

And with *al-Nasā'ī* is a ḥadīth of Abū Hurayrah (ﷺ); "Whoever ties a knot then blows into, he has performed magic, and whoever performs magic he has committed *shirk*, and whoever depends upon something he is entrusted to it."[67]

وعن ابن مسعود رضي الله عنه أن رسول الله صلى الله عليه وسلم قال: (ألا هل أنبئكم ما الغضة؟ هي النميمة، القالة بين الناس) [رواه مسلم].

He explained, "*Ṭarq* is lines etched in the earth." This is explained in *al-Nihāyah*; "The etching that women do with pebbles." There is an English word for it; geomancy. It is also known as *'Ilm al-Raml*; "Divination by means of figures or lines drawn in the sand." (Hans Wehr Dictionary of Modern Written Arabic, 3rd Ed. 1976) A similar explanation follows from Ibn Taymiyyah where he defines the word *a'rāf* and he includes the word *ramāl*, or the one who practices this form of prediction.

[65] Shaykh Sulaymān notes that the report from al-Ḥasan is not found with the compilers mentioned, Abū Dāwūd in particular. However the ḥadīth is quoted by Ibn Kathīr with the same quotes after it. But he says, "And like this has been reported by Abū Dāwūd in his *Sunan*, al-Nasā'ī, and Ibn Abū Ḥātim in his *tafsīr*..." Regarding the "saying" of al-Ḥasan, Shaykh 'Abdul-Raḥmān bin Ḥasan notes a report from Ibn Mufliḥ about the scream of *Iblīs* in Baqiy bin Mukhlid's *tafsīr*, a report from Sa'īd bin Jubayr about the screaming of *Iblīs*, recorded by Ibn Abū Ḥātim, and a report from Ibn 'Abbās about the scream of *Iblīs* in *al-Mukhtārah* by *al-Ḍiyā'*. See *Fatḥ al-Majīd*.

[66] It was also recorded by Aḥmad and Ibn Mājah. Al-Albānī labeled the ḥadīth's chain as good [*jayyid*]. See *al-Ṣaḥīḥah* no. 793. See also *Ṣaḥīḥ al-Jāmi'*; no. 6074.

[67] Shaykh Sulaymān says, 'The author mentioned this ḥadīth of Abū Hurayrah, attributing it to al-Nasā'ī but he did not clarify if it is *mawqūf* or *marfū'*. Al-Nasā'ī recorded it as *marfū'*. And the author mentioned from al-Dhahabī that he said, 'Not authentic.' and Ibn Mufliḥ graded it *ḥasan*.' This is what he said. Al-Albānī has graded it weak in *Ḍa'īf al-Jāmi'*; no. 5703, and *Ghāyat al-Marām* no. 288.

And from Ibn Mas'ūd that Allāh's Messenger (ﷺ) said, "Shall I not inform you about *al-ghaḍah:* It is slander; gossiping among the people." Recorded by Muslim.

ولهما عن ابن عمر رضي الله عنهما، ان رسول الله صلى الله عليه وسلم قال: (إن من البيان لسحراً).

Ibn 'Umar (ﷺ) narrates that Allāh's Messenger (ﷺ) said, "Surely some eloquence is but magic."[68]

فيه مسائل:

الأولى: أن العيافة والطرق والطيرة من الجبت.

الثانية: تفسير العيافة والطرق.

الثالثة: أن علم النجوم نوع من السحر.

الرابعة: أن العقد مع النفث من ذلك.

الخامسة: أن النميمة من ذلك.

السادسة: أن من ذلك بعض الفصاحة.

Important Points

1. That *'iyāfah*, *ṭarq* and omens are from *jibt*.
2. The explanation of *'iyāfah* and *ṭarq*.
3. That knowledge of the stars is a type of magic.
4. Blowing into knots is also from that.
5. That slander is also from that.
6. That some eloquence is also from that.

[68] Recorded by al-Bukhārī, Mālik, Aḥmad and others.

Commentary by *ʿAllāmah* al-Saʿdi

Clarifying some Points about the different types of magic

Magic is included among the topics of *tawḥīd* because in most cases the magician relies upon some form of *shirk* or *tawassul* with satanic spirits. So the worshipper's *tawḥīd* will not be complete until he avoids all types of magic, whether a little or a lot. For such reasons the *sharīʿah* has mentioned it in accompaniment with *shirk*.

It falls under the category of *shirk* from the view of seeking the service of the *shayāṭīn* and depending upon them. Additionally, the one requesting the service of the *shayāṭīn* may be ensnared into doing what they want him to do. Such behaviour claims a knowledge of the unseen and a partner with Allāh in what He knows, or beliefs that result in that. All of this is a branch of *shirk* and *kufr*.

It also results in other prohibited or repulsive behaviour such as murder, separating loved ones, recalcitrance or unlawful compassion, employing tactics that confuse ones ability to properly reason. Such behaviour falls under the category of detestable prohibited matters, whereas the previous category falls under *shirk* and what leads to it. It is for these reasons - because of the detriment and harm that he causes - that the magician is to be killed.

Among the types of magic popularly employed among people is slander, by which they share a common trait with the evil of the magician, because in both cases they are separating people, changing the hearts of loved ones, and sowing the seeds of evil. So there are different categories and levels of magic, some of them more base and vile than others.

Chapter 26

ما جاء في الكهان ونحوهم
What is said about fortunetellers and their like

روى مسلم في صحيحه، عن بعض أزواج النبي صلى الله عليه وسلم عن النبي صلى الله عليه وسلم قال: «من أتى عَرَّافاً فسأله عن شيء فصدقه، لم تقبل له صلاة أربعين يوماً».

In his *Ṣaḥīḥ*, Muslim records from some of the wives of the Prophet (ﷺ) who said, "Whoever comes to a psychic to ask about something, believing in what he says, his *ṣalāh* is not accepted from him for forty days."[69]

وعن أبي هريرة رضي الله عنه، عن النبي صلى الله عليه وسلم قال: «من أتى كاهناً فصدقه بما يقول، فقد كفر بما أنزل على محمد صلى الله عليه وسلم» رواه أبو داود.

وللأربعة، والحاكم وقال: صحيح على شرطهما،

Abū Hurayrah (ﷺ) reports that the Prophet (ﷺ) said, "Whoever comes to a fortuneteller, believing in what he says, then he has disbelieved in what was revealed to Muḥammad (ﷺ)." Recorded by Abū Dāwūd.[70] And from the four

---

[69] "Believing in what he says" is not with Muslim, but with Aḥmad.

[70] Abū Dāwūd's Shaykh was not sure about the wording. Shaykh Sulaymān says, "Recorded also by al-Tirmidhī, al-Nasā'ī, and Ibn Mājah similarly. ... Al-Baghawī said its chain is weak, and al-Dhahabī said, 'Its chain is not established.'" Al-Tirmidhī said, "Muḥammad (al-Bukhārī) graded it weak due to its chain." In *Ghāyat al-Marām*, after discussing the ḥadīth's chain as noted by al-Mundhirī, al-Albānī says, "The ḥadīth is *ṣaḥīḥ*. It has been transmitted from Abū Hurayrah via three routes which I have shown in *al-Irwā'* no. 2006." He also included it in *Ṣaḥīḥ al-Jāmi'*, and *Ṣaḥīḥ Sunan Al-Tirmidhī*.

as well as al-Ḥākim, who said, "It is *ṣaḥīḥ* according to their conditions [al-Bukhāræ and Muslim];

عن (أبي هريرة من أتى عرافاً أو كاهناً فصدقه بما يقول، فقد كفر بما أنزل على محمد صلى الله عليه وسلم». ولأبي يعلى بسند جيد عن ابن مسعود موقوفاً.

"Whoever comes to a psychic or a fortuneteller believing in what he says, then he has disbelieved in what has been revealed to Muḥammad(ﷺ)." [71]Abū Ya'la reports similar as a saying of Ibn Mas'ūd with a good chain.[72]

وعن عمران بن حصين رضي الله عنه مرفوعاً: «ليس منا من تَطير أو تُطير له أو تَكهن أو تُكهن له أو سَحر أو سُحر له، ومن أتى كاهناً فصدقه بما يقول، فقد كفر بما أنزل على محمد صلى الله عليه وسلم) رواه البزار بإسناد جيد، ورواه الطبراني في الأوسط بإسناد حسن من حديث ابن عباس دون قوله: «ومن أتى..» الخ.

From 'Imrān bin Ḥuṣayn (ﷺ) [from the Prophet (ﷺ)]; "He is not one of us who interprets an omen or has one interpreted for him. Nor he who tells a fortune or has one told for him, or who performs magic or has it done for him. And whoever goes to a fortuneteller believing in what he says, then he has disbelieved in what was revealed to Muḥammad (ﷺ)." Recorded by al-Bazzār with a good chain. And al-Ṭabarānī recorded it in *al-Awsaṭ*, with a *ḥasan* chain from Ibn 'Abbās without the words, "Whoever goes..." to the end.[73]

قال البغوي: العراف: الذي يدعي معرفة الأمور بمقدمات يستدل بها على المسروق ومكان الضالة ونحو ذلك وقيل: هو الكاهن والكاهن هو الذي يخبر عن المغيبات في المستقبل وقيل: الذي يخبر عما في الضمير.

Al-Baghawī explained, "The *a'rāf*, is the one who claims to know matters of the past which are used to know about something that was stolen, or where to find something that is lost, etc." And they say that this is the *ḳāhin*. And the *ḳāhin* is the one who tells the hidden matters of the future. And they say he is the one who reads minds.

[71] This is a variant version of the same ḥadīth above, this wording recorded by Aḥmad.

[72] Shaykh Sulaymān says that this report is also recorded by al-Bazzār with a chain that meets the criteria of Muslim.

[73] The grading mentioned in the text seems to come from al-Mundhirī. Al-Albānī graded the ḥadīth of 'Imrān bin Ḥuṣayn (up to but not including "whoever goes to...") *ṣaḥīḥ* in *Ṣaḥīḥ al-Jāmi'* no. 5435, noting *al-Ṣaḥīḥah* 2195 for its discussion.

وقال أبو العباس ابن تيمية: العراف: اسم للكاهن والمنجم والرمال ونحوهم ممن يتكلم في معرفة الأمور بهذه الطرق.

Abū al-ʿAbbās Ibn Taymiyah said; "*Aʿrāf* is the name for the *kāhin*, the *munajim*, the *ramāl* and any other who is said to know a matter through such means."

وقال ابن عباس –في قوم يكتبون (أبا جاد) وينظرون في النجوم –: ما أرى من فعل ذلك له عند الله من خلاق.

Regarding the people who practice numerology and utilise the zodiac, "One who does that will find no good for himself with Allāh."[74]

فيه مسائل:

الأولى: لا يجتمع تصديق الكاهن مع الإيمان بالقرآن.

الثانية: التصريح بأنه كفر.

الثالثة: ذكر من تُكهن له.

الرابعة: ذكر من تُطير له.

الخامسة: ذكر من سحر له.

السادسة: ذكر من تعلم أبا جاد.

السابعة: ذكر الفرق بين الكاهن والعراف.

Important Points

1. Believing a fortuneteller and faith in the Qur'ān will not coexist in someone.
2. The clarification that this is *kufr*.
3. The mention of the one who has his fortune told.
4. The mention of the one who has an omen read.

---

[74] Shaykh Sulaymān says, "It is recorded by al-Ṭabarānī from Ibn ʿAbbās *marfūʿ*, and its chain is weak..."Al-Ḥaythamī said, "In its chain is Khālid bin Yazīd al-ʿAmri and he lies." (*Majmaʿ al-Zawāʾid* 5:118). Al-Albānī graded it weak in *Ḍaʿīf al-Jāmiʿ*, and he indicated that it may be fabricated in *al-Ḍaʿīfah* no. 417.

5. The mention of the one who has some spell performed for him.
6. The mention of the one who learns numerology.
7. The mention of the difference between the fortuneteller [*kāhin*] and the psychic [*aʿrāf*].

Commentary by *ʿAllāmah* al-Saʿdī

What is said about Fortunetellers and their Like

That is anyone who claims to know the unseen regardless of the method, for Allāh (ﷻ) is the sole knower of the unseen. So whoever claims a share in any matter of that, whether by telling fortunes, being a psychic, etc., or whoever believes one who makes such claims, then he has associated something that is solely for Allāh, and he has lied against Allāh and His Messenger.

Most fortunetelling utilises the *shayāṭīn*, believing them to have a share with Allāh in knowing the unseen, or using them as mediators with Him. So this is *shirk* from the view of claiming partners with Allāh in an area of knowledge which is His alone, as well as from the view of seeking nearness to other than Allāh. The *sharīʿah* came to cleanse the religion of futile superstitions and to remove their harm from the reasoning of the creatures.

Chapter 27

ما جاء في النشرة

What is said about *nushrah*

عن جابر رضي الله عنه أن رسول الله صلى الله عليه وسلم سئل عن النشرة فقال: «هي من عمل الشيطان» رواه أحمد بسند جيد. وأبو داود، وقال: سئل أحمد عنها فقال: ابن مسعود يكره هذا كله.

From Jābir, "Allāh's Messenger (ﷺ) was asked about *nushrah*. He said, 'It is from the works of *shayṭān*.'" Recorded by Aḥmad with a good chain as well as Abū Dāwūd, and he said, "I asked Aḥmad about it. He said, 'Ibn Mas'ūd disliked all of it.'"[75]

وفي «البخاري» عن قتادة: قلت لابن المسيب: رجل به طب أو يؤخذ عن امرأته، أيحل عنه أو ينشر؟ قال: لا بأس به، إنما يريدون به الإصلاح، فأما ما ينفع فلم ينه عنه. أ.هـ.

And with al-Bukhārī from Qatādah, "I said to Ibn Mūsayyab, 'If a man is under a spell, or he is cold [sexually] to his wife, can he undo this, or use *nushrah*?' He said, 'There is no harm in it, they are only intending some good by it, there is no prohibition for what there is benefit in.'"[76]

وروى عن الحسن أنه قال: لا يحل السحر إلا ساحر.

---

[75] "Recorded by Aḥmad, and Abū Dāwūd records it from him in his *Sunan*, and al-Faḍl bin Ziyād in *al-Masā'il* [*isnād*] from Jābir...Ibn Mufliḥ said, 'Its chain is good [*jayyid*].' And al-Ḥāfiẓ graded its chain *ḥasan*, and this grade was endorsed by al-Arnā'ūṭ. It was also recorded by Ibn Abū Shaybah and Abū Dāwūd has a *marfū'* report for it from *al-ḥasan* in *al-Marāsīl*; "*Nushurah* is the work of *Shayṭān*." Al-Albānī included it in *Ṣaḥīḥ Sunan Abū Dāwūd* no. 3277.

[76] Mentioned in *mu'allaq* form by al-Bukhārī. It was connected by Abū Bakr al-Athrām in his *Sunan* [via two routes] from Qatādah with similar meaning. (*Taysīr al-'Azīz*)

It is reported from al-Ḥasan that he said, "None can undo magic except the magician."[77]

قال ابن القيم: النشرة: حل السحر عن المسحور، وهي نوعان:

إحداهما: حل بسحر مثله، وهو الذي من عمل الشيطان، وعليه يحمل قول الحسن، فيتقرب الناشر والمنتشر إلى الشيطان بما يحب، ويبطل عمله عن المسحور.

Ibn al-Qayyim said, "*Nushrah* is to undo a magic spell. There are two types; the first is undoing the magic with what is similar to it, and this is the work of *shayṭān* which the saying of *al-Ḥasan* refers to. So the one seeking the *nāshir* and the one performing it go to a *shayṭān* giving him what he wants in exchange for what will remove the spell.

والثاني: النشرة بالرقية والتعوذات والأدوية والدعوات المباحة، فهذا جائز.

The second is *nushrah* through *ruqyah*, *ta'awudhāt*, medicine, and permissible supplication. This is allowed."

فيه مسألتان:

الأولى: النهي عن النشرة.

الثانية: الفرق بين المنهي عنه والمرخص فيه مما يزيل الأشكال.

Important Points

1. The prohibition of *nushrah*.
2. The distinction between what is prohibited of it, and that which removes harm that an exception has been made for.

---

[77] This is not a statement of approval, but if it is correct from him it means that only a magician would deal with magic. Shaykh Sulaymān says; "This report is mentioned by Ibn al-Jawzi in *Jāmi' al-Musānīd* without a chain, with the wording 'None breaks the magic [spell] except the magician.' Ibn Jarīr recorded it in *al-Tahdhīb* by way of Yazīd bin Zuray' from Qatādah from Sa'īd bin al-Mūsayab that he did not see any harm in a man under a spell to go to one who can break it for him. He said, 'This is doing good.' Qatādah said, "And al-Ḥasan rejected that saying, 'This is only known by the magician.' He said, 'Sa'īd bin Mūsayyib said, "Allāh only forbade from what harms, he did not forbid what benefits." (*Taysīr al-'Azīz*)

Commentary by *ʿAllāmah* al-Saʿdī

What is said about *nushrah*

That is removal of the spell from the spellbound. The passage from Ibn al-Qayyim that the author mentioned is sufficient in explaining the difference between what is allowed of it and what is not.

Chapter 28

ما جاء في التطير

What is said about omens

وقول الله تعالى: (ألا إنما طائرهم عند الله ولكن أكثرهم لا يعلمون) .

وقوله: (قالوا طائركم معكم) .

Allāh (ﷻ) said; "...Rather, their (evil beliefs based on their) omens are about Allāh, but most of them do not know." (*al-Aʿrāf* 7:131) And; "They (the messengers) said, 'Your omens are for you.'" (*Yā Sīn* 36:19)[78]

عن أبي هريرة رضي الله عنه، أن الرسول صلى الله عليه وسلم قال: (لا عدوى، ولا طيرة، ولا هامة، ولا صفر) أخرجاه. زاد مسلم: (ولا نوء، ولا غول).

Abū Hurayrah (رضي الله عنه) said that Allāh's Messenger (ﷺ) said, "There is no *ʿadwā*, nor *ṭiyarah*, nor *hāmah*, nor *ṣafar*." Recorded by al-Bukhārī and Muslim. Muslim adds, "No *naw'a*, nor *ghūl*."[79]

ولهما عن أنس رضي الله عنه قال: قال رسول الله صلى الله عليه وسلم: (لا عدوى ولا طيرة، ويعجبني الفأل) قالوا: وما الفأل؟ قال: (الكلمة الطيبة).

Anas relates that Allāh's Messenger (ﷺ) said, "There is no *ʿadwā*, nor *ṭiyarah*, but *fa'l* [optimism] is more a marvel to me." They said, "What is *fa'l*?" He said, "A good word." Collected by al-Bukhārī and Muslim.

---

[78] As if they were saying, "The evil hesitation that you have derived from these omens, causing you to reject Allāh's messengers, is only an indication of just how evil you actually are."

[79] See "The *Ghūl*" an adaptation of *Mashhūr Ḥasan Salmān's* book, in *Hudā* v.5 no.3.

ولأبي داود بسند صحيح عن عقبة بن عامر رضي الله عنه قال: ذكرت الطيرة عند رسول الله صلى الله عليه وسلم فقال: (أحسنها الفأل، ولا ترد مسلماً فإذا رأى أحدكم ما يكره فليقل: اللهم لا يأتي بالحسنات إلا أنت، ولا يدفع السيئات إلا أنت، ولا حول ولا قوة إلا بك).

And from Abū Dāwūd with a *ṣaḥīḥ* chain from ʿUqbah[80] bin ʿĀmir who said, "*Ṭiyarah* was mentioned to Allāh's Messenger, he said, 'The best of it is *fa'l*. It does not harm a Muslim. So when one of you sees what he dislikes then let him say, "O Allāh none brings good but You! None defends from evil but You! There is no might or power except by You.!"

وعن ابن مسعود رضي الله عنه مرفوعاً: «الطيرة شرك، الطيرة شرك، وما منا إلا ، ولكن الله يذهبه بالتوكل» رواه أبو داود، والترمذي وصححه، وجعل آخره من قول ابن مسعود.

Ibn Masʿūd reported [that the Prophet (ﷺ) said]; "*Ṭiyarah* is *shirk*, *ṭiyarah* is *shirk*, it will not be among us but Allāh would remove it through *tawakkul*." Recorded by Abū Dāwūd and *al-Tirmidhī* who said it was *ṣaḥīḥ*, but he quoted the end of it from Ibn Masʿūd.[81]

ولأحمد من حديث ابن عمرو: (من ردته الطيرة عن حاجة فقد أشرك) قالوا: فما كفارة ذلك؟ قال: (أن تقول: اللهم لا خير إلا خيرك، ولا طير إلا طيرك، ولا إله غيرك).

And with Aḥmad is a ḥadīth from Ibn ʿAmr, "Whoever is prevented from what he is in need of because of an omen [*ṭiyarah*] he has committed *shirk*." They said, "What is the atonement for it?" He said, To say, 'O Allāh there is no good except for Your good, there is no omen except your omen, and none worthy of worship other than You.'"[82]

وله من حديث الفضل بن عباس رضي الله عنهما: إنما الطيرة ما أمضاك أو ردك.

[80] That is ʿUrwah. It is not clear if he was a companion. And its chain was labeled weak by ʿAbd al-Qādir al-Arnā'ūṭ in his notes on *Fatḥ al-Majīd*, as well as al-Albānī; no. 843 of *Ḍaʿīf Sunan Abū Dāwūd*.

[81] It was also recorded by Ibn Mājah, al-Nasā'ī, Aḥmad and others. Al-Tirmidhī noted that he heard al-Bukhārī saying that his Shaykh Sulaymān bin Ḥarb said that the addition is from Ibn Masʿūd. Al-Albānī graded it *ṣaḥīḥ* no. 1314 *Ṣaḥīḥ Sunan Al-Tirmidhī*.

[82] Recorded by Aḥmad and al-Ṭabarānī from ʿAbdullāh bin ʿAmr *marfūʿ*. Its chain contains Ibn Luhīʿah who al-Ḥaythamī noted is weak. Al-Albānī included it up to "he has committed *shirk*", in *Ṣaḥīḥ al-Jāmiʿ* no. 6264, see its discussion in *al-Ṣaḥīḥah* no. 1065.

Also collected by Aḥmad is a ḥadīth from al-Faḍl bin ʿAbbās (ﷺ), "*Ṭiyarah* is only if you proceed or refrain [because of it]."[83]

فيه مسائل:

الأولى: التنبيه على قوله: (ألا إنما طائرهم عند الله) مع قوله: (طائركم معكم).

الثانية: نفي العدوى.

الثالثة: نفي الطيرة.

الرابعة: نفي الهامة.

الخامسة: نفي الصفر.

السادسة: أن الفأل ليس من ذلك بل مستحب.

السابعة: تفسير الفأل.

الثامنة: أن الواقع في القلوب من ذلك مع كراهته لا يضر بل يذهبه الله بالتوكل.

التاسعة: ذكر ما يقول من وجده.

العاشرة: التصريح بأن الطيرة شرك.

الحادية عشرة: تفسير الطيرة المذمومة.

Important Points

1. Explaining the saying of Allāh, "...Rather, their (evil beliefs based on their) omens are about Allāh, but most of them do not know" with "Your omens are for you."
2. The negation of ʿ*adwā*.
3. The negation of *ṭiyarah*.
4. The negation of *hāmah*.

[83] Al-Musnad. It's chain is weak and disconnected according to al-Arnāʾūṭ.

5. The negation of *ṣafar*.
6. That *fa'l* is not included, rather it is recommended.
7. The explanation of *fa'l*.
8. Any hesitation that occurs in the hearts [due to omens] will not actually cause harm, rather Allāh would remove it if *tawakkul* is present.
9. Mentioning what should be said by one in such case.
10. The clarification that *ṭiyarah* is *shirk*.
11. The explanation of the blameworthy *ṭiyarah*.

Commentary by *ʿAllāmah* al-Saʿdī

What is said about omens

That is pessimism due to omens, or names or expressions or locations etc. The *sharīʿah* has prohibited pessimism due to omens and it censures the omen readers, whereas *fa'l* is recommended and omens are rejected.

The difference between them; the good *fa'l* does not effect people's creed nor reasoning, nor does it require the heart to depend upon other than Allāh. Rather it encourages beneficial activity and happiness, and it encourages the soul in the pursuit of what is beneficial.

An example is when the worshipper has decided to travel, or marry, or to agree to a contract, or such important circumstance. Then he sees something which encourages him to do it, or he hears words that encourage him, like someone saying to him, "O *Rāshid* [one who was guided aright], or O *Sālim* [unobstructed] or *Ghānim* [successful]." So he is encouraged, and his desire to see the matter through that he has already decided to do will intensify. All of this is good and results in good things, there being nothing of precaution in that.

As for the omen, that is when one decides to do some beneficial religious or worldly matter, but he sees or hears something that causes him to hesitate over that. This results in one of two cases, one of which is worse than the other;

1. He gives in to that premonition, avoiding what he had decided to do, or vice versa. So he becomes pessimistic because of it, retreating from something that he already decided on. So, as can be seen by this, his heart becomes utterly dependant and acts upon this bad feeling. This bad feeling, in turn, changed his intention, his decision, and his action. There is no doubt that in such a case there is an effect on his faith, damaging his *tawḥīd* and *tawakkul*. Not to mention the weakness of the heart and the fear of creatures that has arisen in it his heart. All of this causes him to depend upon matters that there is no reason for, cutting off his heart's dependence upon Allāh. This is a sign of the weaknesses of *tawḥīd* and *tawakkul*, and it is one of the paths of *shirk* and the routes leading to it, as well as being among the superstitions abhorrent to reason.

2. That he does not accept that premonition, yet it fills his heart with stress, sadness and grief. So even though this is not the same as the first, it is still evil and harmful for the worshipper, weakening the heart and diminishing *tawakkul*. Sometimes his bad feelings prove true, so thinking that it was because of that omen, it intensifies his pessimism, and sometimes it will reach the level of the first case.

So this is an elaboration to explain why the *sharī'ah* shows an abhorrence for pessimism, why it censures it, and how such pessimism negates *tawḥīd* and *tawakkul*. It is necessary for anyone who senses something like this, fearing that he may be overcome and follow the premonition, that he struggle to defend himself and seek help from Allāh for this, and not depend upon such premonitions, thinking that they will protect him from evil.

Chapter 29

ما جاء في التنجيم

What is said about astronomy/astrology

قال البخاري في «صحيحه»: قال قتادة: خلق الله هذه النجوم لثلاث: زينة للسماء ورجوماً للشياطين، وعلامات يهتدى بها. فمن تأول فيها غير ذلك اخطأ، وأضاع نصيبه، وتكلف ما لا علم له به. أ.هـ.

In his *Ṣaḥīḥ*, al-Bukhārī said, "Qatādah said, 'Allāh created these stars for three [things]; decorating the heavens, stoning the *shayāṭīn*, and signs for navigation. Whoever interprets other than that about them is mistaken and missed his share, and mentioned what he has no knowledge of.'"[84]

وكره قتادة تعلم منازل القمر، ولم يرخص ابن عيينة فيه، ذكره حرب عنهما، ورخص في تعلم المنازل أحمد وإسحاق.

Qatādah disliked learning about the moon's orbit, Ibn 'Uyaynah did not make a concession for it, Ḥarb mentioned this from them. Aḥmad and Isḥāq made exception for it.[85]

وعن أبي موسى قال: قال رسول الله صلى الله عليه وسلم: (ثلاثة لا يدخلون الجنة: مدمن الخمر، وقاطع الرحم، ومصدق بالسحر) رواه أحمد وابن حبان في صحيحه.

---

[84] This was mentioned in *mu'allaq* form by al-Bukhārī. Ibn Ḥājar (*Fatḥ al-Bārī*) said that it was connected by 'Abd bin Ḥumayd via Shaybān. It was also recorded by 'Abdul-Razzāq, Ibn Jarīr, Ibn al-Mundhir and others.

[85] Ḥarb bin Ismā'īl, Abū Muḥammad al-Karmāni a companion of Aḥmad and Isḥāq bin Rahuyah.

From Abū Mūsa who said that Allāh's Messenger said, "Three will not enter Paradise, the one addicted to *ḳhamr*, one who cuts the relations of kinship, and the believer in magic." Recorded by Aḥmad and Ibn Ḥibbān in his *Ṣaḥīḥ*.[86]

فيه مسائل:

الأولى: الحكمة في خلق النجوم.

الثانية: الرد على من زعم غير ذلك.

الثالثة: ذكر الخلاف في تعلم المنازل.

الرابعة: الوعيد فيمن صدق بشيء من السحر ولو عرف أنه باطل.

Important Points

1. The wisdom in creating the stars.
2. The refutation of whoever claims contrary to that.
3. The mention of the difference over learning about orbits.
4. The threat for whoever finds truth in any kind of magic even if he knows that it is false.

Commentary by *ʿAllāmah* al-Saʿdī

What is said about astronomy/astrology

There are two types of astronomy;

1. The type called knowledge of the effects [i.e., astrology]. That is deducing universal occurrences from astronomical conditions. This is falsehood, and it is a claim of sharing with Allāh in knowing the unseen, a knowledge of which He is alone in. Or, it amounts to having faith in the one who makes such claims. This negates *tawḥīd* because of the falsehood that such claims amount to, and since the

[86] This ḥadīth is also recorded by al-Ṭabarānī and al-Ḥākim. Due to its routes all going through Abū Harīr, ʿAbdullāh bin al-Ḥuṣayn al-Azadi, it is weak. See *Ḍaʿīf Jāmiʿ al-Ṣaghīr* no. 2598., and *Ḍaʿīf Mawārid al-Ẓamān* no. 171 no. 163

heart depends on other than Allāh, and since it contains that which contradicts reason. Such claims traverse the paths of falsehood, giving credence to them, corrupting reason and religion.

2. Facilitating knowledge; that is determining the *qiblah*, the time, or the direction due to the sun, moon or the stars. This type contains no harm. Rather most of it is beneficial. The *sharī'ah* laid some emphasis on it since it is a way to know the time for acts of worship, or a means to follow proper directions.

So it is necessary to distinguish between what the *sharī'ah* prohibits and deems unlawful, and that which it allows, recommends and obliges. The first category is the kind that negates *tawḥīd*, not the second.

Chapter 30

ما جاء في الاستسقاء بالأنواء

What is said about seeking rain by *anwā'*

وقول الله تعالى: (وتجعلون رزقكم أنكم تكذبون) .

Allāh (ﷻ) said; "Rather than (thanking Allāh) for the provision He gives you, you deny (Him)?" (*al-Wāqi'ah* 56:82)

عن أبي مالك الأشعري رضي الله عنه أن رسول الله صلى الله عليه وسلم قال: (أربعة في أمتي من أمر الجاهلية لا يتركونهن: الفخر بالأحساب، والطعن في الأنساب، والاستسقاء بالنجوم، والنياحة) وقال: (النائحة إذا لم تتب قبل موتها تقام يوم القيامة وعليها سربال من قطران ودرع من جرب). رواه مسلم.

Abū Mālik al-Ash'arī (رضي الله عنه) reported that the Messenger of Allāh (ﷺ) said; "There are four matters of *jāhilīyyah* in my *ummah* that they will not leave; pride of ancestry, abusing lineage, seeking rain by the stars, and wailing."

And he said; "When the wailing woman does not repent before her death, she will be raised on the Day of Resurrection with a coat of tar and skin of leprosy." Recorded by Muslim.

ولهما عن زيد بن خالد رضي الله عنه قال: صلى لنا رسول الله صلى الله عليه وسلم صلاة الصبح بالحديبية على إثر سماء كانت من الليل، فلما انصرف أقبل على الناس فقال: (هل تدرون ماذا قال ربكم؟) قالوا: الله ورسوله أعلم. قال: (قال: أصبح من عبادي مؤمن بي وكافر، فأما من قال: مطرنا بفضل الله ورحمته، فذلك مؤمن بي كافر بالكوكب، وأما من قال: مطرنا بنوء كذا وكذا، فذلك كافر بي مؤمن بالكواكب).

Zayd bin Khālid (رضي الله عنه) reports; "The Prophet (ﷺ) lead us in the morning prayer at al-Ḥudaybiyah after a night of rain. When he finished, he faced the people and said;

'Do you know what your Lord has said?' They said, 'Allāh and His Messenger (ﷺ) know better.' He said, 'He said; "This morning some of my servants have believed in Me and others have disbelieved. As for the believer he said, 'We received rain from Allāh's bounty.' That is the believer in Me and the disbeliever in the stars. As for the one who said, 'We received rain because the position of the stars was like this and this' that is the disbeliever in Me and the believer in the stars." (Al-Bukhārī and Muslim).

ولهما من حديث ابن عباس بمعناه وفيه قال بعضهم: لقد صدق نوء كذا وكذا، فأنزل الله هذه الآيات: (فلا أقسم بمواقع النجوم) إلى قوله: (وتجعلون رزقكم أنكم تكذبون) .

And for them[87]is a ḥadīth from Ibn 'Abbās (رضي الله عنه) with this meaning. In it; "Some said, 'Such and such positioning proved right.'" So Allāh revealed these *āyāt*; "But no! I swear by the setting star, and it is a tremendous oath if you but knew, that it is a honoured Qur'ān, in a protected book, none touches it but the pure, revealed from the Lord of the worlds. Is this the news that you deny and rather than (thanking Allāh) for the provision He gives you, you deny (Him)?" (*al-Wāqi'ah* 56:75-82)

فيه مسائل:

الأولى: تفسير آية الواقعة.

الثانية: ذكر الأربع من أمر الجاهلية.

الثالثة: ذكر الكفر في بعضها.

الرابعة: أن من الكفر ما لا يخرج عن الملة.

الخامسة: قوله: (أصبح من عبادي مؤمن بي وكافر) بسبب نزول النعمة.

السادسة: التفطن للإيمان في هذا الموضع.

السابعة: التفطن للكفر في هذا الموضع.

الثامنة: التفطن لقوله: (لقد صدق نوء كذا وكذا).

التاسعة: إخراج العالم للمتعلم المسألة بالاستفهام عنها، لقوله: (أتدرون ماذا قال ربكم؟).

العاشرة: وعيد النائحة.

[87] Recorded by Muslim.

Important Points

1. Explanation of the *āyah* of *al-Wāqi'ah*.
2. Mention of four matters of *jāhilīyyah*.
3. Mentioning disbelief in the case of some of them.
4. That among disbelief is that which does not remove one from the *millah*.
5. His saying, "This morning some of my servants believed in Me and others disbelieved" because of the favours [that Allāh alone] sent down.
6. The importance of faith in this context.
7. The importance of disbelief in this context.
8. The importance of saying, "Such and such positioning proved true."
9. The knowledgeable teaching the seeker of knowledge by asking, "Do you know what your Lord has said?"
10. The threat of punishment for wailing.

Commentary by *'Allāmah* al-Sa'dī

Seeking rain by *anwā'*

Since it is part of *tawḥīd* to recognise that Allāh is the sole provider of favours and protector against affliction, and sayings and beliefs related to this are attributed to Him out of obedience to Him, then the saying, "We received rain because the positions were like this and this" negates this objective via the severest negation because it attributes the rain to the position [of planets or stars].

The obligation is to attribute the rain and other such favours to Allāh, for He is the one who dispenses this to His worshippers. As for the *anwā'*, this is by no means the reason that rain comes down. The reasons are only related to the love and mercy from Allāh, due to His worshippers being in need and their requesting it from their Lord, either because of their conditions, or their requests for it. So He sends the rains down on them in His wisdom and mercy depending upon their needs and necessities.

So the worshipper's *tawḥīd* is not complete until he recognises the external and internal favours that Allāh grants to him and all creatures, attributing these favours to Him, seeking them while worshipping Him, remembering Him, and being grateful to Him.

This is a case of the fulfilment of *tawḥīd*, and with this, what completes faith and what nullifies it will be known.

Chapter 31

قول الله تعالى: ومن الناس من يتخذ من دون الله أنداداً

Allāh (ﷻ) said; "and among people are those who have taken other than Allāh as equals"

قول الله تعالى: (ومن الناس من يتخذ من دون الله أنداداً يحبونهم كحب الله) الآية. وقوله: (قل إن كان ءاباؤكم وأبناؤكم). إلى قول تعالى: (أحب إليكم من الله ورسوله) الآية.

Allāh (ﷻ) said; "And among people are those who have taken other than Allāh as equals whom they love as they love Allāh." (*al-Baqarah* 2:102). And He (ﷻ) said; "Say; 'If your fathers, and your children, and your brothers, and your wives and your relatives, and the wealth that you have acquired, and the businesses you fear decline in, and your pleasant dwellings are more loved to you than Allāh, His Messenger, and *jihād* in His cause - then wait until Allāh brings His command."(*al-Tawbah* 9:24)

عن أنس رضي الله عنه، أن رسول الله صلى الله عليه وسلم قال: (لا يؤمن أحدكم حتى أكون أحب إليه من ولده ووالده والناس أجمعين) أخرجاه.

Anas (ﷺ) reported that Allāh's Messenger (ﷺ) said, "None of you believes until I am more loved to him than his children his parents and all of humanity." They have [al-Bukhārī and Muslim] recorded it.

ولهما عنه قال: قال رسول الله صلى الله عليه وسلم: (ثلاث من كن فيه وجد بهن حلاوة الإيمان: أن يكون الله رسوله أحب إليه مما سواهما، وأن يحب المرء لا يحبه إلا لله، وأن يكره أن يعود في الكفر بعد إذ أنقذه الله منه كما يكره أن يقذف في النار)، وفي رواية: (لا يجد أحد حلاوة الإيمان حتى ..) إلى آخره.

And from al-Bukhārī and Muslim, "Allāh's Messenger (ﷺ)said, 'There are three things that for whomever they are present, he has the delight of faith;

That Allāh and His Messenger are more loved to him than anyone else, that he loves a person - not loving him for other than Allāh, and that he hates to return to disbelief after Allāh has saved him from it, just as he would hate to be thrown into the Fire."

In one narration[88]; "None shall have the delight of faith until..." until the end.

وعن ابن عباس رضي الله عنهما قال: من أحب في الله، وأبغض في الله، ووالى في الله، وعادى في الله، فإنما تنال ولاية الله بذلك، ولن يجد عبد طعم الإيمان وإن كثرت صلاته وصومه حتى يكون كذلك. وقد صارت عامة مؤاخاة الناس على أمر الدنيا، وذلك لا يجدي على أهله شيئا. رواه بن جرير، وقال ابن عباس في قوله تعالى: (وتقطعت بهم الأسباب) قال: المودة.

And from Ibn ʿAbbās (ﷺ); "Whoever loves for Allāh, hates for Allāh, befriends for Allāh, shows enmity for Allāh's sake - this is the only way for Allāh's friendship. There will not be a person tasting faith even though he increases his prayer, his fasting, until he is like that. In general, the case is that people are brothers in matters of the world, and that will not bring anything for its people." Recorded by Ibn Jarīr.[89] And explaining the saying of Allāh (ﷻ) "And their ties of kinship are cut." (*al-Baqarah* 2:166) he [Ibn ʿAbbās] said, "Love."[90]

فيه مسائل:

الأولى: تفسير آية البقرة.

الثانية: تفسير آية براءة.

الثالثة: وجوب محبته صلى الله عليه وسلم على النفس والأهل والمال.

الرابعة: أن نفي الإيمان لا يدل على الخروج من الإسلام.

الخامسة: أن للإيمان حلاوة قد يجدها الإنسان وقد لا يجدها.

---

[88] Al-Bukhārī in the *Book of Adab* from Anas.

[89] Also recorded by Aḥmad. Al-Arnā'ūṭ labeled it weak. The first part is also recorded by Ibn Abū Shaybah and Ibn Abū Ḥātim.

[90] "This report was recorded by ʿAbd bin Ḥumayd, Ibn Jarīr, Ibn al-Mundhir, and Ibn Abū Ḥātim and al-Ḥākim, who graded it *ṣaḥīḥ*" (*Fatḥ al-Majīd*). "And al-Dhahabī agreed, and it is as he said" Al-Arnā'ūṭ. Yet in other books, al-Dhahabī graded one of its narrators -ʿĪsa bin Abī ʿĪsa- beeble of even worse, as did many others including Shaykh Muqbil in his notes on *al-Mustadrak* (no. 3135) and al-Albānī in many places.

السادسة: أعمال القلب الأربعة التي لا تنال ولاية الله إلا بها، ولا يجد أحد طعم الإيمان إلا بها.

السابعة: فهم الصحابي للواقع: أن عامة المؤاخاة على أمر الدنيا.

الثامنة: تفسير: (وتقطّعت بهم الأسباب) .

التاسعة: أن من المشركين من يحب الله حباً شديداً.

العاشرة: الوعيد على من كانت الثمانية أحب إليه من دينه.

الحادية عشرة: أن من اتخذ نداً تساوي محبته محبة الله فهو الشرك الأكبر.

Important Points

1. Explanation of the *āyah* of *Sūrah al-Baqarah*.
2. Explanation of the *āyah* of *Sūrah al-Barā'ah* (*al-Tawbah*)
3. The obligation of loving him (ﷺ) more than the self, one's family and wealth.
4. The negation of faith is not proof of the removal from Islām.
5. That there is a delightful taste to faith, for some it is present, and for others it is not.
6. Four deeds of the heart for which there will not occur friendship of Allāh without them, nor will there be one who has tasted faith without them.
7. The understanding of the companion that in general, people form bonds of brotherhood based on matters of the world.
8. The explanation of; "And their ties of relationship are cut."
9. That among the *mushrikīn* are those who have a strong love for Allāh.
10. The threat of punishment for anyone who loves the eight things mentioned more than his religion.
11. That to take a rival, loving him equally as one loves Allāh, is major *shirk*.

Commentary by *ʿAllāmah* al-Saʿdi

The Saying of Allāh; "And among people are those who have taken other than Allāh as equals whom they love as they love Allāh." (*al-Baqarah* 2:102)

The foundation and essence of *tawḥīd* is rendering one's love sincerely to Allāh alone, and this is the basis of deifying Him and servitude to Him. Rather it is the reality of worship. *Tawḥīd* is not complete until the worshipper's love for his Lord is complete, and until his love for Him surpasses and overcomes that of all whom he loves, and that all of those that he loves are loved only in proportion to the extent of their love for Allāh. For this is how strength and happiness may be obtained.

Among the branches and signs of completion of love for Allāh's sake, is that the worshipper loves the deeds and qualities that Allāh loves, and he hates the deeds and qualities that Allāh hates, and he befriends His (ﷻ) friends and is an enemy of His (ﷻ) enemies. By this the worshipper perfects his faith and *tawḥīd*.

As for taking equals who are loved as Allāh is loved, and choosing their obedience over obedience to Allāh, and dedicating oneself to their remembrance and calling upon them, this is major *shirk*, the kind that Allāh does not pardon for. The heart of the one who practices this *shirk* is devoid of love for Allāh (ﷻ) and dependant upon others besides Him who have no control over anything. This is the same useless dependence that occurs among the *mushrikīn*, for which, on the Day of Resurrection, they will be cut off completely from what they worshipped. This love and friendship will have turned into hatred and enmity.

Know that love is divided into three categories;

1. Love of Allāh which is the foundation of faith and *tawḥīd*.

2. Love for Allāh's sake; loving Allāh's prophets, His messengers, and following them, and loving the deeds that Allāh loves, and the times and places, etc., and this follows the love of Allāh and perfects it.

3. Love with Allāh. This is the love of the *mushrikīn* for their gods and their equals among trees, stones, humans, angels, etc., and it is the foundation of *shirk* and its root.

Here there is also a fourth category of love, that is the natural love which depends upon what a person likes and dislikes of food, drink, marrying, clothes, comradary etc., and this, when it is allowed, then it falls under the larger category of loving Allāh and obedience to Him, and it enters into the category of worship. But if it departs from this, and leads one to what Allāh does not love, then it will either cross over into the prohibited things, or remain among the lawful. And Allāh knows best.

Chapter 32

قول الله تعالى: إنما ذلكم الشيطان يخوف أولياءه

The saying of Allāh (ﷻ); "It is only Shayṭān who suggests fearing of his friends"

قول الله تعالى: (إنما ذلكم الشيطان يخوف أولياءه فلا تخافوهم وخافون إن كنتم مؤمنين).
وقوله: (إنما يعمر مساجد الله من آمن بالله واليوم الآخر وأقام الصلاة وآتى الزكاة و لم يخش إلا الله) الآية.

وقوله: (ومن الناس من يقول ءامنا بالله فإذا أوذي في الله جعل فتنة الناس كعذاب الله) الآية.

The saying of Allāh (ﷻ); "It is only *shayṭān* who suggests fearing of his friends, do not fear them, but fear Me if you are indeed believers." (*Āl ʿImrān* 3:175) And He (ﷻ) said; "The *masjids* of Allāh are only to be maintained by those who believe in Allāh and the Last Day, establish prayer, pay *zakāh*, and do not fear except Allāh, it is only those that can be among the guided." (*al-Tawbah* 9:18) And; "Among people are those who say, 'We believe in Allāh.' But when they are tested by Allāh, they equate the trials of man to Allāh's punishment." (*al-ʿAnkabūt* 29:10)

عن أبي سعيد رضي الله عنه مرفوعا: (إن من ضعف اليقين: أن ترضى الناس بسخط الله، وأن تحمدهم على رزق الله، وأن تذمهم على ما لم يؤتك الله، إن رزق الله لا يجره حرص حريص، ولا يرده كراهية كاره).

From Abū Saʿid al-Khudri (رضي الله عنه) *marfūʿ*; "Among the weakening of certainty is to please the people by displeasing Allāh, and to praise them for what Allāh provided, and to blame them for what Allāh did not give you, Allāh's providing is not due to wishful desires nor is it withheld by the loathing of one who hates it."[91]

وعن عائشة رضي الله عنها: أن رسول الله صلى الله عليه وسلم قال: (من التمس رضى الله بسخط الناس رضي الله عنه وأرضى عنه الناس، ومن التمس رضى الناس بسخط الله سخط الله عليه وأسخط عليه الناس) رواه ابن حبان في صحيحه.

From 'Ā'ishah (🌸) that Allāh's Messenger (🌸) said, "Whoever seeks Allāh's pleasure at the expense of the displeasure of people, then Allāh will be pleased with him and the people will be pleased with him. And whoever seeks the pleasure of the people at the expense of the displeasure of Allāh, Allāh will be displeased with him and the people will be displeased with him." Recorded by Ibn Ḥibbān in his *Ṣaḥīḥ*.[92]

فيه مسائل:

الأولى: تفسير آية آل عمران.

الثانية: تفسير آية براءة.

الثالثة: تفسير آية العنكبوت.

الرابعة: أن اليقين يضعف ويقوى.

الخامسة: علامة ضعفه، ومن ذلك هذه الثلاث.

السادسة: أن إخلاص الخوف لله من الفرائض.

السابعة: ذكر ثواب من فعله.

الثامنة: ذكر عقاب من تركه.

---

[91] "This ḥadīth was recorded by Abū Nu'aym in *al-Ḥilyah*, and al-Bayhaqī in *Shu'b al-Imān* who saw it as deficient due to Muḥammad bin Marwān al-Suddī, he said, 'Weak.'..."(*Taysīr*) there are also problems with other narrators in its chain. Al-Arnā'ūṭ said, "It is a weak ḥadīth." Al-Albānī graded it weak in *Ḍa'īf al-Jāmi'* no. 2009, and there is a reference there for it in *al-Ḍa'īfah* (no. 482) but the number is incorrect.

[92] It is recorded by Abū Nu'aym, and al-Tirmidhī, and it was graded *ṣaḥīḥ* by Al-Albānī (no. 1967) *Ṣaḥīḥ Sunan Al-Tirmidhī*.

Important Points

1. The explanation of the *āyah* of *Sūrah Āl ʿImrān*.
2. The explanation of the *āyah* of *Sūrah al-Barāʾah*.
3. The explanation of the *āyah* of *Sūrah al-ʿAnkabūt*.
4. That certainty weakens and strengthens.
5. Signs of its weakening, and these three are among them.
6. That sincere fear for Allāh is among the obligations.
7. Mentioning the reward of he who achieves it.
8. Mentioning the punishment of he who avoids it.

Commentary by *ʿAllāmah* al-Saʿdī

The saying of Allāh (ﷻ);"It is only *shayṭān* who suggests fearing of his friends, do not fear them, but fear Me if you are indeed believers." (*Āl ʿImrān* 3: 175)

By this chapter the author, may Allāh have mercy upon him, is reminding of the obligation of one to rely with his fear on Allāh alone, the prohibition of directing that to creatures, and clarifying that *tawḥīd* is not complete otherwise.

Some details are necessary here for clarification and to remove any confusion. Know that fear and dread sometimes occurs out of worship, and sometimes naturally and habitually, and that depends upon the causes and related conditions.

So if the fear and dread causes deification, worship and seeking to be nearer to the one feared, and it inwardly encourages obedience and fearing him secretly, such that it prevents him from disobeying the one feared, then directing it to Allāh is among the greatest of the obligations of faith, and directing it to other than Allāh is the major *shirk* that Allāh does not forgive. Because this is an act associating this worship - which is among the greatest obligations of the heart - to other than Allāh along with Allāh, and sometimes it increases his fear of the others more than his fear of Allāh.

Also, whoever fears Allāh alone, in this way, he is sincere in his *tawḥīd*, and whoever fears other than Him, then he has made an equal to Allāh in his fearing, just like one who makes an equal to Allāh in love. This is like a person who fears earning the anger or displeasure of someone in a grave. So he cancels the favour or whatever occurs by his worshipping the grave.

If the fear is natural, like one who fears his enemy or a predator or a snake etc., then what he fears is the obvious harm. So this type is not worship, it will happen to many of the believers, and it does not negate their faith. When he is fearing that which warrants such fear - depending upon the cause - then this fear is not the blameworthy type.

If his fear and hesitation is due to one whom there is no reason to fear at all, or there is a poor reason for it, then this is the blameworthy type which leads its doer to cowardice. The Prophet (ﷺ) sought refuge in Allāh from cowardice because it is among the evil qualities. Complete faith, *tawakkul*, and courage all defend against cowardice, making the believers sincere, strengthening them, turning their fear to the One who can give them security and tranquility, strengthening their faith and the courage in their hearts, perfecting their reliance upon Him (ﷻ). And this topic is discussed in the next chapter.

Chapter 33

قول الله تعالى: وعلى الله فتوكلوا إن كنتم مؤمنين

Allāh's (ﷻ) saying; "Depend upon Allāh, if you are indeed believers."

قول الله تعالى: (وعلى الله فتوكلوا إن كنتم مؤمنين) . وقوله: (إنما المؤمنون الذين إذا ذكر الله وجلت قلوبهم) الآية وقوله (يا أيها النبي حسبك الله ومن اتبعك من المؤمنين) وقوله (ومن يتوكل على الله فهو حسبه) .

Allāh's (ﷻ) saying; "Depend upon Allāh, if you are indeed believers." (*al-Mā'idah* 5:23) And; "The believers are only those who when Allāh is mentioned, their hearts shudder with fear." (*al-Anfāl* 18:2) And; "O Prophet! Sufficient for you is Allāh and [for] those who follow you among the believers." (*al-Anfāl* 8: 64) And; "And whoever dependeds upon Allāh, then He is sufficient for him." (*al-Ṭalāq* 65:3)

عن ابن عباس رضي الله عنهما قال: (حسبنا الله ونعم الوكيل) . قالها إبراهيم عليه السلام حين ألقي في النار، وقالها محمد صلى الله عليه وسلم حين قالوا له: (إن الناس قد جمعوا لكم فاخشوهم فزادهم إيماناً وقالوا حسبنا الله ونعم الوكيل) رواه البخاري والنسائي.

Ibn 'Abbās (ﷺ) said, "'Sufficient unto us is Allāh and He is the best to depend upon.' This was said by Ibrāhīm (ﷺ) when he faced the fire, and Muḥammad (ﷺ) said it when they said to him; 'The people have gathered against you, so fear them.' Their faith only increased and they said, 'Allāh is sufficient for us and the best to depend upon.'" Recorded by al-Bukhārī and al-Nasā'ī.[93]

---

[93] Recorded by al-Bukhārī in the *Book of Tafsīr* in his *Ṣaḥīḥ*.

فيه مسائل:

الأولى: أن التوكل من الفرائض.

الثانية: أنه من شروط الإيمان.

الثالثة: تفسير آية الأنفال.

الرابعة: تفسير الآية في آخرها.

الخامسة: تفسير آية الطلاق.

السادسة: عظم شأن هذه الكلمة، وأنها قول إبراهيم ومحمد صلى الله عليهما وسلم في الشدائد.

Important Points

1. That *tawakkul* is among the obligations.
2. That it is among the conditions of faith.
3. The explanation of the *āyah* of *Sūrah al-Anfāl*.
4. The explanation of the *āyah* that comes later after it.
5. The explanation of the *āyah* of *Sūrah al-Ṭalāq*.
6. The great importance of this saying, that it was said by Ibrāhīm and Muḥammad (ﷺ) during their hardest times.

Commentary by ʿ*Allāmah* al-Saʿdī

Allāh's (ﷻ) saying; "Depend upon Allāh, if you are indeed believers." (*al-Mā'idah* 5:23)

Tawakkul upon Allāh is one of the most important obligations of *tawḥīd* and faith. The worshipper's faith strengthens and his *tawḥīd* is completed, according to the degree of the strength of his dependence upon Allāh. The worshipper is compelled to depend upon Allāh and seek His aid in all that he intends to do or avoid doing in his worldly or religious affairs.

The reality of *tawakkul* upon Allāh is that the worshipper knows every matter is from Allāh. And that whatever Allāh wills will certainly be, and what He does not will cannot be. And that He is the benefactor, the malefactor, the giver, the withholder, and that there is no power nor might but by Allāh. So after having this knowledge, his heart depends upon his Lord to bring him the benefit in his religious and worldly affairs, and to protect him from harm. Then he has the utmost trust in his Lord to bring about what he seeks. By this he has made every possible effort for those means that bring benefit.

So when the worshipper maintains this knowledge, this reliance, and trust, then he is depending upon Allāh in reality, and for him is good news and the promises of Allāh for the people of *tawakkul*. And when he depends in this way on other than Allāh, then he is a *mushrik*, and whoever depends or relies upon other than Allāh, then he is entrusted to that, and he has lost his way.

Chapter 34

قول الله تعالى: أفأمنوا مكر الله

Allāh's (ﷻ) saying; "Are they secure from Allāh's plan?"

قول الله تعالى: (أفأمنوا مكر الله فلا يأمن مكر الله إلا القوم الخاسرون) وقوله: (ومن يقنط من رحمة ربه إلا الضالون) .

Allāh's (ﷻ) saying; "Are they secure from Allāh's plan? None feels safe from Allāh's planning but the doomed." (*al-Aʿrāf* 7:99) And; "And who despairs of his Lords mercy but the misguided?" (*al-Ḥijr* 15:56)

عن ابن عباس رضي الله عنهما، أن رسول الله صلى الله عليه وسلم سئل عن الكبائر، فقال: (الشرك بالله، واليأس من روح الله، والأمن من مكر الله).

وعن ابن مسعود رضي الله عنه قال: (أكبر الكبائر: الإشراك بالله، والأمن من مكر الله، والقنوط من رحمة الله، واليأس من روح الله) رواه عبد الرزاق.

Ibn ʿAbbās (ﷺ) said, "Allāh's Messenger (ﷺ) was asked about the major sins. He said, '*Shirk* with Allāh, despair of hope in Allāh and feeling secure from Allāh's planning."[94] Ibn Masʿūd (ﷺ) said, " The greatest of major sins are *shirk* with Allāh, feeling secure [from Him], feeling despair of His mercy, and giving up hope in Allāh." Recorded by ʿAbdul-Razzāq.[95]

---

[94] "This ḥadīth was recorded by al-Bazzār, and Ibn Abū Ḥātim by way of Shabīb bin Bishr, from ʿIkrimah from Ibn ʿAbbās. Its narrators are trustworthy except for Shabīb bin Bishr..." (*Fatḥ al-Majīd*) "Al-Ḥaythamī mentioned it in *Majmaʿ al-Zawāʾid* (1/104) from the ḥadīth of Ibn ʿAbbās (ﷺ), saying at the end of it, 'Recorded by al-Bazzār and al-Ṭabarānī and their narrators are trustworthy." Al-Arnāʾūṭ.

[95] "It was recorded by Ibn Jarīr with a correct chain from Ibn Masʿūd (ﷺ)." (*Fatḥ al-Majīd*) "And Al-Ḥaythamī mentioned it in *Majmaʿ al-Zawāʾid* (1:104) reporting it from al-Ṭabarānī in *al-Kabīr*. He said, 'Its chain is *ṣaḥīḥ*.'" (Al-Arnāʾūṭ)

فيه مسائل:

الأولى: تفسير آية الأعراف.

الثانية: تفسير آية الحجر.

الثالثة: شدة الوعيد فيمن أمن مكر الله.

الرابعة: شدة الوعيد في القنوط.

Important Points

1. The explanation of the *āyah* of *Sūrah al-Aʿrāf*.
2. The explanation of the *āyah* of *Sūrah al-Ḥijr*.
3. The severity of the threat for whoever feels secure from Allāh's planning.
4. The severity of the threat for despair.

Commentary by *ʿAllāmah* al-Saʿdī

Allāh's (ﷻ) saying; "Are they secure from Allāh's plan? None feels safe from Allāh's planning but the doomed." (*al-Aʿrāf* 7:99)

The intent of this discussion is that it is necessary for the worshipper to fear Allāh, as well as hope in Him with desire and fear. If he looks at his sins and Allāh's justice, and His severity in punishment, then he becomes frightened and is in a state of anxiety over his Lord. If he looks at His favours both general and specific, and His encompassing forgiveness, then he hopes in Him. If he was obedient he hopes from his Lord to complete that favour and accept his acts of obedience from him, fearing His rejection of it because he may not have fulfilled all of its requirements. And if he falls into disobedience, he hopes that his Lord will accepts his repentance and erases his faults, and he fears the deficiency of his repentance and repeating the sins that he would be punished for.

Whenever he is blessed and facilitated he hopes that Allāh will continue this and increase him in this way, and he hopes that he has properly demonstrated his gratitude for it, and he fears a deficiency in his gratitude that would ruin it. When he is upset and distressed, he hopes that Allāh will protect him, and he awaits relief from that situation.

When he confronts a situation, he hopes that Allāh will strengthen his patience, he fears the effect of trials that will cause him to miss the desired rewards, making the situation even worse because it was not undertaken with the necessary patience.

So it is necessary for the believer, the one of *tawḥīd*, that he has fear and hope in every situation. This is what is obligatory as well as what is beneficial, and with this, happiness results.

Here, there are two grave dangers for the worshipper;

1. That his fear overcomes him to the degree that he despairs of Allāh's mercy and care.

2. That he becomes too liberal with hope, such that he feels a sense of security from Allāh's planning and His punishing.

So when the situation reaches such proportions, then one loses the obligatory fear and hope which are among the greatest foundations of *tawḥīd* and the greatest obligations of faith.

As for despairing of Allāh's mercy and losing hope of His concern, there are two cases to beware of;

1. That the worshipper transgresses against himself, and he engages in the prohibited, becoming resolved in it, submersed in acts of disobedience, cutting off all of his hope in Allāh's mercy because he knows that he has engaged in things that prevent His mercy. Then he continues in such behaviour until this description becomes his reality. This is the prime objective of *shayṭān* for the worshipper, and when it reaches this level then there is no way of return to what is good for him except by sincere repentance with a strong sense of will to turn away from it.

2. That the worshipper's fear is overpowering due to the crimes that he has committed, and due to his weak knowledge about Allāh's encompassing mercy and forgiveness to the extent that he thinks - in his ignorance - that Allāh would not forgive him nor have mercy on him even if he repented and turned away from

these acts. His will weakens him to despair of Allāh's mercy. This is one of the gravely dangerous effects of his poor knowledge about His Lord and His (ﷻ) true worth, as well as a sign of a weak and paralyzed soul. If he really knew about His Lord, and he did not linger in negligence about such knowledge, then he would know to rush to His Lord, to His mercy, His gentleness and kindness.

There are also two destructive ends that result from feeling secure of Allāh's displeasure:

1. The worshipper neglects his religion, he is heedless of knowing His Lord and His worth, remaining remiss in that. His negligence and heedlessness continues to make him decrease in performing his obligations, increasing him in the unlawful, until fear of Allāh is removed from his heart, and nothing remains of it, for faith is supported by fear of Allāh and fear of His punishment in this life and the Hereafter.

2. That the worshipper is an ignorant servant who is astonished by, and deluded with his own deeds. He will not cease in his ignorance until he becomes proud of his deeds, until fear of Allāh is removed from his heart, and he thinks that he has a special status with Allāh. So he feels secure from Allāh's displeasure, leaning on his weak despicable soul. Anyone who has reached this point, then he has forsaken the way to guidance since he is the one whom he depends upon.

So these are the details of how these matters negate *tawḥīd*.

Chapter 35

من الإيمان بالله الصبر على أقدار الله

Among faith in Allāh is patience in what Allāh has decreed.

وقول الله تعالى: (ومن يؤمن بالله يهد قلبه) .

Allāh (ﷻ) said, "And whoever believes in Allāh, He guides his heart." (*al-Taghābun* 64:11)

قال علقمة: هو الرجل تصيبه المصيبة فيعلم أنها من عند الله، فيرضى ويسلم.

'Alqamah said; "He is the man who is stricken by an affliction, but he knows that it is from Allāh, so he accepts it and submits."[96]

وفي صحيح مسلم عن أبي هريرة رضي الله عنه، أن رسول الله صلى الله عليه وسلم قال: (اثنتان في الناس هما بهم كفر: الطعن في النسب، والنياحة على الميت).

In *Ṣaḥīḥ* Muslim, from Abū Hurayrah (ﷺ), "Allāh's Messenger (ﷺ) said, 'There are two things that indicate disbelief when present in people; Abusing lineage and wailing over the dead.'"

ولهما عن ابن مسعود مرفوعاً: (ليس منا من ضرب الخدود، وشق الجيوب، ودعا بدعوى الجاهلية).

[96] Reported in *mu'allaq* form by al-Bukhārī up to Ibn Mas'ūd with this meaning. Ibn Ḥājar says it was connected up to 'Alqamah by 'Abdul-Razzāq (*Fatḥ al-Bārī*), via that route it is with Ibn Jarīr, as well as a similar statement from Ibn 'Abbās, and Ibn Ḥājar mentions that al-Barqāni recorded similar with a different chain to Ibn Mas'ūd. See *Fatḥ al-Majīd* with notes by al-Arnā'ūṭ.

And for them from Ibn Mas'ūd *marfū'*; "He is not from us who strikes his cheek, tears his garment, and calls with the call of *jāhilīyyah*."[97]

وعن أنس رضي الله عنه، أن رسول الله صلى الله عليه وسلم قال: (إذا أراد الله بعبده الخير عجل له العقوبة في الدنيا، وإذا أراد بعبده الشر أمسك عنه بذنبه حتى يوافي به يوم القيامة)

From Anas (ﷺ); "Allāh's Messenger (ﷺ) said, 'When Allāh wants good for His servant He hastens his punishment in this world, and when He intends bad for His servant, He delays His sins until he faces it on the Day of Resurrection.'"[98]

وقال النبي صلى الله عليه وسلم: (إن عظم الجزاء مع عظم البلاء، وإن الله تعالى إذا أحب قوماً ابتلاهم، فمن رضي فله الرضي، ومن سخط فله السخط) حسنه الترمذي.

And he (ﷺ) said, "The greater reward is with the greater trial. When Allāh (ﷻ) loves a people He tries them, so whoever is pleased, then for him is the pleasure [of Allāh], and whoever is displeased, then for him is the displeasure [of Allāh]." Al-Tirmidhī graded it *ḥasan*.[99]

فيه مسائل:

الأولى: تفسير آية التغابن.

الثانية: أن هذا من الإيمان بالله.

الثالثة: الطعن في النسب.

الرابعة: شدة الوعيد فيمن ضرب الخدود وشق الجيوب ودعا بدعوى الجاهلية.

الخامسة: علامة إرادة الله بعبده الخير.

السادسة: إرادة الله به الشر.

السابعة: علامة حب الله للعبد.

الثامنة: تحريم السخط.

التاسعة: ثواب الرضي بالبلاء.

[97] Al-Bukhārī in the *Book of Funerals*.

[98] Recorded by al-Tirmidhī and others. It was graded *ḥasan ṣaḥīḥ* by Al-Albānī in *Ṣaḥīḥ Sunan al-Tirmidhī* no. 1953.

[99] It is in *Ṣaḥīḥ Sunan al-Tirmidhī* no. 1954.

Important Points

1. The explanation of the *āyah* of *Sūrah al-Taghābun*.
2. That this is part of faith in Allāh.
3. Abusing lineage.
4. Making a severe warning for whoever strikes his cheeks, tears his clothes, and calls with the calling of *jāhilīyyah*.
5. Signs that Allāh intends good for His servant.
6. And when Allāh intends bad for him.
7. Indicating love of Allāh for His worshipper.
8. The prohibition of displeasure.
9. The gift of the pleasure with the trial.

Commentary by *ʿAllāmah* al-Saʿdī

Among faith in Allāh is patience in what Allāh has decreed

As for patience in obedience to Allāh, and patience in the face of disobedience to Him, it is clear to everyone that these are elements of faith, even that they are among its foundations and branches. Because faith, all of it, is being patient with what Allāh loves and is pleased with, and with what brings one closer to Him, and being patient in staying away from what Allāh has prohibited.

Certainly, the religion is built upon three foundations; trusting the information from Allāh and His Messenger (ﷺ), implementing the commands of Allāh and His Messenger (ﷺ), and staying away from what Allāh and His Messenger forbade.

Patience with what Allāh has decreed falls under these general categories, but in specific cases the need to be aware of it and act upon it is stronger.

So when the worshipper knows that an affliction occurs by Allāh's leave, and that Allāh's wisdom is complete in having decreed it, and that He gives ample favours to His servants when decreeing it, then He is pleased with what Allāh has decreed for him and he submits to His command, being patient with what troubles him, drawing nearer to Allāh, and hoping for His rewards, and fearing His punishment. He has embraced the best of conduct, so his heart is tranquil and his faith and *tawḥīd* are strong.

Chapter 36

ما جاء في الرياء

What is said about *riyā'*

وقول الله تعالى: (قل إنما أنا بشر مثلكم يوحى إليَّ أنما إلهكم إله واحد) الآية.

Allāh (ﷻ) said, "Say: 'I am but a human like you, it has been revealed to me that your god is one.'" (*al-Kahf* 18:110)

عن أبي هريرة مرفوعاً: (قال الله تعالى: أنا أغنى الشركاء عن الشرك، من عمل عملاً أشرك معي فيه غيري تركته وشركه). رواه مسلم.

From Abū Hurayrah (ﷺ) that the Prophet (ﷺ) said; "Allāh said, 'I am most independant and free from needing partners. Whoever does a deed associating something in it with Me, he and his *shirk* are forsaken." Recorded by Muslim.

وعن أبي سعيد مرفوعاً: (ألا أخبركم بما هو أخوف عليكم عندي من المسيح الدجال؟) قالوا: بلى يا رسول الله! قال: (الشرك الخفي، يقوم الرجل فيصلي، فيزيّن صلاته، لما يرى من نظر رجل). رواه أحمد.

From Abū Sa'īd al-Khudri that the Prophet (ﷺ) said; "Shall I not inform you of what I fear more for you than *al-Masīḥ al-Dajjāl*?" They said, "Yes O Messenger of Allāh!" He said, "Hidden *shirk*. A mans stands to pray, so he beautifies his prayer when he notices someone looking at him." Recorded by Aḥmad.[100]

---

[100] It is a *ḥasan* ḥadīth. Also recorded by Ibn Mājah, and similar was recorded by al-Bayhaqī. See *Ṣaḥīḥ al-Jāmi'* no. 2607.

فيه مسائل:

الأولى: تفسير آية الكهف.

الثانية: الأمر العظيم في رد العمل الصالح إذا دخله شيء لغير الله.

الثالثة: ذكر السبب الموجب لذلك، وهو كمال الغنى.

الرابعة: أن من الأسباب، أنه تعالى خير الشركاء.

الخامسة: خوف النبي صلى الله عليه وسلم على أصحابه من الرياء.

السادسة: أنه فسر ذلك بأن يصلي المرء لله، لكن يزينها لما يرى من نظر رجل إليه.

Important Points

1. The explanation of the *āyah* of *Sūrah al-Kahf*.
2. The importance of the case of rejecting the righteous deeds when they are done for other than Allāh.
3. Mentioning the reason necessitating that i.e., perfect independence.
4. That among the reasons is that He is exalted above the best of partners.
5. The Prophet's (ﷺ) fear of *riyā'* for his companions.
6. He explained it, that a man prays to Allāh, but he beautifies his prayer when he sees someone looking at him.

For *ʿAllāmah* al-Saʿdī's Commentary Refer to the Next Chapter

Chapter 37

من الشرك إرادة الإنسان بعمله الدنيا

Intending deeds in the world for the sake of humans is a type of *shirk*

وقول الله تعالى: (من كان يريد الحياة الدنيا وزينتها نوف إليهم أعمالهم فيها وهم فيها لا يبخسون أولئك الذين ليس لهم في الآخرة إلا النار وحبط ما صنعوا فيها وباطل ما كانوا يعملون) الآيتين.

Allāh (ﷻ) said, "Whoever seeks the life of this world and its glitter, We will confer upon them their deeds without diminishing them. These are those for whom there is nothing in the Hereafter but the Fire, and what they did for that is disgraced, and what they were doing was in vain." (*Hūd* 11:15-16)

وفي الصحيح عن أبي هريرة رضي الله عنه قال: قال رسول الله صلى الله عليه وسلم: (تعس عبد الدينار، تعس عبد الدرهم، تعس عبد الخميصة، تعس عبد الخميلة، إن أعطي رضي، وإن لم يعط سخط، تعس وانتكس وإذا شيك فلا انتقش، طوبى لعبد أخذ بعنان فرسه في سبيل الله، أشعث رأسه، مغبرة قدماه، إن كان في الحراسة كان في الحراسة، وإن كان في الساقة كان في الساقة، إن استأذن لم يؤذن له، وإن شفع لم يشفع).

In the *Ṣaḥīḥ* (al-Bukhārī,) from Abū Hurayrah (رضي الله عنه), that he said, "Allāh's Messenger (ﷺ) said; "Ruin for the worshipper of the *dīnār*! Ruin for the worshipper of the *dirham*! Ruin for the worshipper of the *khamīṣah*! Ruin for the worshipper of the *khamīlah*! If he is given, he is pleased, and if he is not given he is displeased. Ruin and humiliation! He can not even find relief from the slightest prick!

But *ṭūbā* is for the worshipper taking the reins of his horse in the cause of Allāh; his hair flying, his feet dusty. If he is assigned the watch, then he remains on watch. If he is assigned the rear guard, he guards the rear. Yet if he asks permission, he is not permitted, and if he intercedes, his intercession is not granted."[101]

فيه مسائل:

الأولى: إرادة الإنسان الدنيا بعمل الآخرة.

الثانية: تفسير آية هود.

الثالثة: تسمية الإنسان المسلم: عبد الدينار والدرهم والخميصة.

الرابعة: تفسير ذلك بأنه إن أعطي رضي، وإن لم يعط سخط.

الخامسة: قوله (تعس وانتكس).

السادسة: قوله: (وإذا شيك فلا انتقش).

السابعة: الثناء على المجاهد الموصوف بتلك الصفات.

Important Points

1. People do deeds of the Hereafter while intending only the world.
2. Explanation of the *āyah* of *Sūrah Hūd*.
3. Calling a Muslim, "Worshipper of the *dīnār*, or *dirhām* or *khamīṣah*".
4. The explanation of that, that if he is given he is pleased, and if he is not given he is displeased.
5. His saying, "Ruin and humiliation!"
6. Saying, "He can not even find relief from the slightest prick!."
7. Praising the kind of *mujāhid* described.

[101] Al-Bukhari and a shorter version with Ibn Maajah. The examples given in this hadeeth are intended to be clear opposites; the first person can only be pleased by things, and he is never satisfied. The second remains in the utmost sincerity for Allaah, without any complaint, although he is the kind of person whose requests are not commonly granted by people, nor his intercession. In this way, he is the opposite of the person who is always used to getting his way, doing all that he does with that goal in mind.

Commentary by *ʿAllāmah* al-Saʿdī

What is said about *riyā'* and- intending deeds in the world for the sake of humans is a type of *shirk*

Know that sincerity for Allāh is the foundation of the religion, and the essence of *tawḥīd* and worship. It is when the worshipper intends all of his deeds for the Face of Allāh, for His rewards, and His favours. So he maintains the six foundations of faith, the five signs of Islām, and the fulfilment of faith - *iḥsān* - as well as the rights of Allāh and the rights of His worshippers. In this way his intention is perfected for the Face of Allāh and for the abode of the Hereafter. He does not intend by this to be seen, nor to be heard of, nor does he do it for position, or for worldly matters. By this he will have completed his faith and *tawḥīd*.

Among the worst behaviours that diminish sincerity is to perform deeds just to be seen by people, for their praise, or to honour them, or doing deeds for the sake of worldly matters. This degrades sincerity and *tawḥīd*.

There are some details about *riyā'*:

If a worshipper does a deed with the goal of having people see it, and he remains with this evil intention, then his deed is disgraced, and he commits minor *shirk*, and he runs the risk of it leading him to major *shirk*.

If the worshipper does a deed intending the Face of Allāh and with that, he is also intending it for the sight of people - if he does not remove the *riyā'* from his deed - then the texts are clear that this deed is also false.

When the worshipper does a deed for the Face of Allāh alone, but *riyā'* surfaces for an instant during his deed, if he wards it off and purifies his sincerity for Allāh, then there is no harm in that deed. But if he settles for that - becoming tranquil with it - then the value of the deed diminishes, resulting in a weakening of his faith in proportion to the amount of *riyā'* that survived in his heart. Still, the deed remains for Allāh, but whatever portion of it he mixed up and was confused about is *riyā'*.

Riyā' is a dangerous disease which requires the soul to hasten to disciplining itself in sincerity, to wage war in defence against the destruction caused by *riyā'*, to oppose its assault, seeking Allāh's help to defend against it, so that perhaps Allāh will purify the worshipper's faith and complete his *tawḥīd*.

As for deeds done merely for worldly reasons or for the attainment of things in the world: if the worshipper's intent is always for this goal, without having the objective of doing things for the Face of Allāh and the abode of the Hereafter, then there will be no reward for him in the Hereafter for these acts.

Acts characterised in this manner will not be found in the hearts of the believer, for the believer - even if his faith is weak - will certainly bring the goal of Allāh and the abode of the Hereafter to mind.

As far as the one who does such acts for Allāh's Face, as well as for the sake of the world, these objectives being equal or approximately so, then these will - if he is a believer - diminish his faith, *tawḥīd* and sincerity. His deeds will be diminished because he has forsaken complete sincerity in them.

One who does a deed for Allāh alone and he is most sincere in his deed - having complete sincerity in it - but for that deed he receives wages designated to help in work for the religion, wages that are to be spent on good deeds - such as the *mujāhid* who deserves some spoils of war or provisions for his struggling, or like in the case of an endowment that is responsible for paying the salaries of those who work in the *masjids*, schools and other religious positions - then there is no harm on the worshipper's faith and *tawḥīd* to accept such wages, since it is not being used for worldly work, it is only intended for the religion, and the objective is that the individual who receives it does work in the religion.

For this reason Allāh designated a great portion of the *sharī'ah* wealth, like *zakāh* and the spoils of war, for those who work for religious endowments, as well as helping to benefit in the world. This topic is well known.

The previous examples help to make the rulings for these many important issues clearer for you, it is up to you to judge similar cases in their proper light. And Allāh knows best.

Chapter 38

من أطاع العلماء والأمراء في تحريم ما أحل الله

أو تحليل ما حرم الله فقد اتخذهم أرباباً من دون الله

Whoever obeys the scholars and leaders in prohibiting what Allāh allowed or allowing what Allāh prohibits, then he has taken them as lords besides Allāh.

وقال ابن عباس: يوشك أن تنزل عليكم حجارة من السماء، أقول: قال رسول الله صلى الله عليه وسلم، وتقولون: قال أبو بكر وعمر؟!

Ibn ʿAbbās (راضي) said, "Stones are about to rain down upon you from the heavens! I tell you, 'Allāh's Messenger (ﷺ) said' and you people say, 'Abū Bakr said and ʿUmar said.'"

وقال الإمام أحمد: عجبت لقوم عرفوا الإسناد وصحته، يذهبون إلى رأي سفيان، والله تعالى يقول: (فليحذر الذين يخالفون عن أمره أن تصيبهم فتنة أو يصيبهم عذاب أليم) أتدري ما الفتنة؟ الفتنة: الشرك، لعله إذا رد بعض قوله أن يقع في قلبه شيء من الزيغ فيهلك.

Imām Aḥmad said, "I am amazed at the people who are aware of the correctness of an *isnād*, yet they would go to Sufyān's opinion. Allāh (ﷻ) said, 'Warn those who oppose his command that they will be stricken with a *fitnah* or they will suffer a lasting punishment.' (al-Nūr 24:63) Don't you know what this *fitnah* is? The *fitnah* is *shirk*. Perhaps when one rejects some of his sayings (ﷺ) there occurs in his heart something of a desire to be destroyed."[102]

---

[102] The previous statement of Ibn ʿAbbās was narrated with slightly different wording in Musnad Aḥmad (1:337). Shaykh Aḥmad Shākir said it is *ṣaḥīḥ*. This statement of Aḥmad or similar, was reported by al-Faḍl bin Ziyād and Abū Ṭālib according to Ibn Taymiyah. See *Taysīr al-ʿAzīz* or *Fatḥ al-Majīd*.

عن عدي بن حاتم: أنه سمع النبي صلى الله عليه وسلم يقرأ هذه الآية: (اتخذوا أحبارهم ورهبانهم أرباباً من دون الله) الآية. فقلت له: إنا لسنا نعبدهم قال: (أليس يحرمون ما أحل الله فتحرمونه ويحلّون ما حرم الله، فتحلونه؟) فقلت: بلى. قال فتلك عبادتهم) رواه أحمد، والترمذي وحسنه.

From 'Adī bin Ḥātim, "That he heard the Prophet (ﷺ) reciting this *āyah*; 'They have taken their priests and monks as Lords besides Allāh.' [*al-Tawbah* 9:11]

So I said to him, 'We did not worship them.' He said, 'Did they not prohibit what Allāh allowed so you prohibited it, and did they not allow what Allāh prohibited so you allowed it.' I said, 'Yes.' He said, 'That was your worship of them.'" Recorded by Aḥmad and al-Tirmidhī who graded it *ḥasan*.[103]

فيه مسائل:

الأولى: تفسير آية النور.

الثانية: تفسير آية براءة.

الثالثة: التنبيه على معنى العبادة التي أنكرها عدي.

الرابعة: تمثيل ابن عباس بأبي بكر وعمر، وتمثيل أحمد بسفيان.

الخامسة: تغيّر الأحوال إلى هذه الغاية، حتى صار عند الأكثر عبادة الرهبان هي أفضل الأعمال، وتسمى الولاية، وعبادة الأحبار هي العلم والفقه ثم تغيرت الحال إلى أن عبد من دون الله من ليس من الصالحين، وعبد بالمعنى الثاني من هو من الجاهلين.

Important Points

1. The explanation of the *āyah* of *Sūrah al-Nūr*.

2. The explanation of the *āyah* of *Sūrah al-Barā'ah*.

3. About the meaning of worship, which 'Adī had rejected.

---

[103] It is recorded by al-Tirmidhī, Ibn Jarīr. Al-Suyūti mentioned it in *al-Dur al-Manthūr* and he also attributed it to Ibn Sa'd al-Ṭabarānī and a number of others. Ibn Kathīr attributed it also to Aḥmad. Al-Albānī graded it *ḥasan* in *Ṣaḥīḥ Sunan al-Tirmidhī* no. 2471.

4. The example of Ibn 'Abbās with Abū Bakr and 'Umar, and the example of Aḥmad with Sufyān.
5. These conditions changed such that most of the worship of the priests was considered the best of deeds, but it was termed '*al-wilāyah*', and they referred to worshipping the monks as "knowledge" and "*fiqh*". Then the situation changed so that the those that were worshipped besides Allāh were not even among the righteous. And with the second meaning, even the ignorant are worshipped.

For '*Allāmah* al-Sa'dī's Commentary Refer to the Next Chapter

Chapter 39

قول الله تعالى: ألم تر إلى الذين يزعمون

Allāh (ﷻ) said; “Have you not seen those who claim...”

قول الله تعالى: (ألم تر إلى الذين يزعمون أنهم ءامنوا بما أنزل إليك وما أنزل من قبلك يريدون أن يتحاكموا إلى الطاغوت وقد أمروا أن يكفروا به ويريد الشيطان أن يضلهم ضللاً بعيدا) الآيات. وقوله: (وإذا قيل لهم لا تفسدوا في الأرض قالوا إنما نحن مصلحون) وقوله: (ولا تفسدوا في الأرض بعد إصلاحها) الآية. وقوله: (أفحكم الجاهلية يبغون) الآية.

Allāh (ﷻ) said; “Have you not seen those who claim that they believe in what has been revealed to you and what was revealed before you, they intend to judge according to the *ṭāghūt*, yet they were ordered to disbelieve in him. And *shayṭān* intends to lead them far astray.” (*al-Nisā’* 4:60) And He (ﷻ) said, “And when it is said to them, ‘Do not spread corruption in the land’, they say, ‘We are only those who bring about good.’” (*al-Baqarah* 2:11) And; “And do not spread corruption in the land after it has been set in order.” (*al-Aʿrāf* 7:56) And; “Is it the *jāhilīyyah* rule that you seek?” (*al-Mā’idah* 5:50)

عن عبد الله بن عمرو رضي الله عنهما، أن رسول الله صلى الله عليه وسلم قال: (لا يؤمن أحدكم حتى يكون هواه تبعاً لما جئت به) قال النووي: حديث صحيح، رويناه في كتاب «الحجة» بإسناد صحيح.

ʿAbdullāh bin ʿAmr (رضي الله عنه) reported that Allāh’s Messenger (ﷺ) said, “None of you is a believer until his desires follow that which I have been sent with.” Al-Nawawī said, “This ḥadīth is *ṣaḥīḥ*, it was reported to us in *Kitāb al-Hujjah* with a *ṣaḥīḥ* chain."[104]

وقال الشعبي: كان بين رجل من المنافقين ورجل من اليهود خصومة؛ فقال اليهودي: نتحاكم إلى محمد ــ لأنه عرف أنه لا يأخذ الرشوة ــ وقال المنافق: نتحاكم إلى اليهود ــ لعلمه أنهم يأخذون الرشوة - فاتفقا أن يأتيا كاهناً في جهينة فيتحاكما إليه، فنزلت: ﴿ ألم تر إلى الذين يزعمون ﴾ الآية.

Al-Sha'bī said, "There was a disagreement between a man among the hypocrites and a man from the Jews. The Jew said, 'We will have Muḥammad judge.' Because he knew that he would not take a bribe. The hypocrite said, 'We should have a Jew judge.' Because he knew that they would take a bribe. So finally they agreed to go to a fortuneteller in Juhaynah to have him judge. So the following *āyah* was revealed; "Have not you seen those who claim..."(4:60)

وقيل: نزلت في رجلين اختصما، فقال أحدهما: نترافع إلى النبي صلى الله عليه وسلم، وقال الآخر: إلى كعب بن الأشرف، ثم ترافعا إلى عمر، فذكر له أحدهما القصة. فقال للذي لم يرض برسول الله صلى الله عليه وسلم: أكذلك؟ قال: نعم، فضربه بالسيف فقتله.

They also say it was revealed about two disputing men, one of whom said, 'Let us go to the Prophet (ﷺ).' The other said, 'But to Ka'b bin al-Ashraf.' Then finally the case went to 'Umar. So one of them narrated the incident to him. So he said to the one who did not accept going to Allāh's Messenger (ﷺ), 'Is this so?' He said, 'Yes.' So he struck him, killing him with his sword."[105]

---

[104] "This ḥadīth was recorded by Shaykh Abū al-Fataḥ Naṣr bin Ibrāhīm al-Maqdisī al Shāfi'ī in his book "*al-Hujjah 'alal-Muhajjah*", with an authentic chain as the author, may Allāh have mercy upon him stated from al-Nawawī. It was also recorded by Al-Ṭabarānī and..." (*Taysīr*) This is ḥadīth number 41 in *Jāmi' al-'Ulūm wa al-Ḥikam* by Ibn Rajab, and he indicates it weakness. It was also graded weak by Salīm al-Hilālī in his *al-Muntaqā man Jāmi' al-'Ulūm wa al-Ḥikam*, and Al-Albānī in *Ẓalālil-Junnah fī Takhrīj al-Sunnah* no. 15, and al-Arnā'ūṭ in his notes on *Fatḥ al-Majīd*. Yet, as the author of *Taysīr al-'Azīz* has pointed out, the meaning of the ḥadīth is well testified to through the Qur'ān.

[105] These were recorded by al-Kulabi in his *Tafsīr*, and their chains are deemed weak by Ibn Ḥājar in *Fatḥ al-Bārī*. Ibn Kathīr quotes a chain from al-Ṭabarānī to Ibn 'Abbās saying, "Abū Barzah al-Aslami was a fortuneteller who arbitrated for the disputes among the Jews, so some people among the *mushrikīn* went to him for arbitration. Then Allāh (ﷻ) revealed the *āyah*..." This ḥadīth was mentioned by al-Wāhidi in his book *Asbāb al-Nuzūl*. About its chain al-Ḥaythamī said (*Majma' Al-Zawā'id* 7:6). Recorded by al-Ṭabarānī and its men are *ṣaḥīḥ*." Shaykh Muqbil bin Hādī said, "I could not find a biography of al-Ṭabarānī's Shaykh [in this narration], but according to al-Wāhidi he is

فيه مسائل:

الأولى: تفسير آية النساء وما فيها من الإعانة على فهم الطاغوت.

الثانية: تفسير آية البقرة: (وإذا قيل لهم لا تفسدوا في الأرض) .

الثالثة: تفسير آية الأعراف (ولا تفسدوا في الأرض بعد إصلاحها) .

الرابعة: تفسير: (أفحكم الجاهلية يبغون) .

الخامسة: ما قال الشعبي في سبب نزول الآية الأولى.

السادسة: تفسير الإيمان الصادق والكاذب.

السابعة: قصة عمر مع المنافق.

الثامنة: كون الإيمان لا يحصل لأحد حتى يكون هواه تبعاً لما جاء به الرسول صلى الله عليه وسلم.

Important Points

1. The explanation of the *āyah* of *Sūrah al-Nisā'* and what it contains indicating the meaning of *al-ṭāghūt*.
2. The explanation of the *āyah* of *Sūrah al-Baqarah*, "And when it is said to them, 'Do not spread corruption in the land...'"
3. The explanation of the *āyah* of *Sūrah al-A'rāf*, "And do not spread corruption in the land after it has been set in order..."
4. The explanation of, "Is it the judgement of *jāhilīyyah* that you seek?"
5. What al-Sha'bī said about the circumstances of the revelation of the first *āyah*.

followed up by Ibrāhīm bin Sa'īd al-Jawharī." (*Ṣaḥīḥ al-Musnad min Asbāb al-Nuzūl* p. 79) This al-Jawharī is a narrator of the six ḥadīth compilers except for al-Bukhārī. So it seems according to the statement of Shaykh Muqbil that its grade is at least *ḥasan*. And Allāh knows best. This narration, it should be indicated, does not contain the story of 'Umar killing the hypocrite.

6. The explanation of the true faith and the false kind.
7. The story of 'Umar and the hypocrite.
8. Faith will not be achieved until one's desires are in accord with what the Messenger (ﷺ) came with.

Commentary by *'Allāmah* al-Sa'dī

Whoever Obeys the Scholars and Leaders in Prohibiting what Allāh Allowed or Allowing what Allāh Prohibits, then He has taken them as Lords besides Allāh. "Have you not seen those who claim that they believe in what has been revealed to you." (*al-Nisā'* 4:60)

The point that the author mentioned is clear. The Lord, the God, is the only one worthy of judgement, of legislative rule, and penal rule. He is the one deified and worshipped alone, there is no partner for Him. He is to be obeyed with absolute obedience, so the absence of disobedience depends upon the degree to which obedience is defined as obedience to Him.

When the worshipper views scholars or leaders in this way, considering obedience to them the primary obedience, and obedience to Allāh and His Messenger (ﷺ) comes next, then he has taken them as lords besides Allāh, deifying them, rendering judgement to them, and putting their rule ahead of the rule of Allāh and His Messenger. This is the epitome of *kufr*. All rule is for Allāh, just as all worship is for Allāh.

So it is obligatory upon everyone to not take other that Allāh as the ruler, and that he refers every matter of division among people to Allāh and His Messenger. In this way all of the worshipper's religion will be for Allāh, and his *tawḥīd* will be sincerely for Allāh's Face.

Anyone who judges with other than the judgement of Allāh and His Messenger, then he has rendered his judgement to the *ṭāghūt*, and if he claims that he is a believer then he is a liar.

Faith is not correct nor complete except according to the judgements of Allāh and His Messenger, both in the foundations of religion and its branches, regarding all cases, as the author mentions in the following chapter.

So whoever has judged according to the rule of other than Allāh and His Messenger, then he has taken that one as a lord, and he has judged according to the *ṭāghūt*.

Chapter 40

من جحد شيئاً من الأسماء والصفات

Whoever denies any of the Names or Attributes

وقول الله تعالى: (وهم يكفرون بالرحمن) الآية.

Allāh (ﷻ) said, "They are rejecting *'Al-Raḥmān'*."(*al-Ra'd* 13:30)

وفي صحيح البخاري قال علي: (حدثوا الناس بما يعرفون، أتريدون أن يكذب الله ورسوله؟).

From *Ṣaḥīḥ al-Bukhārī*, 'Alī said, "Speak to the people about what they know. Do you want Allāh and His Messenger to be rejected?"[106]

وروى عبد الرزاق عن معمر عن ابن طاوس عن أبيه عن ابن عباس: أنه رأى رجلاً انتفض — لما سمع حديثاً عن النبي صلى الله عليه وسلم في الصفات، استنكاراً لذلك — فقال: (ما فرق هؤلاء؟ يجدون رقة عند محكمه، ويهلكون عند متشابهه) انتهى.

'Abdul-Razzāq reported from Ma'mar from Ibn Ṭāwus from his father from Ibn 'Abbās, "That he saw a man objecting and showing his displeasure when he heard a ḥadīth from the Prophet (ﷺ) about the attributes. He said, "What is the problem with these people? They are agreeable when it comes to what is *muḥkamah*, and they perish when it comes to the *mutashābihah*." End quote.[107]

ولما سمعت قريش رسول الله صلى الله عليه وسلم يذكر: (الرحمن) أنكروا ذلك. فأنزل الله فيهم: (وهم يكفرون بالرحمن) .

[106] Recorded by al-Bukhārī in the Book of Knowledge of his *Ṣaḥīḥ*. However it does not contain the second half of the quote.

[107] "This chain is *ṣaḥīḥ*." Al-Arnā'ūṭ.

And when the *Quraysh* heard Allāh's Messenger mentioning '*Al-Raḥmān*' they rejected that. So it was about them that Allāh revealed, "And they reject, '*al-Raḥmān*.'"[108]

فيه مسائل:

الأولى: عدم الإيمان بجحد شيء من الأسماء والصفات.

الثانية: تفسير آية الرعد.

الثالثة: ترك التحديث بما لا يفهم السامع.

الرابعة: ذكر العلة أنه يفضي إلى تكذيب الله ورسوله، ولو لم يتعمد المنكر.

الخامسة: كلام ابن عباس لمن استنكر شيئاً من ذلك، وأنه هلك.

Important Points

1. The absence of faith when denying any of the Names or attributes.
2. The explanation of the *āyah* of *Sūrah al-Ra'd*.
3. To avoid speaking about what the listener will not understand.
4. Giving the reason for that; it leads to rejecting Allāh and His Messenger, even if such rejection is not done on purpose.
5. The saying of Ibn 'Abbās about whoever rejects any of this, and that he is the most ruined.

Commentary by '*Allāmah* al-Sa'dī

Whoever Denies any of the Names or Attributes

The basis of faith and its foundational guidelines are belief in Allāh, in His Names, and His attributes.

The stronger one's knowledge of these while worshipping Allāh, the stronger his *tawḥīd*. So when he knows that Allāh is

[108] Ibn Kathīr says, "This was said by Qatādah and the ḥadīth is recorded by al-Bukhārī."

singled out by the perfect attributes, alone in His magnificence, majesty and splendor, there being no comparison to Him in His perfection, then it becomes more realistic that by this means he will know and fulfil his belief that He is the true God, and divinity other than His is false.

So whoever denies any of Allāh's Names or attributes, he initiates what contradicts and nullifies *tawḥīd*, and this is a branch of disbelief.

Chapter 41

قول الله تعالى: يعرفون نعمت الله ثم ينكرونها

Allāh (ﷻ) said; "They recognise Allāh's favours, then they reject them."

قول الله تعالى: (يعرفون نعمت الله ثم ينكرونها) .

Allāh (ﷻ) said; "They recognise Allāh's favours, then they reject them." *al-Nahl* 16:83)

قال مجاهد ما معناه: هو قول الرجل: هذا مالي، ورثته عن آبائي.

About the meaning, Mujāhid said, "It is the statement of a person, 'This is my money, I inherited it from my forefathers.'"

وقال عون بن عبد الله: يقولون: لولا فلان لم يكن كذا.

ʿAwn bin ʿAbdullāh said, "They say, 'If not for so and so, it would not be like this.'"[109]

وقال ابن قتيبة: يقولون: هذا بشفاعة آلهتنا.

Ibn Qutaybah said, "They say, 'This is due to the intercession of our gods.'"

وقال أبو العباس – بعد حديث زيد بن خالد الذي فيه: (إن الله تعالى قال: أصبح من عبادي مؤمن بي وكافر..) الحديث، وقد تقدم ــ وهذا كثير في الكتاب والسنة، يذم سبحانه من يضيف إنعامه إلى غيره، ويشرك به.

---

[109] The report from ʿAwn is recorded by al-Ṭabarī.

قال بعض السلف: هو كقولهم: كانت الريح طيبة، والملاح حاذقاً، ونحو ذلك مما هو جارٍ على ألسنة كثير.

After the ḥadith of Zayd bin Khālid, mentioning that Allāh (ﷻ) said, "This morning some of My servants have believed in Me and others have disbelieved. As for the believer he said, 'We received rain from Allāh's bounty.' That is the believer in Me and the disbeliever in the stars. As for the one who said, 'We received rain because the position of the stars was like this and this' that is the disbeliever in Me and the believer in the stars." (Al-Bukhārī and Muslim)." Abū al-'Abbās [Ibn Taymiyah] said, "This occurs often in the Book and the Sunnah. He (ﷻ) rebukes anyone who attributes His favours to other than Him, making partners for Him.

Some of the *salaf* said that he is like those who say, 'The wind was good', 'The navigator was proficient' and other such sayings are common on the tongues of many."

فيه مسائل:

الأولى: تفسير معرفة النعمة وإنكارها.

الثانية: معرفة أن هذا جارٍ على ألسنة كثير.

الثالثة: تسمية هذا الكلام إنكاراً للنعمة.

الرابعة: اجتماع الضدين في القلب.

Important Points

1. The explanation of recognising the favours and rejecting them.
2. Recognising that this is common upon many tongues.
3. Referring to this type of speech as, "Rejecting the favours."
4. The coexistence of two opposites in the heart.

Commentary by *'Allāmah* al-Sa'dī

Allāh (ﷻ) said; "They recognise Allāh's favours, then they reject them. Most of them are disbelievers." (*al-Naḥl* 16:83)

It is obligatory for the creatures to attribute the favours to Allāh, in both saying and recognition as preceded, and with this *tawḥīd* can be completed. So whoever rejects Allāh's favour by his heart or tongue, that is a disbeliever, nothing of the religion remains with him.

Whoever acknowledges in his heart that all favours come from Allāh alone, but sometimes he attributes a favour to Allāh, and sometimes he attributes it to himself and his work, or to the work of someone else - as is commonly done upon the tongue of many people - then in such case it is obligatory for the worshipper to repent and to stop claiming that the favours come from others besides the One worthy of it, and to struggle with himself in this struggle. His faith will not be fulfilled without realising that the favours are from Allāh, both by saying and recognition.

Gratitude, which is the head of faith, is built upon three pillars;

1 The soul's recognition of the favours that Allāh granted it as well as those He granted for others.

2. To recall this fact, and to praise Allāh for it.

3. Utilising the favours to help in the obedience and worship of the One who granted them. And Allāh knows best.

Chapter 42

. قول الله تعالى: فلا تجعلوا لله أنداداً وأنتم تعلمون

Allāh's (ﷻ) saying; "So do not knowingly make equals for Allāh."

قول الله تعالى: (فلا تجعلوا لله أنداداً وأنتم تعلمون) .

Allāh's (ﷻ) saying; "So do not knowingly make equals for Allāh." (*al-Baqarah* 2:22)

قال ابن عباس في الآية: الأنداد: هو الشرك أخفى من دبيب النمل على صفاة سوداء في ظلمة الليل؛ وهو أن تقول: والله، وحياتك يا فلان وحياتي، وتقول: لولا كليبة هذا لأتانا اللصوص، ولولا البط في الدار لأتانا اللصوص، وقول الرجل لصاحبه: ما شاء الله وشئت، وقول الرجل: لولا الله وفلان. لا تجعل فيها فلاناً هذا كله به شرك) رواه ابن أبي حاتم.

Ibn ʿAbbās (ﷺ) said about this *āyah*; "*Andād* [equals]: That is *shirk*. It is more inconspicuous than a crawling ant on a black rock in the darkness of night. It is the saying, 'By Allāh and by your life O so and so,' and 'By my life.' And to say, 'If it was not for this dog then the thieves would have come...' or 'If it was not for the duck in the yard then the thief would have come...' And a man saying to his companion, 'As Allāh and you have willed.' And a man saying, 'If not for Allāh and so and so' Do not include 'so and so' in it, all of this contains *shirk*." Recorded by Ibn Abū Ḥātim.[110]

---

[110] According to the chain cited from Ibn Abū Ḥātim by Ibn Kathīr, this report is *ḥasan*.

وعن عمر بن الخطاب رضي الله عنه: أن رسول الله صلى الله عليه وسلم قال: (من حلف بغير الله فقد كفر أو أشرك) رواه الترمذي وحسنه، وصححه الحاكم.

'Umar bin al-Khaṭṭāb[111] (ﷺ) reported that Allāh's Messenger (ﷺ) said, "Whoever swears by other than Allāh than he has committed disbelief, or *shirk*." Recorded by Al-Tirmidhī who graded it *ḥasan*, and al-Ḥākim graded it *ṣaḥīḥ*.[112]

وقال ابن مسعود: لأن أحلف بالله كاذباً أحب إليّ من أن أحلف بغيره صادقاً.

Ibn Mas'ūd said, "Swearing falsely by Allāh is more beloved to me than to have sworn by other than Him truthfully."

وعن حذيفة رضي الله عنه، عن النبي صلى الله عليه وسلم قال: (لا تقولوا: ما شاء الله وشاء فلان، ولكن قولوا: ما شاء الله ثم شاء فلان) رواه أبو داود بسند صحيح.

And from Ḥudhayfah (ﷺ) from the Prophet (ﷺ) who said, "Do not say, 'As Allāh has willed and as so and so willed.' Rather say, 'As Allāh has willed, then so and so willed.'" Recorded by Abū Dāwūd with a *ṣaḥīḥ* chain.[113]

وجاء عن إبراهيم النخعي، أنه يكره أن يقول: أعوذ بالله وبك، ويجوز أن يقول: بالله ثم بك. قال: ويقول: لولا الله ثم فلان، ولا تقولوا: لولا الله وفلان.

It is report from Ibrāhīm al-Nakha'ī; "That he dislikes for one to say, 'I seek refuge with Allāh and with you.' He permitted one to say, 'With Allāh, then with you.' And he said, "Say; 'If not for Allāh, then so and so.' But do not say, 'If not for Allāh and so and so.'"

فيه مسائل:

الأولى: تفسير آية البقرة في الأنداد.

الثانية: أن الصحابة رضي الله عنهم يفسرون الآية النازلة في الشرك الأكبر بأنها تعم الأصغر.

---

[111] The statement of 'Umar, as well as the three quotes including the ḥadīth after it, were left out of *al-Qawl al-Sadīd*. They have been added since they are part of *Kitāb al-Tawḥīd*.

[112] The ḥadīth with al-Tirmdhi was narrated by Ibn 'Umar, it was graded *ṣaḥīḥ* by al-Albānī no. 1241, *Ṣaḥīḥ Sunan al-Tirmidhī*. There are two narrations before it from 'Umar about the prohibition of swearing by other than Allāh, and after this particular one, al-Tirmidhī quotes one of them again for explanation.

[113] Recorded also by Aḥmad and others. Its chain is *ṣaḥīḥ*.

الثالثة: أن الحلف بغير الله شرك.

الرابعة: أنه إذا حلف بغير الله صادقاً، فهو أكبر من اليمين الغموس.

الخامسة: الفرق بين الواو وثم في اللفظ.

Important Points

1. The explanation of the *āyah* of *Sūrah al-Baqarah* about *al-andād*.
2. That the companions used an *āyah* revealed about major *shirk* to explain minor *shirk*.
3. That swearing by other than Allāh is *shirk*.
4. That swearing truthfully by other than Allāh is worse than perjury.
5. The distinction between using the expression "and" versus "then".

Commentary by ʿ*Allāmah* al-Saʿdī

Allāh's (ﷻ) saying; "So do not knowingly make equals for Allāh." (*al-Baqarah* 2:22)

A discussion preceded over Allāh's (ﷻ) saying;

وَمِنَ ٱلنَّاسِ مَن يَتَّخِذُ مِن دُونِ ٱللَّهِ أَندَادًا

"And among people are those who have taken others as equals to Allāh."
(al-Baqarah 2:165)

And that it deals with major *shirk* because of making an equal to Allāh in worship, whether love, fear, hope, or other types of worship.

This discussion mentions it about minor *shirk*, like the *shirk* via utterances, as in the case of swearing by other than Allāh, combining Allāh with one of His creatures in expressions such as, "If not for Allāh and so and so", and, "This, by Allāh and by you...", and like attributing the occurrence of something to other than Allāh, as in, "If not for the guard then the thieves would have come..." "If not for so and so's medicine I would have perished", "If not for the proficiency of so and so in his work then this wouldn't have..." All of this negates *tawḥīd*.

The obligation is to attribute all matters - their occurrence, and their beneficial results - to Allāh's decree and initiation, and to remember with this, the importance of the effect and its benefits. So by saying, "If not for Allāh..." then it is known that the effects result from Allāh's decree and His will.

So the worshipper's *tawḥīd* will not be complete until he does not make any equals for Allāh in his heart, his sayings, or his actions.

Chapter 43

ما جاء فيمن لم يقنع بالحلف بالله

What is said about one who is not satisfied with another swearing by Allāh.

عن ابن عمر رضي الله عنهما، أن رسول الله صلى الله عليه وسلم قال: (لا تحلفوا بآبائكم، من حلف بالله فليصدق، ومن حلف له بالله فليرض. ومن لم يرض فليس من الله)، رواه ابن ماجه بسند حسن.

Ibn 'Umar (ﷺ) reported that Allāh's Messenger (ﷺ) said; "Do not swear by your forefathers, whoever swears by Allāh, then trust him, and whoever swears by Allāh then accept it from him. And whoever does not accept it then he is not from Allāh." Recorded by Ibn Mājah with a *ḥasan* chain.[114]

فيه مسائل:

الأولى: النهي عن الحلف بالآباء.

الثانية: الأمر للمحلوف له بالله أن يرضى.

الثالثة: وعيد من لم يرض

Important Points

1. The prohibition of swearing by ones forefathers.
2. The command for one to accept one who swears to him by Allāh.

[114] It was graded *ṣaḥīḥ* by al-Albānī in *Ṣaḥīḥ al-Jāmi'*; no. 7247, see also *al-Irwā'* no. 2698.

3. The threat for whoever does not accept it.

Commentary by *ʿAllāmah* al-Saʿdī

What is said about one who is not Satisfied with another Swearing by Allāh.

This refers to when you are faced with an oath by your opponent and his overall truthfulness is known, or his good nature and trustworthiness is apparent. Then it is necessary for you to accept it and be content with his oath. This is so, because there is no definitive reason which would warrant rejecting his apparent truthfulness. In any case where the Muslims feel required to swear by Allāh, the honour of their Lord, and His majesty, then it is required upon you to accept their oath.

If he is given an oath by Allāh, but he does not accept it without making conditions for his opponent, like making him swear by a divorce, or requiring his opponent to make a *duʿā* for himself to be punished if he were untrue, then this falls under the threat, because that is evil conduct, dishonouring Allāh and a refusal to follow the ruling of Allāh and His Messenger.

In the case of one who is known to be an open sinner or liar, and he is making an oath in a matter that one is certain he is lying about, then rejecting such oath does not fall under the threat mentioned, due to the knowledge of his lying and because his heart does not contain the honour of Allāh that would make the people feel safe in accepting his oath. In this case, the threat is removed due to the impossibility of determining his accuracy. And Allāh knows best.

Chapter 44

قول: ما شاء الله وشئت

Saying "What Allāh willed and what you willed."

عن قتيلة، أن يهودياً أتى النبي صلى الله عليه وسلم فقال: إنكم تشركون، تقولون ما شاء الله وشئت، وتقولون: والكعبة، فأمرهم النبي صلى الله عليه وسلم إذا أرادوا أن يحلفوا أن يقولوا: (ورب الكعبة، وأن يقولوا: ما شاء الله ثم شئت) رواه النسائي وصححه.

From Qutaylah; "A Jew came to the Prophet (ﷺ) saying, 'You [people] have made *shirk*. You say, "As Allāh has willed and you have willed." And they say, "By the Ka'bah!"' So the Prophet (ﷺ) ordered that when intending to swear you say, 'By the Ka'bah's Lord' And , 'As Allāh willed, then you willed." Recorded by al-Nasā'ī who graded it *ṣaḥīḥ*.[115]

وله أيضاً عن ابن عباس رضي الله عنهما: أن رجلاً قال للنبي صلى الله عليه وسلم: ما شاء الله وشئت، فقال: (أ جعلتني لله نداً؟ ما شاء الله وحده).

He also recorded from Ibn 'Abbās (رضي الله عنه) saying, "A man came to the Prophet (ﷺ) saying, 'As Allāh has willed and you have willed.' He (ﷺ) said, 'Are you making me an equal to Him? As Allāh has willed alone."[116]

---

[115] Also recorded by Aḥmad , al-Ḥākim and others. It was graded *ṣaḥīḥ* by al-Albānī in *Ṣaḥīḥ Sunan al-Nasā'ī* no. 3533, and al-*Ṣaḥīḥah* no. 136.

[116] Recorded by al-Bukhārī in *al-Adab al-Mufrad*, al-Nasā'ī in *'Amal al-Yawm wal-Laylah* with similar wording. As well with Aḥmad, Ibn Mājah and others. See *al-Ṣaḥīḥah* no. 139 where al-Albānī grades it *ḥasan*.

ولابن ماجه عن الطفيـــل أخـــي عائشة لأمهـــا قال: رأيت كأني أتيت على نفر من اليهود، فقلت: إنكم لأنتم القوم، لولا أنكم تقولون: عزير ابن الله. قالوا: وإنكم لأنتم القوم لولا أنكم تقولون: ما شاء الله وشاء محمد. ثم مررت بنفر من النصارى فقلت: إنكم لأنتم القوم، لولا أنكم تقولون: المسيح ابن الله، قالوا: وإنكم لأنتم القوم، لولا أنكم تقولون: ما شاء الله وشاء محمد. فلما أصبحت أخبرت بها من أخبرت، ثم أتيت النبي صلى الله عليه وسلم فأخبرته. قال: (هل أخبرت بها أحداً؟) قلت: نعم. قال: فحمد الله وأثنى عليه، ثم قال: (أما بعد؛ فإن طفيلاً رأى رؤيا، أخبر بها من أخبر منكم، وإنكم قلتم كلمة كان يمنعني كذا وكذا أن أنهاكم عنها. فلا تقولوا: ما شاء الله وشاء محمد، ولكن قولوا: ما شاء الله وحده).

With Ibn Mājah; from al-Ṭufayl, the brother of ʿĀ'ishah through her mother, he said, "I dreamt that I came upon a group of Jews, I said to them, 'You would be the people [you claim] if you hadn't said that ʿUzair was the son of Allāh.' They replied, 'You would be the people [you claim] if you didn't say, 'as Allāh willed and as Muḥammad willed.' Then I passed a group of Christians so I said, 'You would be the people [you claim] if you hadn't said that *al-Masīḥ* was the son of Allāh.' They replied, 'You would be the people [you claim] if you didn't say, 'as Allāh willed and as Muḥammad willed.'

The following morning I informed the incident to some others. Then I came to the Prophet (ﷺ) and told him. He said, 'Have you informed this to anyone?' I said, 'Yes.' Then he praised Allāh and glorified Him and said, "To proceed; Ṭufayl had a dream, and he has narrated to some of you what he saw in it. You have been saying a statement that I have been prevented from prohibiting because of this and that. Do not say "as Allāh willed and as Muḥammad willed." But say, "As Allāh willed" alone.'"[117]

فيه مسائل:

الأولى: معرفة اليهود بالشرك الأصغر.

الثانية: فهم الإنسان إذا كان له هوى.

الثالثة: قوله صلى الله عليه وسلم: (أجعلتني لله نداً؟) فكيف بمن قال:

[117] This narration is recorded by Ibn Mājah, Aḥmad and others. It was graded *ṣaḥīḥ* by al-Albānī, see *al-Ṣaḥīḥah* no. 137 & 138.

يا أكرم الخلق ما لي من ألوذ به سواك . . . .

والبيتين بعده.

الرابعة: أن هذا ليس من الشرك الأكبر، لقوله: (يمنعني كذا وكذا).

الخامسة: أن الرؤيا الصالحة من أقسام الوحي.

السادسة: أنها قد تكون سبباً لشرع بعض الأحكام.

Important Points

1. The Jews awareness of minor *shirk*.
2. The condition of people's understanding when their desire effects an issue.
3. His saying, "Are you making me an equal to Him?" So how about the one who says, "I have none to recourse to but him (i.e. the Prophet (ﷺ))...." and the rest of the verses of that poem.
4. That this is not from major *shirk* due to his saying, "I have been prevented by this or that..."
5. That true dreams are a type of revelation.
6. That it was the means for explaining some legislation.

For *ʿAllāmah* al-Saʿdī's Commentary Refer to the Next Chapter

Chapter 45

من سب الدهر فقد آذى الله

Whoever curses time, he has offended Allāh

وقول الله تعـــالى: ﴿ وقالوا ما هي إلا حياتنا الدنيا نموت ونحيا وما يهلكنا إلا الدهر﴾ الآية.

Allāh (ﷻ) said, "They say, 'There is but our life in the world. We die and we live. Nothing causes us to perish except for time." (*al-Jāthiyah* 45:24)

في الصحيح عن أبي هريرة، عن النبي صلى الله عليه وسلم قال: (قال الله تعالى: يؤذيني ابن آدم، يسب الدهر، وأنا الدهر، أقلب الليل والنهار)

In the *Ṣaḥīḥ*, from Abū Hurayrah, the Prophet (ﷺ) said, "Allāh (ﷻ) said, 'The son of Ādam has offended Me, he curses time, but I am the time; I turn the night and the day."

وفي رواية: (لا تسبوا الدهر، فإن الله هو الدهر).

And in one narration, "Do not curse time, for Allāh is surely the time."[118]

فيه مسائل:

الأولى: النهي عن سب الدهر.

الثانية: تسميته أذى لله.

[118] The first is with al-Bukhārī and Muslim, and the second with Muslim and Aḥmad. "Al-Shāfi'ī, Abū 'Ubayd and others among the Imāms explained the meaning of 'Do not curse time for surely Allāh is time.' that when the Arabs during *jāhilīyyah* suffered adversity, trials or troubles, they would say, 'O frustrating time!' So they would link this occurrence to time and curse it, when in fact it was really Allāh who caused the event, so they were actually cursing Him..." (*Fatḥ al-Majīd*) This is supported by a similar narration recorded by al-Bukhārī in *al-Adab al-Mufrad*.

الثالثة: التأمل في قوله: (فإن الله هو الدهر).

الرابعة: أنه قد يكون سابا ولو لم يقصده بقلبه.

Important Points

1. The prohibition of cursing time.
2. Calling this "offending Allāh."
3. Noting his saying, "For Allāh is surely the time."
4. That cursing can occur even if it is not intended in the heart.

Commentary by ʿ*Allāmah* al-Saʿdī

Whoever Curses Time, He has Offended Allāh

This occurred often during *jāhilīyyah*, and many of the evil people, the libertines, and the foolish followed them when they engaged it changing time and altering the seasons. Contrary to what they intended, they were insulting time and sometimes cursing it. This behaviour arose from a weakness in religion, from foolishness and from tremendous ignorance.

Time is not a matter that they have any control over. For surely the arrangement and organisation of the events of time is maintained by Allāh *al-ʿAzīz al-Ḥakīm*, so in reality, their philandering and insults are directed at the One who truly controls it.

Just as this behaviour erodes away at religion, it also contradicts reason, since by it calamities are increased, their scale becomes larger, and the door to the necessary patience is closed. And this negates *tawḥīd*.

As for the believer, he knows that the events of time occur by the decree, power, and wisdom of Allāh, so he would not toy with something that Allāh or His Messenger never asked him to be responsible for, rather he accepts what Allāh arranges, and submits to His commands, and by that he completes his *tawḥīd* and his sense of tranquility.

Chapter 46

التسمي بقاضي القضاة ونحوه
The Name Judge of Judges, and the like

في الصحيح عن أبي هريرة رضي الله عنه، عن النبي صلى الله عليه وسلم قال: (إن أخنع اسم عند الله: رجل تسمى ملك الأملاك، لا مالك إلا الله).

In the *Ṣaḥīḥ*, from Abū Hurayrah, the Prophet (ﷺ) said, "The most despicable name to Allāh is a man called King of Kings. There is no King but Allāh."

قال سفيان: مثل (شاهان شاه).

Sufyān said, "Similar is Shah of Shahs."[119]

وفي رواية: (أغيظ رجل على الله يوم القيامة وأخبثه).

And in one narration, "The most infuriating man to Allāh on the Day of Resurrection, and the most filthy to Him..."[120]

قوله (أخنع) يعني أوضع.

His saying, "*Akhnaʿa* [despicable]" means the most despicable.

فيه مسائل:

الأولى: النهي عن التسمي بملك الأملاك.

الثانية: أن ما في معناه مثله، كما قال سفيان.

الثالثة: التفطن للتغليظ في هذا ونحوه، مع القطع بأن القلب لم يقصد معناه.

الرابعة: التفطن أن هذا لإجلال الله سبحانه.

---

[119] Recorded by al-Bukhārī, Muslim, Abū Dāwūd, and al-Tirmidhī and others.

[120] Recorded by Muslim and Aḥmad.

Important Points

1. The prohibition of the title king of kings.
2. As well as what has a similar meaning as Sufyān said.
3. Realising the emphasis on this matter and its like, even in the abstract sense when the heart does not intend such meaning.
4. Realising that this is for Allāh (ﷻ) only.

For ʿ*Allāmah* al-Saʿdī's Commentary Refer to the Next Chapter

Chapter 47

احترام أسماء الله وتغيير الاسم لأجل ذلك
The Sacredness of Allāh's (ﷻ) Names, changing ones name because of that.

عن أبي شريح: أنه كان يكنى أبا الحكم؛ فقال له النبي صلى الله عليه وسلم: (إن الله هو الحكم، وإليه الحكم) فقال: إن قومي إذا اختلفوا في شيء أتوني، فحكمت بينهم، فرضي كلا الفريقين فقال: (ما أحسن هذا فمالك من الولد؟) قلت: شريح، ومسلم، وعبد الله. قال: (فمن أكبرهم؟) قلت: شريح، قال: (فأنت أبو شريح)، رواه أبو داود وغيره.

From Abū Shurayḥ, "That his *kunyā* was Abūl-Ḥakam, so the Prophet (ﷺ) said to him, 'Allāh is *al-Ḥakam* [the Judge], and to Him is the judgement.' He said, 'But when my people differ over something they have me judge between them, and each group accepts.' He (ﷺ) said, 'What is better than this, what children do you have?' He said, 'Shurayḥ, Muslim and ʿAbdullāh.' He asked, 'Who is the eldest?' I said, 'Shurayḥ', he said, 'So you are Abū Shurayḥ.'" Recorded by Abū Dāwūd and others.[121]

فيه مسائل:

الأولى: احترام أسماء الله وصفاته ولو لم يقصد معناه.

الثانية: تغيير الاسم لأجل ذلك.

الثالثة: اختيار أكبر الأبناء للكنية.

---

[121] Also al-Nasā'ī, al-Ḥākim and Ibn Ḥibbān. Shaykh Sulaymān said, "Ibn Muflih said, 'Its chain is good [*jayd*]'" and al-Albānī graded it *ṣaḥīḥ* in *Ṣaḥīḥ al-Jāmiʿ* no. 1845.

Important Points

1. The sanctity of Allāh's Names and attributes, even if one does not intend their meanings.
2. Changing the name for the sake of that.
3. Choosing the eldest of sons for the *kunyā*.

Commentary by *ʿAllāmah* al-Saʿdī

The Name Judge of Judges, and the like & The Sacredness of Allāh's Names, and Changing a Name because of that

These two discussions are branches of the preceding chapters. That is, it is obligatory that no equals be made for Allāh in intention, saying, or deed. So one is not to be called with a name that implies some type of partnership with one of Allāh's Names or attributes, like the judge of judges, the king of kings etc. Or, the Ruler of rulers, or Abū al-Ḥakam [the father of rule] etc. All of this is out of precaution for *tawḥīd* and Allāh's names and attributes, and defending against what leads to *shirk*, to the extent of even refraining from expressions which it is feared may bring about the thought that they imply a partnership with Allāh in any of His rights or what is specific to Him.

Chapter 48

من هزل بشيء فيه ذكر الله أو القرآن أو الرسول

Whoever jokes about anything that Allāh has mentioned, the Qur'ān, or the Messenger.

وقول الله تعالي: (ولئن سألتهم ليقولن إنما كنا نخوض ونلعب) الآية.

Allāh (ﷻ) said, "But if you were to ask them they would say, 'We were only joking and playing." (*al-Tawbah* 9: 65)

عن ابن عمر، ومحمد بن كعب، وزيد بن أسلم، وقتادة – دخل حديث بعضهم في بعض – : أنه قال رجل في غزوة تبوك: ما رأينا مثل قرائنا هؤلاء، أرغب بطوناً، ولا أكذب ألسناً، ولا أجبن عند اللقاء ـــ يعني رسول الله صلى الله عليه وسلم وأصحابه القرّاء ـــ فقال له عوف بن مالك: كذبت، ولكنك منافق، لأخبرن رسول الله صلى الله عليه وسلم. فذهب عوف إلى رسول الله صلى الله عليه وسلم ليخبره فوجد القرآن قد سبقه. فجاء ذلك الرجل إلى رسول الله صلى الله عليه وسلم وقد ارتحل وركب ناقته، فقال: يا رسول الله! إنما كنا نخوض ونتحدث حديث الركب، نقطع به عنا الطريق. فقال ابن عمر: كأني أنظر إليه متعلقاً بنسعة ناقة رسول الله صلى الله عليه وسلم، وإن الحجارة تنكب رجليه – وهو يقول: إنما كنا نخوض ونلعب – فيقول له رسول الله صلى الله عليه وسلم: (أبالله وآياته ورسوله كنتم تستهزءون) ما يتلفت إليه وما يزيده عليه.

From Ibn ʿUmar, Muḥammad bin Kaʿb, Zayd bin Aslam, and Qatādah - each of them narrated similar - that during the battle of *Tabūk* a man said, "We have not seen of our reciters similar to these people, none more greedy in appetite, nor false in speech, nor cowardly in battle." He was referring to the reciting of the companions of Allāh's Messenger (ﷺ). ʿAwf bin Mālik said to him, "You have lied. Rather, you are a *munāfiq*. We will tell Allāh's Messenger (ﷺ)." So

ʿAwf went to tell Allāh's Messenger (ﷺ), but some Qur'ān [revealed about this incident it] preceded him. That man came to Allāh's Messenger (ﷺ), while he (ﷺ) was mounted upon his camel. He said, "O Messenger of Allāh! we were only joking and we were saying things to pass the time for us on the road." Ibn ʿUmar said, "It is as if I am looking at him; clinging to the saddle of the Messenger of Allāh's camel, stones battering his feet, saying, 'We were only joking and playing!' So Allāh's Messenger (ﷺ) said, 'Is it with Allāh, His *āyāt*, and His Messenger that you are amused? They are not excused, they have disbelieved after their faith.'

He did not say any more nor any less to him." [122]

فيه مسائل:

الأولى: وهي العظيمة: أن من هزل بهذا فهو كافر.

الثانية: أن هذا هو تفسير الآية فيمن فعل ذلك كائناً من كان.

الثالثة: الفرق بين النميمة والنصيحة لله ولرسوله.

الرابعة: الفرق بين العفو الذي يحبه الله وبين الغلظة على أعداء الله.

الخامسة: أن من الأعذار ما لا ينبغي أن يقبل.

Important Issues

1. An extremely important point, that whoever jokes like this, then he is a disbeliever.
2. That this is the explanation of the *āyah*, so whoever does it then it applies.
3. The difference between gossip, and between *naṣīḥah* to Allāh and His Messenger.
4. The difference between pardoning which Allāh loves, and between being severe with Allāh's enemies.
5. That it is not necessary to accept some excuses.

---

[122] Recorded by Ibn Abū Ḥātim, Ibn Jarīr al-Ṭabarī and similar with others. Shaykh Muqbil bin Hādī included it in *Ṣaḥīḥ al-Musnad min Asbāb al-Nuzūl* (p.122), grading it *ḥasan*.

Commentary by ʿ*Allāmah* al-Saʿdī

Whoever Jokes about anything that Allāh has mentioned, the Qur'ān, or the Messenger.

Meaning that this is something that entirely negates faith, and removes one from the religion, because the bases of the religion is faith in Allāh, His Books, and His Messengers.

And faith requires honouring this, and it is well known that mocking and joking about something of these matters is among the worst kinds of sheer disbelief. Because this disbelief increases disdain and contempt.

The disbelievers are of two types; passive and antagonistic. The antagonistic is the one at war with Allāh and His Messenger, attacking Allāh, His religion, and His Messenger with the sternest rejection and the worst falsehood. And mockery is a tactic from this category.

Chapter 49

ما جاء في قول الله تعالى: ولئن أذقناه رحمةً منا من بعد ضراء

Allāh's (ﷻ) saying; "And if We give him a taste of Our mercy after touching him with adversity"

ما جاء في قول الله تعالى: (ولئن أذقناه رحمةً منا من بعد ضراء مسته ليقولن هذا لي) الآية.

Allāh's (ﷻ) saying; "And if We give him a taste of Our mercy after touching him with adversity, then he says, 'This is from me...'" (*Fuṣṣilat* 41:50)

قال مجاهد: هذا بعملي وأنا محقوق به. وقال ابن عباس: يريد من عندي.

Mujāhid said, "(Meaning,) this is from my deeds and I deserve it." Ibn ʿAbbās said, "Meaning, that which is with me."

وقوله: (قال إنما أوتيته على علم عندي)

And He (ﷻ) said, "He says, 'It only came to me because of the knowledge with me." (*al-Qaṣaṣ* 28:78)

قال قتادة: على علم مني بوجوه المكاسب. وقال آخرون: على علم من الله أني له أهل. وهذا معنى قول مجاهد: أوتيته على شرف.

Qatādah said, "From my knowledge of profiting." And others said, "From Allāh's knowledge, I am the best who knows it."

And this is the meaning of Mujāhid's statement, "It came to me out of honour."

وعن أبي هريرة رضي الله عنه أنه سمع رسول الله صلى الله عليه وسلم يقول: (إن ثلاثة من بني إسرائيل: أبرص، وأقرع، وأعمى. فأراد الله أن يبتليهم، فبعث إليهم ملكاً، فأتى الأبرص، فقال: أي شيء أحب إليك؟ قال: لون حسن، وجلد حسن، ويذهب عني الذي قد قذرني الناس به قال: فمسحه، فذهب عنه قذره، وأعطي لوناً حسناً وجلداً حسناً، قال: فأي المال أحب إليك؟ قال: الإبــل أو البقر ــ شك إسحاق ــ فأعطي ناقة عشراء، وقال: بارك الله لك فيها. قال: فأتى الأقرع، فقال أي شيء أحب إليك قال: شعر حسن، ويذهب عني الذي قد قذرني الناس به فمسحه، فذهب عنه، وأعطي شعراً حسناً، فقال: أي المال أحب إليك؟ قال: البقر، أو الإبل، فأعطي بقرة حاملاً، قال: بارك الله لك فيها. فأتى الأعمى، فقال: أي شيء أحب إليك؟ قال: أن يرد الله إلي بصري؛ فأبصر به الناس، فمسحه، فرد الله إليه بصره، قال: فأي المال أحب إليك؟ قال: الغنم، فأعطي شاة والداً؛ فأنتج هذان وولد هذا، فكان لهذا وادٍ من الإبل، ولهذا وادٍ من البقر، ولهذا وادٍ من الغنم، قال: ثم إنه أتى الأبرص في صورته وهيئته. فقال: رجل مسكين، قد انقطعت بي الحبال في سفري، فلا بلاغ لي اليوم إلا بالله ثم بك، أسألك بالذي أعطاك اللون الحسن، والجلد الحسن، والمال، بعيراً أتبلغ به في سفري، فقال: الحقوق كثيرة. فقال له: كأني أعرفك، ألم تكن أبرص يقذرك الناس، فقيراً، فأعطاك الله عز وجل المال؟ فقال: إنما ورثت هذا المال كابراً عن كابر، فقال: إن كنت كاذباً فصيّرك الله إلى ما كنت. قال: وأتى الأقرع في صورته، فقال له مثل ما قال لهذا، وردّ عليه مثل ما ردّ عليه هذا، فقال: إن كنت كاذباً فصيّرك الله إلى ما كنت. وأتى الأعمى في صورته، فقال: رجل مسكين وابن سبيل، قد انقطعت بي الحبال في سفري، فلا بلاغ لي اليوم إلا بالله ثم بك. أسألك بالذي ردّ عليك بصرك شاة أتبلغ بها في سفري، فقال: كنت أعمى فردّ الله إليَّ بصري، فخذ ما شئت ودع ما شئت، فوالله لا أجهدك اليوم بشيء أخذته لله. فقال: أمسك مالك، فإنما ابتليتم فقد رضي الله عنك، وسخط على صاحبيك) أخرجاه.

From Abū Hurayrah that he heard Allāh's Messenger (ﷺ) saying, "Once there were three men from the children of Isrā'īl, a leper, a blind man and a bald man; whom Allāh wanted to test, so He sent an angel to them. The angel asked the leper, 'What would you most like to have?' The leper said, 'Good complexion and good skin, because the people consider me to be filthy.' Then the angel touched him and he was cured. He was given a good complexion and good skin. Then the angel said, 'Which property would you most like to have?' The leper said, 'Camels.' So he was given a pregnant camel, and the angel said, 'May Allāh bless you with it.' Then the angel came to the bald man and said, 'What would you most like to have?' He said, 'Nice hair, and I wish to be cured from this disease because people find me repulsive.' The angel touched him, and he was given nice hair. Then the angel said, 'Which property would you most like to have?' He said, 'Cows.' so the angel gave him a pregnant cow that had plenty of milk. The angel said to him,'May Allāh bless you with it.' The angel came to the blind man and said, 'What would you most like to have?' He said, 'I wish Allāh would restore my sight so I can see the people.' He touched his eyes and Allāh gave him his sight back. The angel said, 'Which property would you most like to have?' He said, 'Sheep.' So the angel gave him a pregnant sheep. Later, all three pregnant animals gave birth to their young. They multiplied and brought forth so many (animals) that one of the men had a herd of camels filling a valley, one had a herd of cows filling a valley, and the other one had a flock of sheep filling a valley. Then the angel, disguised to appear as a leper, visited the leper and said, 'I am a poor man, who has lost all means of livelihood while on a journey. So none will satisfy my need except Allāh and then you. In the Name of Him Who has given you such nice complexion, such beautiful skin, and so much property, I ask you to give me a camel so that I may reach my destination.' The man replied, 'I have many obligations (so I cannot give any to you).' The angel said, 'I think I know you, were you not a leper who the people shunned? Weren't you a poor man and then Allāh gave this to you?' He replied, 'I inherited this from my family.' The angel said, 'If you are lying, then let Allāh make you as you were before.' Then the angel, disguised as a bald man, went to the bald man and said the same as he had to the leper. He too answered the same way. The angel told him, 'If you are lying, then let Allāh make you as you were before.' Then the angel, disguised as a blind man, visited the blind man and said, 'I am a poor man and a traveller, whose means of livelihood have been exhausted while on a journey. I have nobody to help me except Allāh, and after Him, you yourself. I ask you in the name of Him who has given you back your eyesight to give me a sheep, so that with its help, I may complete my journey.' The man said, 'I was once blind, and Allāh returned my sight to me, I was once poor and Allāh made me rich. So take anything you like from what I have. By Allāh, I will not praise you for leaving anything (you need) of my property which you may take for Allāh's sake.' The angel replied, 'Keep your property. You (three men) have been tested. Allāh is pleased with you, but He is angry with your two companions.'" They (al-Bukhārī and Muslim), recorded it.

فيه مسائل:

الأولى: تفسير الآية.

الثانية: ما معنى: (ليقولن هذا لي) .

الثالثة: ما معنى قوله: (أوتيته على علم عندي).

الرابعة: ما في هذه القصة العجيبة من العبر العظيمة.

Important Points

1. The explanation of the *āyah*.
2. The meaning of "'This is from me...'" (*Fuṣṣilat* 41:50)
3. The meaning of "It only came to me because of the knowledge with me." (*al-Qaṣaṣ* 28:78)
4. The numerous important lessons from this story.

Commentary by *ʿAllāmah* al-Saʿdī

Allāh's (ﷻ) saying; "And if We give him a taste of Our mercy after touching him with adversity, then he says, 'This is from me...'" (*Fuṣṣilat* 41:50)

The objective of this discussion, is that all one claims he receives of favours and provisions by his own hand, skill, or intellect, or because he deserves that, thinking that he has some right over Allāh for it, then this negates *tawḥīd*. Because the believer is obliged to recognise internally and externally that the favours come from Allāh and that the praise is due to Allāh for that, and to recognise that these are from His favours and beneficence, to utilise these favours in acts of obedience to Allāh, not to think that he has some right for these things over Allāh. Rather Allāh alone has the right over them, he is simply a servant in every sense. So by this he fulfils his faith and *tawḥīd*. If the opposite occurs, then he achieves only ingratitude for the favour, and amasement with the self, displaying that which is among the most evil of traits.

Chapter 50

قول الله تعالى: فلما آتاهما صالحاً

Allāh's (ﷻ) saying, "And when good came to them"

قول الله تعالى: (فلما آتاهما صالحاً جعلا له شركاء فيما آتاهما) الآية.

Allāh's (ﷻ) saying, "And when good came to them they made *shirk* in what they received." (*al-A'rāf* 7:190)

قال ابن حزم: اتفقوا على تحريم كل اسم معبّد لغير الله؛ كعبد عمر، وعبد الكعبة، وما أشبه ذلك، حاشا عبد المطلب.

Ibn Ḥazm said, "The prohibition of every name of servitude to other than Allāh is agreed upon, like 'Abd 'Amr for example, or 'Abd al-Ka'bah, and the like, with the exception of 'Abd al-Muṭṭālib."

وعن ابن عباس رضي الله عنه في الآية قال: لما تغشاها آدم حملت، فأتاهما إبليس فقال: إني صاحبكما الذي أخرجتكما من الجنة لتطيعاني أو لأجعلن له قرني أيل، فيخرج من بطنك فيشقه، ولأفعلن ولأفعلن — يخوفهما — سّمياه عبد الحارث، فأبيا أن يطيعاه، فخرج ميتاً، ثم حملت، فأتاهما، فقال مثل قوله، فأبيا أن يطيعاه، فخرج ميتاً، ثم حملت، فأتاهما، فذكر لهما فأدركهما حب الولد، فسمياه عبد الحارث فذلك قوله تعالى: (جعلا له شركاء فيما آتاهما) رواه ابن أبي حاتم.

About the *āyah*, Ibn 'Abbās (ﷺ) said; "When Ādam [learned of his wife's pregnancy] *Iblīs* came to them. He said, 'I am your companion who had you removed from Paradise. Obey me or I will make him have two horns like a deer which will rip your insides when it comes out. I will, I will [etc.]' in order to frighten them into calling the child ʿAbd al-Ḥārith. But they refused to obey him. Then the child was still-born. Then she became pregnant again, so he came saying as he had before. They still did not obey him, and the child was still-born again. Then she was pregnant again, so he came to talk to them again. This time out of their sense of love for their child, they called him ʿAbd al-Ḥārith. That is why Allāh said, "they made *shirk* in what they received." Recorded by Ibn Abū Ḥātim.[123]

وله بسند صحيح عن قتادة قال: شركاء في طاعته، ولم يكن في عبادته.

And also [from Ibn Abū Ḥātim] with a *ṣaḥīḥ* chain from Qatādah who said, "*Shirk* in obeying Him, not in worshipping Him."

وله بسند صحيح عن مجاهد في قوله: (لئن آتيتنا صالحاً) قال: أشفقا ألا يكون إنساناً، وذكر معناه عن الحسن وسعيد وغيرهما.

And [from Ibn Abū Ḥātim] with a *ṣaḥīḥ* chain from *Mujāhid* about Allāh's (ﷻ) saying, "And when good came to them..." he said, "Give us of good" he said, "They were afraid that it would not be a human." And this meaning was mentioned by al-Ḥasan, Saʿīd, and others.

فيه مسائل:

الأولى: تحريم كل اسم معبّد لغير الله.

الثانية: تفسير الآية.

الثالثة: أن هذا الشرك في مجرد تسمية لم تقصد حقيقتها.

الرابعة: أن هبة الله للرجل البنت السوية من النعم.

الخامسة: ذكر السلف الفرق بين الشرك في الطاعة، والشرك في العبادة.

Important Points

1. Prohibition of every name denoting servitude to other than Allāh.

2. The explanation of the *āyah*.

---

[123] Recorded by Aḥmad, al-Tirmidhī, al-Ḥākim and others. Ibn Kathīr considered it among the disparaged reports from the people of the Book, and al-Arnā'ūṭ graded it weak in his notes on *Fatḥ al-Majīd*, and al-Albānī graded it weak, no. 4769 *Ḍaʿīf al-Jāmiʿ*; and no. 342 *Silsilat al-Aḥadīth al-Ḍaʿīfah*.

3. That this *shirk* was simply by the name, not the objective in reality.
4. That Allāh's gift to man of a healthy child is among His favours.
5. The *salaf* mentioned the distinction between *shirk* in obedience and *shirk* in worship.

Commentary by *ʿAllāmah* al-Saʿdī

Allāh's (ﷻ) saying, "And when good came to them they made *shirk* in what they received. Allāh is exalted above what they associate with Him." (*al-Aʿrāf* 7:190)

The objective here is that children were among Allāh's favours for them, and Allāh completed the favour for them by making them have healthy bodies.

Therefore they must be healthy in their religion. This requires them to be grateful to Allāh for the favour He granted them, and that requires that their children not be servants of other than Allāh, nor are they to attribute the favour to other than Allāh. This is a rejection of the favours that would negate *tawḥīd*.

Chapter 51

قول الله تعالى: ولله الأسماء الحسنى فادعوه بها

Allāh (ﷻ) said, "Allāh's are the most beautiful Names, so call Him by them"

قول الله تعالى: ﴿ ولله الأسماء الحسنى فادعوه بها وذروا الذين يلحدون في أسمائه﴾ الآية:

Allāh (ﷻ) said, "Allāh's are the most beautiful Names, so call Him by them, and avoid those who are heretical with His Names." (*al-A'rāf* 7: 180)

ذكر ابن أبي حاتم عن ابن عباس رضي الله عنهما (يلحدون في أسماءه): يشركون.

Ibn Abū Ḥātim mentioned from Ibn 'Abbās, "those who are heretical with His names," are those who make *shirk* [with them].[124]

وعنه: سموا اللات من الإله، والعزى من العزيز.

And from him; "*Al-Lāt* is from *al-Ilāh*, and *al-'Uzza* from is *al-'Azīz*."[125]

وعن الأعمش: يدخلون فيها ما ليس منها.

And from al-A'mash; "They give it meanings that are not included in them."

---

[124] Shaykh Sulaymān said, "Ibn Abū Ḥātim did not record this report from Ibn 'Abbās, rather only from Qatādah." (*Taysīr al-'Azīz*) Similar is quoted by Ibn Kathīr.

[125] That is from Ibn 'Abbās, recorded by Ibn Abū Ḥātim. However, Ibn Kathīr has this statement, "From Ibn Jurayj, from Mujāhid."

فيه مسائل:

الأولى: إثبات الأسماء.

الثانية: كونها حسنى.

الثالثة: الأمر بدعائه بها.

الرابعة: ترك من عارض من الجاهلين الملحدين.

الخامسة: تفسير الإلحاد فيها.

السادسة: وعيد من ألحد.

Important Points

1. Confirming the Names.
2. They are beautiful.
3. The command to call Him by them.
4. Avoiding the ignorant heretics who oppose them.
5. The explanation of *ilḥād* [heresy].
6. The threat against heresy.

Commentary by ʿ*Allāmah* al-Saʿdī

Allāh (ﷻ) said, "Allāh's are the most beautiful Names, so call Him by them and avoid those who are heretical with His Names." (*al-Aʿrāf* 7: 180)

Tawḥīd is founded upon confirming what Allāh has affirmed for Himself, or what His Messenger (ﷺ) affirmed of His beautiful Names. It is to have the beautifying awareness of the majestic meanings that are inclusive of the Names, to worship Allāh by them, and call upon Him with them.

So every matter that the worshipper seeks from His Lord - whether related to this life or religion - then he seeks it by the beautiful Names of Allāh related to that.

So whoever calls upon Him to bring him sustenance, he asks Him by His Name *al-Razzāq*. For the result of mercy and forgiveness, then by His name *al-Rahīm, al-Raḥmān, al-Barr, al-Karīm, al-ʿAfu, al-Ghafūr, al-Tawāb* or others.

What is even better than this, is that calling upon Him by His Names and attributes is a form of worship if the meanings of His beautiful Names are realised, and their effect is in the heart, such that the heart is effected by the understanding and implications of these names, and it is motivated by that awareness.

Similar is the case with the Names of greatness, and pride, majesty and granduer and the Names that inspire fear, motivating the heart to honour Allāh and recognise His majesty.

The Names with the meanings of beauty, righteousness, beneficence, mercy and kindness - all of these motivate the heart to love Allāh, longing for Him, praising Him and feeling grateful to Him.

The Names of might, wisdom, knowledge and power motivate the hearts to submit in awe and fear before Him.

The Names of knowledge, informing, omnipresence, watchfulness, witnessing - all of these motivate the heart to be aware that Allāh is watching every motion and moment of stillness, making one guard against evil thoughts and harmful intentions.

The Names *al-Ghani*, and *al-Laṭif* make the hearts realise their need and dependence upon Him, making them rely upon Him all of the time and in every situation.

This awareness results in the hearts due to the servant's awareness of the Names and attributes. By the servant worshipping Allāh with them, he is not seeking the outcome of the world, nor to master it or perfect it. It is the best form of obedience to worship Him with, and it is the essence of *tawḥīd* and worship. By opening this door, he has opened the door of the ultimate *tawḥīd*, and the perfect faith that is not realised except by the perfection achieved by the people of *tawḥīd*. Affirming the Names and attributes is the foundation of this most exalted goal.

As for *ilḥād* [heresy] in Allāh's Names and attributes, it is the utmost negation of this grand goal.

There are different kinds of *Ilḥād*:

If the heretic negates the meanings of the Names or attributes, as is done by the *Jāhimīyah* and their successors. Or by resembling them to the attributes of creatures, as the *mushabihah* among the *Rawāfiḍ* and others do.

Or by calling the creatures by His Names as the *mushrikīn* did with the name *al-Lāt* from *al-Illāh*, *al-ʿUzza* from *al-ʿAzīz*, and *al-Manāt* from *al-Manān*, deriving them from the beautiful Names of Allāh. So they likened them to Allāh then they sanctioned worshipping them, which is solely Allāh's right alone.

So the reality of heresy in Allāh's Names is altering them, either in expression or meaning, explanation or interpretation, or changing them. All of this negates *tawḥīd* and faith.

Chapter 52

لا يقال: السلام على الله

Not to say "*Al-Salām ʿalā Allāh*"

في الصحيح عن ابن مسعود رضي الله عنه قال: كنا إذا كنا مع النبي صلى الله عليه وسلم في الصلاة قلنا: السلام على الله من عباده، السلام على فلان، فقال النبي صلى الله عليه وسلم: (لا تقولوا السلام على الله، فإن الله هو السلام).

In the *Ṣaḥīḥ* from Ibn Masʿūd (ﷺ), who said, "When we were with the Prophet (ﷺ) in prayer we were saying, '*Al-Salāmu ʿalā Allāh* (*Al- Salam* be upon Allāh) from His worshippers, *al-salāmu ʿalā* so and so.;" So the Prophet (ﷺ) said, 'Do not say "*Al-salāmu ʿalā Allāh*", for Allāh is *al-Salām*.'"[126]

فيه مسائل:

الأولى: تفسير السلام.

الثانية: أنه تحية.

الثالثة: أنها لا تصلح لله.

الرابعة: العلة في ذلك.

الخامسة: تعليمهم التحية التي تصلح لله.

---

[126] Recorded by al-Bukhārī, Muslim, Al-Tirmidhī and al-Nasāʾī.

Important Issues

1. The explanation of *al-Salām*.
2. That it is a greeting.
3. That it is not a befitting greeting for Allāh.
4. The reason for this.
5. His (ﷺ) teaching them the greeting that befits Allāh.

Commentary by *ʿAllāmah* al-Saʿdī

Not to Say "*Al-Salām ʿalā Allāh*"

He (ﷺ) has explained this meaning by his saying, "For Allāh is *al-Salām*." So He (ﷻ) is *al-Salām*, the one secure from every defect and shortcoming, secure from any of His creatures resembling Him. He is the one utterly secure from His servants. So the servant will never be capable of causing any harm to Him, nor can they ever bring Him any benefit, rather they are all in dire need of Him, dependant upon Him in all of their circumstances, and He is the Free, the one worthy of praise.

Chapter 53

قول: اللهم اغفر لي إن شئت

Saying: "O Allāh! Forgive me if You Will."

في الصحيح عن أبي هريرة رضي الله عنه، أن رسول الله صلى الله عليه وسلم قال: (لا يقل أحدكم: اللهم اغفر لي إن شئت، اللهم ارحمني إن شئت، ليعزم المسألة، فإن الله لا مكره له).

In the *Ṣaḥīḥ* from Abū Hurayrah that Allāh's Messenger (ﷺ) said, "None of you may say, 'O Allāh forgive me if you will.' O Allāh have mercy on me if you will.' But be resolved on the issue, for there is no difficulty for Allāh."[127]

ولمسلم: (وليعظم الرغبة، فإن الله لا يتعاظمه شيء أعطاه).

And with Muslim, "But let your hope be great, for nothing is too great for Allāh to give it."

فيه مسائل:

الأولى: النهي عن الاستثناء في الدعاء.

الثانية: بيان العلة في ذلك.

الثالثة: قوله: (ليعزم المسألة).

الرابعة: إعظام الرغبة.

الخامسة: التعليل لهذا الأمر.

[127] Al-Bukhārī and Muslim.

Important Points

1. The prohibition of this kind of condition in supplications.
2. Explaining the reason for that.
3. His saying, "But be resolved on the issue."
4. Heightening one's hopes.
5. The reasoning for this order.

Commentary by ʿ*Allāmah* al-Saʿdī

Saying: "O Allāh! Forgive me if You Will."

Every occurrence is by Allāh's will and intent. So when seeking a religious matter, like asking for mercy or forgiveness, or when seeking something related to this life, like good health, provisions, and the like, then the worshipper is ordered to ask for it from his Lord in a manner imploring Him of its urgency, and being certain about it. This kind of seeking is the core and marrow of ʿ*ubūdiyah*.

This will not be complete unless the request is a certain one, without conditioning it by "if you will", and the matter must be something that is good, having no harm in it. Allāh (ﷻ) is not one whom something is too grand for.

Here there is a clear distinction between this general request, and cases of asking for something specific. Like asking for things that may not bring about any benefit or good, or its result is not a positive good for the worshipper. So the worshipper asks his Lord, and he relies upon his Lord to chose the best matter for him, like in the case of the *duʿā*; "O Allāh cause me to live while living is good for me, and take me when You know that death is better for me." Or like the *duʿā* of *istikhārah*.

So understand this difference, the subtle importance of the distinction between seeking good things that are well known for their benefit, being free of any harm, and the supplicant is resolved when seeking it, not being uncertain about it - and seeking a matter which the worshipper is not sure if there may be a punishment for it, nor can he be sure of the benefit over the harm of it. So the supplicant leaves the choice to his Lord, the one who encompasses everything in His knowledge, control, mercy and beneficence.

Chapter 54

لا يقول: عبدي وأمتي

Not to say, "My slave or my slave girl."

في الصحيح عن أبي هريرة رضي الله عنه، أن رسول الله صلى الله عليه وسلم قال: (لا يقل أحدكم: أطعم ربك، وضىء ربك، وليقل: سيدي ومولاي، ولا يقل: عبدي وأمتي، وليقل: فتاي وفتاتي، وغلامي).

In *Ṣaḥīḥ al-Bukhārī* from Abū Hurayrah (ﷺ), that Allāh's Messenger (ﷺ) said, "Let one of you not say, 'Feed your lord' 'Clean your lord' Let him call you 'my master', 'my patron', and let none of you say, 'My slave or my slave girl' let him say, 'My young man', 'my young woman' or 'my boy.'"[128]

فيه مسائل:

الأولى: النهي عن قول: عبدي وأمتي.

الثانية: لا يقول العبد: ربي، ولا يقال له: أطعم ربك.

الثالثة: تعليم الأول قول: فتاي وفتاتي وغلامي.

الرابعة: تعليم الثاني قول: سيدي ومولاي.

الخامسة: التنبيه للمراد، وهو تحقيق التوحيد حتى في الألفاظ.

---

[128] Al-Bukhārī, Muslim and Aḥmad.

Important Points

1. The prohibition of saying, “My slave and my slave-girl.”
2. That the servant does not say, “My lord.” and he is not to be told, “Feed your lord.”
3. Teaching the first to say, “My young man, my young woman, my young boy”
4. Teaching the second to say, “My master, my patron.”
5. Clarifying the reason for this, that is, realising *tawḥīd* even in expressions.

Commentary by *ʿAllāmah* al-Saʿdī

Not to say, “My slave or my slave girl.”

This is from the view that it is recommended for the worshipper of Allāh to change sayings like “my slave”, and “my slave-girl” to “my young man” and “my young woman”. This is a means of protecting oneself from deceptive and dangerous expressions, even if the objective is innocent of that. So this is not because it is unlawful, rather it is to perfect ones etiquette, and to protect his expressions from anything that appears deceptive and dangerous. The manner of expressing oneself is a sign of the perfection of his sincerity, particularly in the case of this kind of expression which has recently been commonly employed.

Chapter 55

لا يرد من سأل الله

Do not turn away the one who asks for the sake of Allāh."

عن ابن عمر رضي الله عنهما قال: قال رسول الله صلى الله عليه وسلم: (من استعاذ بالله فأعيذوه، ومن سأل بالله فأعطوه، ومن دعاكم فأجيبوه، ومن صنع إليكم معروفاً فكافئوه، فإن لم تجدوا ما تكافئونه فادعوا له حتى ترون أنكم قد كافأتموه). رواه أبو داود والنسائي بسند صحيح.

From Ibn 'Umar (ﷺ) that Allāh's Messenger (ﷺ) said, "Whoever asks for Allāh's sake, then give him, whoever seeks your aid for the sake of Allāh then give him, and whoever calls you then answer him, and whoever does good for you then do similar for him. If you cannot do similar for him, then say a *du'ā* for him, until you see that you have." Recorded by Abū Dāwūd and al-Nasā'ī with a *ṣaḥīḥ* chain.[129]

فيه مسائل:

الأولى: إعاذة من استعاذ بالله.

الثانية: إعطاء من سأل بالله.

الثالثة: إجابة الدعوة.

الرابعة: المكافأة على الصنيعة.

---

[129] Recorded also by Aḥmad, al-Bukhārī in *al-Adab al-Mufrad*, Ibn Ḥibbān, al-Ḥākim and others. It was graded *ṣaḥīḥ* by al-Albānī in *Al-Ṣaḥīḥah* no. 254.

الخامسة: أن الدعاء مكافأة لمن لم يقدر إلا عليه.

السادسة: قوله: (حتى ترون أنكم قد كافأتموه).

Important Points

1. Giving refuge to one who seeks your help for the sake of Allāh.
2. Giving one who asks you for the sake of Allāh.
3. Answering the call.
4. Reciprocating the good that one does for you.
5. That the *duʿā* is a way of reciprocating in the case one is not able to do otherwise.
6. His saying, "Until you see that you have reciprocated."

Commentary by *ʿAllāmah* al-Saʿdī

Do not Turn away the one who asks for the sake of Allāh

This chapter about asking deals with an address to the one being asked. That is when one presents himself before people, asking them to fulfil a need via the most honoured means, that is asking "for Allāh's sake." He is to be responded to out of the sacredness and honour that is Allāh's right, and fulfilling the right of his brother since he has laid claim via this the most honoured of possible means.

Chapter 56

لا يسأل بوجه الله إلا الجنة

Not to ask for the sake of Allāh's Face except for Paradise

عن جابر رضي الله عنه قال: قال رسول الله صلى الله عليه وسلم: (لا يسأل بوجه الله إلا الجنة). رواه أبو داود.

From Jābir, Allāh's Messenger (ﷺ) said, "Do not ask for the sake of Allāh's Face except for Paradise." Recorded by Abū Dāwūd.[130]

فيه مسائل:

الأولى: النهي عن أن يسأل بوجه الله إلا غاية المطالب.

الثانية: إثبات صفة الوجه.

Important Points

1. The prohibition from asking for the sake of Allāh's face except for the most important thing sought.
2. Affirming the attribute of the Face.

---

[130] This ḥadīth was graded weak by al-Arnā'ūṭ in his notes on *Fatḥ al-Majīd*, and also by al-Albānī no. 6351 *Ḍa'īf Jāmi' al-Ṣaghīr*. However, the weakness of this particular ḥadīth does not effect the correctness of the second point mentioned by the author.

Commentary by *ʿAllāmah* al-Saʿdī

This chapter about asking deals with an address to the one who asks. It is required that the worshipper hold Allāh's Names and attributes sacred, and that he not ask for anything that he seeks of worldly matters for the sake of Allāh's Face, rather he does not ask via the sake of Allāh's Face except for the most important thing that can be sought, the greatest goal, and that is Paradise because of what it contains of favours and everlasting life, the pleasure of the Lord, gazing at His most splendid Face and relishing His public address. This is the shining goal which is asked for by the sake of Allāh's Face.

As far as seeking other matters of one's religious and worldly life, where the worshipper is not asking for it except from his Lord alone, then he is not to ask Him for it for the sake of His Face.

Chapter 57

ما جاء في اللّو

What is said about "If"

وقول الله تعالى: (يقولون لو كان لنا من الأمر شيء ما قتلنا هاهنا) . وقوله: (الذين قالوا لإخوانهم وقعدوا لو أطاعونا ما قتلوا) الآية.

Allāh (ﷻ) said, "They say, 'If we had anything to do with this matter, then we wouldn't have even been fighting here.' (*Āl ʿImrān* 3:154) And, "those who stayed behind and said about their brothers, 'If they had listened to us they wouldn't have been killed.'" (*Āl ʿImrān* 3:169)

في الصحيح عن أبي هريرة أن رسول الله صلى الله عليه وسلم قال: (احرص على ما ينفعك، واستعن بالله ولا تعجزن، وإن أصابك شيء فلا تقل لو أني فعلت كذا لكان كذا وكذا؛ ولكن قل: قدر الله وما شاء فعل، فإن لو تفتح عمل الشيطان).

In the *Ṣaḥīḥ* from Abū Hurayrah (ﷺ), Allāh's Messenger (ﷺ) said, "Persist in what benefits you, seek Allāh's help and do not behave helplessly. And if something happens to you do not say, 'If I had done this, then that would be.' But say, 'Allāh has decreed, and He has done as He willed." [*Qadar Allāha wa mā shā' faʿla*] because 'if' opens a way for the work of *shayṭān*."[131]

فيه مسائل:

الأولى: تفسير الآيتين في آل عمران.

الثانية: النهي الصريح عن قول: لو، إذا أصابك شيء.

[131] Muslim

الثالثة: تعليل المسألة بأن ذلك يفتح عمل الشيطان.

الرابعة: الإرشاد إلى الكلام الحسن.

الخامسة: الأمر بالحرص على ما ينفع مع الاستعانة بالله.

السادسة: النهي عن ضد ذلك وهو العجز.

Important Points

1. The explanation of the two *āyāt* of *Sūrah Āl ʿImrān*.
2. The clear prohibition from saying "if" when something has happened.
3. The reasoning for this issue, that it opens the way for the work of *shayṭān*.
4. Guidance to a good saying [instead].
5. The command to pursue what benefits, while seeking Allāh's help.
6. The prohibition of the opposite of that, that is behaving helplessly.

Commentary by *ʿAllāmah* al-Saʿdī

What is Said about "If."

Know that the worshipper's usage of the statement "if" falls into two categories, the censured and the praised.

As for that usage which has been censured, it is when he experiences a matter or does something that he does not like so he says, "If I did this then such and such would have happened instead." This is from the works of *shayṭān*, because it contains two dangers;

1. It opens the door to regret, discontentment, and grief, all of which must be removed, since there is no benefit in it.

2. This is bad conduct with Allāh concerning His decree, because every matter that comes up - the important and unimportant - is by the decree of Allāh and His will. So whatever occurs, no doubt occurs by His planning, reversing it is not possible. So if one says,

"If it was like this, or if I had done this, then this would be..." this is a type of resistance and weakness in his faith in Allāh's decree and will.

There is no doubt about the danger of these two matters, and that the worshipper's faith and *tawḥīd* will not be complete without staying away from them.

As for the praiseworthy type, it is when the worshipper says "if" wishing for only good. Like when he (ﷺ) said, "If I had known beforehand what I came to know afterwards, I would not have brought the sacrifice and would have said the *talbiyah* for *ʿumrah.*" [Muslim] And his saying about a man when he expressed his desire to do good, "If I had wealth similar to so and so then I would do similar to what so and so did with it." And "If my brother Mūsā had been patient, then Allāh would have narrated more to us about their story." This was about his story with *al-Khiḍr.*

So the word "if", when it is said expressing the desire for something good, then it is praiseworthy. When it is said in a manner expressing evil than it is censured.

So the usage of "if" depends upon how and what it is used for. If its implication is discontentment, regret and weak faith in the decree and the will of Allāh, or out of desire for something evil, then it is blameworthy.

If the implication is out of the desire for good, guidance, and teaching then it is praiseworthy. This is the case although the author has written the discussion in a way that seems to include both usages.

Chapter 58

النهي عن سب الريح

The prohibition of cursing the wind

عن أبي بن كعب رضي الله عنه أن رسول الله صلى الله عليه وسلم قال: (لا تسبوا الريح، فإذا رأيتم ما تكرهون فقولوا: اللهم إنا نسألك من خير هذه الريح، وخير ما فيها، وخير ما أمرت به، ونعوذ بك من شر هذه الريح، وشر ما فيها، وشر ما أمرت به) صححه الترمذي.

From Ubayy bin Kaʿb (ﷺ) that Allāh's Messenger (ﷺ) said, "Do not curse the wind. When you see what you do not like then say, 'O Allāh we ask you for the good of this wind and the good of what is in it, and the good that you have commanded with it, and we seek refuge in you from the evil of this wind and the evil of what it contains, and the bad that you have commanded it [to do.]" Al-Tirmidhī graded it *ṣaḥīḥ*.[132]

فيه مسائل:

الأولى: النهي عن سب الريح.

الثانية: الإرشاد إلى الكلام النافع إذا رأى الإنسان ما يكره.

الثالثة: الإرشاد إلى أنها مأمورة.

الرابعة: أنها قد تؤمر بخير وقد تؤمر بشر.

---

[132] This grade was endorsed by al-Albānī in *Ṣaḥīḥ Sunan Al-Tirmidhī* no. 1836.

Important Points

1. The prohibition of cursing the wind.
2. Guidance to a beneficial saying when people see what they do not like of it.
3. The understanding that it is fulfilling commands.
4. That it has been commanded with good and it has been commanded with evil.

Commentary by ʿ*Allāmah* al-Saʿdī

The Prohibition of Cursing the Wind

This is a parallel to what preceded about cursing time, except that was a general chapter about cursing the events of time, and this is specific to the wind. While this is prohibited, it is surely done only out of one's weak logic and weak mind. Because the wind only follows a course plotted by Allāh and arranged by Him, so cursing it amounts to cursing Him for the course that He gave it.

In most cases the one who utters the curse upon the wind does not have this meaning in his heart, whereas if that was the case, his situation would be more horrendous than that. But this would scarcely occur in the heart of a Muslim.

Chapter 59

قول الله تعالى: يظنون بالله غير الحق

Allāh (ﷻ) said, "They think other than the truth about Allāh"

قول الله تعالى: ﴿ يظنون بالله غير الحق ظن الجاهلية يقولون هل لنا من الأمر من شيء قل إن الأمر كله لله ﴾ الآية. وقوله: ﴿ الظانين بالله ظن السوء عليهم دائرة السوء ﴾ الآية.

Allāh (ﷻ) said, "They think other than the truth about Allāh, with the *jāhilīyyah* thinking, saying, 'Were we to have had anything to do with the matter' Say; 'The entire matter is up to Allāh.'" (*Āl ʿImrān* 3:154) And; "Those who think about Allāh with evil ideas, it is them that the evil encircles." (*al-Fatḥ* 48:6)

قال ابن القيم في الآية الأولى: فسّر هذا الظن بأنه سبحانه لا ينصر رسوله، وأن أمره سيضمحل، وفسر بأن ما أصابه لم يكن بقدر الله وحكمته، ففسر بإنكار الحكمة، وإنكار القدر، وإنكار أن يتم أمر رسوله، وأن يظهره الله على الدين كله. وهذا هو الظن السوء الذي ظنه المنافقون والمشركون في سورة الفتح، وإنما كان هذا ظن السوء؛ لأنه ظن غير ما يليق به سبحانه، وما يليق بحكمته وحمده ووعده الصادق، فمن ظن أنه يديل الباطل على الحق إدالة مستقرة يضمحل معها الحق، أو أنكر أن يكون ما جرى بقضائه وقدره أو أنكر أن يكون قدره بحكمة بالغة يستحق عليها الحمد، بل زعم أن ذلك لمشيئة مجردة، فذلك ظن الذين كفروا فويل للذين كفروا من النار.

Explaining the first *āyah*, Ibn al-Qayyim said about this thinking of theirs that "It was that He (ﷻ) would not help His Messenger, and that his success would fade, and that the adversity they experienced was not from Allāh's decree and wisdom. They rejected the wisdom and the decree, they rejected the idea that He would complete the mission of His Messenger and manifest His entire religion. This is the evil thinking of the hypocrites and the *mushrikīn* mentioned in *Sūrah al-Fatḥ*. This kind of thinking was evil because it was the kind of thinking about Allāh (ﷻ) that does not suit Him, nor His wisdom, His praise, and His truthful promise.

So whoever thinks that He would grant victory to falsehood over truth, causing it to remain while truth dissipates, or to deny that events occur by His decree and will, or to reject that what He willed was out of a wisdom that is befitting His praise - he rather claims that this just simply happens to occur - then that is the kind of thinking of those who disbelieve, so let those who disbelieve beware of the Fire.

وأكثر الناس يظنون بالله ظن السوء فيما يختص بهم وفيما يفعله بغيرهم، ولا يسلم من ذلك إلا من عرف الله وأسماءه وصفاته وموجب حكمته وحمده.

Most people think evil thoughts about Allāh regarding what happens to them specifically, or what He does to others besides them. None is safe from that except by knowing Allāh, His Names, His attributes, and accepting His wisdom and praising Him.

فليعتن اللبيب الناصح لنفسه بهذا، وليتب إلى الله ويستغفره من ظنه بربه ظن السوء، ولو فتشت من فتشت لرأيت عنده تعنتاً على القدر وملامة له، وأنه كان ينبغي أن يكون كذا وكذا، فمستقل ومستكثر، وفتش نفسك: هل أنت سالم؟

فإن تنج منها تنج من ذي عظيمة　　　وإلا فإني لا إخالك ناجياً

So let the intelligent one who has fallen victim to this take note, and let him repent to Allāh and seek His forgiveness from thinking about his Lord with evil thoughts. If you were to look around, you would find everyone you see annoyed by the *qadr*, blaming it, and that "it should have been like this or that", seeking less or more. So look at yourself. Are you free of this? If you are, then you have been honoured by being saved from it. If not, then you will surely not be saved."

فيه مسائل:

الأولى: تفسير آية آل عمران.

الثانية: تفسير آية الفتح.

الثالثة: الإخبار بأن ذلك أنواع لا تحصر.

الرابعة: أنه لا يسلم من ذلك إلا من عرف الأسماء والصفات وعرف نفسه.

Important Points

1. The explanation of the *āyah* of *Sūrah Āl ʿImrān*.
2. The explanation of the *āyah* of *Sūrah al-Fatḥ*.
3. The information that this can be of many types.
4. That one is not safe from that without knowing the names and attributes and knowing himself.

Commentary by *ʿAllāmah* al-Saʿdī

Allāh (ﷻ) said, "They think other than the truth about Allāh, with the *jāhilīyyah* thinking..." (*Āl ʿImrān* 3: 154)

The worshipper's faith and *tawḥīd* will not be complete until he believes in all that Allāh and His Messenger informed about regarding Allāh's Names, His attributes, and His perfection. This includes trusting all of what He informed about Himself - all that He did, and all that He promised about aiding the religion, fulfilling the truth, and invalidating falsehood. So believing in this is part of faith, and tranquility of the heart with that is part of faith also.

Any kind of thoughts that negate this are from the thinking of *jāhilīyyah* that negate *tawḥīd*. Such thoughts are tantamount to thinking evil thoughts about Allāh, negating His perfection, rejecting His information, and doubting His promise. And Allāh knows best.

Chapter 60

ما جاء في منكري القدر

What is said about the deniers of *qadr*

وقال ابن عمر: والذي نفس ابن عمر بيده، لو كان لأحدهم مثل أحد ذهباً، ثم أنفقه في سبيل الله ما قبله الله منه حتى يؤمن بالقدر. ثم استدل بقول النبي صلى الله عليه وسلم: (الإيمان: أن تؤمن بالله، وملائكته، وكتبه، ورسله، واليوم الآخر، وتؤمن بالقدر خيره وشره). رواه مسلم.

Ibn ʿUmar said, "By the one in whose Hand is Ibn ʿUmar's soul! If one of them had similar to *Uḥud* in gold, then he spent it in the cause of Allāh, Allāh would not accept it from him until he believed in the *qadr*." Then he mentioned the saying of the Prophet (ﷺ), "Faith is to believe in Allāh, His angels, his books, His messengers, the Hereafter, and in the *qadr* - its good and bad." Recorded by Muslim.

وعن عبادة بن الصامت أنه قال لابنه: (يا بني إنك لن تجد طعم الإيمان حتى تعلم أن ما أصابك لم يكن ليخطئك، وما أخطأك لم يكن ليصيبك، سمعت رسول الله صلى الله عليه وسلم يقول: (إن أول ما خلق الله القلم، فقال له: اكتب، فقال: رب، وماذا أكتب؟ قال: أكتب مقادير كل شيء حتى تقوم الساعة) يا بني سمعت رسول الله صلى الله وسلم يقول: (من مات على غير هذا فليس مني).

From ʿUbādah bin al-Ṣāmit, that he said to his sons, "O my sons! You will never experience the taste of faith until you know that what happens to you would never have missed you, and what missed you would never have hit you. I heard Allāh's Messenger (ﷺ) saying, 'The first thing that Allāh created was the pen. He said to it; "Write." It said, "Lord, what do I write?" He said, "Write what has been willed for everything until the Hour."' O my sons! I heard Allāh's Messenger (ﷺ) saying, 'Whoever dies upon other than this [belief] he is not of me.'"[133]

وفي رواية لأحمد: (إن أول ما خلق الله تعالى القلم، فقال له: اكتب، فجرى في تلك الساعة بما هو كائن إلى يوم القيامة).

And in the narration of Aḥmad; "The first thing that Allāh (ﷻ) created was the pen. He said, 'Write.' So all that will be until the Day of Judgement was mentioned at that time."

وفي رواية لابن وهب: قال رسول الله صلى الله عليه وسلم: (فمن لم يؤمن بالقدر خيره وشره أحرقه الله بالنار).

In a narration with Ibn Wahb[134], Allāh's Messenger (ﷺ) said, "Whoever does not believe in the *qadr*, its good and bad, Allāh will incinerate him in the Fire."

وفي المسند والسنن عن ابن الديلمي قال: أتيت أبي بن كعب، فقلت: في نفسي شيء من القدر، فحدثني بشيء لعل الله أن يذهبه من قلبي، فقال: (لو أنفقت مثل أحد ذهباً ما قبله الله منك حتى تؤمن بالقدر، وتعلم أن ما اصابك لم يكن ليخطئك، وما أخطأك لم يكن ليصيبك، ولو مت على غير هذا لكنت من أهل النار). قال: فأتيت عبد الله بن مسعود، وحذيفة بن اليمان، وزيدبن ثابت، فكلهم حدثني بمثل ذلك عن النبي صلى الله عليه وسلم. حديث صحيح رواه الحاكم في صحيحه.

In the *Musnad* and the *Sunan* from Ibn al-Daylamī, he said, "I came to Ubayy bin Ka'b and said, 'There is something I have thought about the *qadr*.' So he narrated something to me that by it, perhaps Allāh would erase that from my heart. He said, 'If you were to spend similar to *Uḥud* in gold, Allāh would not accept it from you until you believed in the *qadr*, and you knew that what happened to you would never have missed you, and that what missed you would have never happened to you. And if you were to die upon other than this, then you would be among the people of the Fire.' He [the narrator said], 'So I came

[133] Wording similar to this is recorded by Abū Dāwūd. Other versions recorded by Al-Tirmidhī, Abū Ya'la and al-Bayhaqī via Aḥmad as follows. It was graded *ṣaḥīḥ* by al-Albānī (*al-Ṣaḥīḥah* no. 133 & and *Ṣaḥīḥ al-Jāmi'* no. 2016-18) and al-Arnā'ūṭ in his notes on *Fatḥ al-Majīd*.

[134] He is al-Ḥāfiẓ 'Abdullāh bin Wahb bin Muslim al-Qurshī al-Miṣrī(197 H.) among whose works was the title *al-Jāmi'*.

to ʿAbdullāh bin Masʿūd, Ḥudhayfah bin al-Yamān, and Zayd bin Thābit, all of them narrated similarly to me from the Prophet (ﷺ), the ḥadīth is *ṣaḥīḥ*." Recorded by al-Ḥākim in his *Ṣaḥīḥ*.[135]

فيه مسائل:

الأولى: بيان فرض الإيمان بالقدر.

الثانية: بيان كيفية الإيمان به.

الثالثة: إحباط عمل من لم يؤمن به.

الرابعة: الإخبار بأن أحداً لا يجد طعم الإيمان حتى يؤمن به.

الخامسة: ذكر أول ما خلق الله.

السادسة: أنه جرى بالمقادير في تلك الساعة إلى قيام الساعة.

السابعة: براءته صلى الله عليه وسلم ممن لم يؤمن به.

الثامنة: عادة السلف في إزالة الشبهة بسؤال العلماء.

التاسعة: أن العلماء أجابوه بما يزيل الشبهة، وذلك أنهم نسبوا الكلام إلى رسول الله صلى الله عليه وسلم فقط.

Important Points

1. Clarifying the obligation of believing in *al-qadr*.
2. Clarifying the how of having faith in *al-qadr*.
3. Abasement of the deeds of the one who does not believe in it.
4. The information that one will not experience the taste of faith until he believes in it.
5. The mention of the first thing that Allāh created.

[135] Recorded by Abū Dāwūd, Ibn Mājah and Aḥmad. It was graded *ṣaḥīḥ* by al-Arnā'ūṭ, and al-Albānī included it in *Ṣaḥīḥ Sunan Abū Dāwūd* no. 3932.

6. That it wrote at that time all that would happen until the Hour.
7. His (ﷺ) declaration of innocence of the one who does not believe in it.
8. To remove any doubts, the *salaf* resorted to asking the knowledgeable.
9. That the knowledgeable ones answered with what removes one's doubts, that is; it was sufficient that they quote the statement of Allāh's Messenger (ﷺ), and that's all.

Commentary by *ʿAllāmah* al-Saʿdī

What is Said about the Deniers of *Qadr*

It has been confirmed by the Book, the Sunnah and the consensus of the *ummah* that belief in the *qadr* is one of the pillars of faith, and that whatever Allāh willed will be, and that whatever He did not will, will not be. So whoever does not believe in this, then he, in reality, does not have faith in Allāh.

It is required that we believe in every category of *qadr*; we believe that Allāh knows everything, and that He wrote in the preserved tablet all that was and would be until the Day of Judgement, and that all matters are from His creating, His will, and His arrangement.

And from the matters that complete faith in the *qadr*; knowing that Allāh did not force His worshippers to do different than what they intend, rather He gave them the choice, so they are either obedient or disobedient.

Chapter 61

ما جاء في المصورين

What is said about imagemakers

عن أبي هريرة رضي الله عنه قال: قال رسول الله صلى الله عليه وسلم: (قال الله تعالى: ومن أظلم ممن ذهب يخلق كخلقي، فليخلقوا ذرة، أو ليخلقوا حبة، أو ليخلقوا شعيرة). أخرجاه.

From Abū Hurayrah (ﷺ) that he said, "Allāh's Messenger (ﷺ) said, 'Allāh (ﷻ) said, "And who is more unjust than one who thinks that he creates as I create? Let them create a grain, let them create a seed, let them create a barley grain." Recorded by al-Bukhārī and Muslim.

ولهما عن عائشة رضي الله عنها، أن رسول الله صلى الله عليه وسلم قال: (أشد الناس عذاباً يوم القيامة الذين يضاهؤون بخلق الله).

From 'Ā'ishah (ﷺ), that Allāh's Messenger (ﷺ) said, "The people punished most severely on the Day of Judgement are those who imitate Allāh's creating." Recorded by al-Bukhārī and Muslim.

ولهما عن ابن عباس رضي الله عنهما: سمعت رسول الله صلى الله عليه وسلم يقول: (كل مصور في النار يجعل له بكل صورة صورها نفس يعذب بها في جهنم).

From Ibn 'Abbās, "I heard Allāh's Messenger (ﷺ) saying, 'Every maker of pictures is in the Fire. Every picture that he made will be given a soul that he will be punished by in *Jahannam*." Recorded by al-Bukhārī and Muslim.[136]

ولهما عنه مرفوعاً: (من صوّر صورة في الدنيا كلّف أن ينفخ فيها الروح، وليس بنافخ).

---

136 Also recorded by Aḥmad.

The Prophet (ﷺ) said, "Whoever makes a picture in the world, he will be responsible for blowing a soul into it and he will not be able to blow." Recorded by al-Bukhārī and Muslim.

ولمسلم عن أبي الهياج قال: قال لي عليّ: (ألا أبعثك على ما بعثني عليه رسول الله صلى الله عليه وسلم؟ ألاَّ تدع صورة إلا طمستها، ولا قبراً مشرفاً إلا سويته).

And with Muslim from Abū al-Hayyāj who said, "'Alī said to me, 'Shall I not dispatch you with what Allāh's Messenger (ﷺ) dispatched me?" That you do not leave any picture without wiping it out, nor an elevated grave without levelling it."[137]

فيه مسائل:

الأولى: التغليظ الشديد في المصورين.

الثانية: التنبيه على العلة، وهو ترك الأدب مع الله لقوله: (ومن أظلم ممن ذهب يخلق كخلقي).

الثالثة: التنبيه على قدرته وعجزهم، لقوله: (فليخلقوا ذرة أو شعيرة).

الرابعة: التصريح بأنهم أشد الناس عذاباً.

الخامسة: أن الله يخلق بعدد كل صورة نفساً يعذب بها المصور في جهنم.

السادسة: أنه يكلف أن ينفخ فيها الروح.

السابعة: الأمر بطمسها إذا وجدت.

Important Points

1. The severe emphasis on picture making.
2. Clarifying its reasons, and that is abandoning all manners with Allāh, as he said, "Who is more unjust that one who thinks that he can create like I create."
3. The clarification about His ability, and their helplessness, by His saying, "Let them create a grain, or a seed, or a kernel of barely."

[137] Also al-Nasā'ī and al-Tirmidhī.

4. Pointing out that they are the people punished the most severely.
5. That Allāh will create a soul for each picture that will punish the picture maker in *Jahannam*.
6. That they will be ordered to blow a soul into them.
7. The order to wipe out pictures when they are found.

Commentary by *ʿAllāmah* al-Saʿdī

What is said about Imagemakers

This is another branch of the topic that preceded elaborating upon the prohibition of making equals to Allāh in the intent, the saying, or the action. And making a picture is an attempt at imitating Allāh's creative ability even if that is not the reason.

So having pictures of living creatures is an attempt at imitating Allāh's creating, as well as a rejection of His divine ability to create, misrepresenting Him, and forgery. It is for these reasons that it is prohibited by the *sharīʿah*.

Chapter 62

ما جاء في كثرة الحلف

What is said about excessive swearing

وقول الله تعالى: (واحفظوا أيمانكم) .

Allāh (ﷻ) said, "And protect your oaths..." (*al-Mā'idah* 5:89)

عن أبي هريرة رضي الله عنه قال: سمعت رسول الله صلى الله عليه وسلم يقول: (الحلف منفقة للسلعة، ممحقة للكسب) أخرجاه.

From Abū Hurayrah (ﷺ), "I heard Allāh's Messenger (ﷺ) saying, "The oath spends the goods, erasing the profits." Recorded by al-Bukhārī and Muslim.[138]

عن سلمان رضي الله عنه أن رسول الله صلى الله عليه وسلم قال: (ثلاثة لا يكلمهم الله ولا يزكيهم ولهم عذاب أليم: أشيمط زان، وعائل مستكبر، ورجل جعل الله بضاعته، لا يشتري إلا بيمينه، ولا يبيع إلا بيمينه) رواه الطبراني بسند صحيح.

From Salmān, that Allāh's Messenger (ﷺ) said, "There are three whom Allāh will not speak to, nor purify them, but they will receive severe punishment; A mature adulterer, a proud poor person, and a man who made his trade out of Allāh; he did not purchase except with an oath, nor did he sell except with an oath." Recorded by al-Ṭabarānī with a *ṣaḥīḥ* chain.[139]

وفي الصحيح عن عمران بن حصين رضي الله عنه قال: قال رسول الله صلى الله عليه وسلم: (خير أمتي قرني، ثم الذين يلونهم ثم الذين يلونهم، قال عمران: فلا أدري أذكر بعد قرنه مرتين أو ثلاثاً؟ ثم إن بعدكم قوماً يشهدون ولا يستشهدون، ويخونون ولا يؤتمنون، وينذرون ولا يوفون، ويظهر فيهم السمن).

---

138 Also recorded by Abū Dāwūd and al-Nasā'ī.

139 Recorded also by others. It was graded *ṣaḥīḥ* by al-Ḥaythamī, al-Arnā'ūṭ, and al-Albānī in *Ṣaḥīḥ al-Jāmi'*; no. 3072

In the *Ṣaḥīḥ* from ʿImrān bin Ḥuṣayn (ﷺ) who said, "Allāh's Messenger (ﷺ) said, 'The best of my *ummah* is my generation, then those who come next, then those who come next...'

ʿImrān said, "I am not sure if he said it two or three times after his generation." '...Then after them are people who testify without their testimony being sought, they will betray though they were not entrusted, and they will vow but not fulfil. Obesity will appear in them.'"[140]

وفيه عن ابن مسعود رضي الله عنه أن النبي صلى الله عليه وسلم قال: (خير الناس قرني، ثم الذين يلونهم، ثم الذين يلونهم، ثم يجيء قوم تسبق شهادة أحدهم يمينه، ويمينه شهادته).

Also [in the *Ṣaḥīḥ*] from Ibn Masʿūd, that the Prophet (ﷺ) said, "The best of people are my generation, then those who come after them, then those who come after them, then those who come after them. Then there will come a people whose testimony will precede their oaths and whose oaths will precede their testimony."

قال إبراهيم: كانوا يضربوننا على الشهادة والعهد ونحن صغار.

Ibrāhīm said, "They would beat us for giving [unrequested] testimony and oaths when we were young."[141]

فيه مسائل:

الأولى: الوصية بحفظ الأيمان.

الثانية: الإخبار بأن الحلف منفقة للسلعة، ممحقة للبركة.

الثالثة: الوعيد الشديد فيمن لا يبيع ولا يشتري إلا بيمينه.

الرابعة: التنبيه على أن الذنب يعظم مع قلة الداعي.

الخامسة: ذم الذين يحلفون ولا يستحلفون.

السادسة: ثناؤه صلى الله عليه وسلم على القرون الثلاثة، أو الأربعة، وذكر ما يحدث بعدهم.

السابعة: ذم الذين يشهدون ولا يستشهدون.

الثامنة: كون السلف يضربون الصغار على الشهادة والعهد.

---

[140] Al-Bukhārī, Abū Dāwūd, and al-Tirmidhī.

[141] Recorded by al-Bukhārī and Muslim.

Important Issues

1. The legacy to keep the oaths.
2. The information that the oath spends the goods, removing the blessings.
3. The severe threat for anyone who does not sell or buy except by use of an oath.
4. The clarification that a sin can be great though few encourage it.
5. Censure of those who swear when their swearing is not requested.
6. His (ﷺ) praise for the three or four generations, and mentioning what would happen after them.
7. Censure of those who give testimony and their testimony is not requested.
8. The *salaf* beat the young for their unrequested testifying and swearing.

Commentary by *ʿAllāmah* al-Saʿdī

What is Said About Excessive Swearing

The basis of swearing is only to bring about certainty for the thing that is being sworn about, and out of honour to the Creator. So it is for this reason that none is sworn by but Allāh, and the oath by other than Him is *shirk*.

Among the matters that complete this honour is that one does not swear by Allāh except truthfully, and that His Name is held too sacred for excessive swearing, because lying and excessive swearing negates this honour which is the essence of *tawḥīd*.

Chapter 63

ما جاء في ذمة الله وذمة نبيه

What is said about Allāh's covenant and His Prophet's covenant

وقول الله تعالى: (وأوفوا بعهد الله إذا عاهدتم ولا تنقضوا الأيمان بعد توكيدها) الآية.

Allāh (ﷻ) said, "And fulfil your covenant with Allāh once you have made a covenant, and do not break your oaths after asserting them." (*al-Naḥl* 16:91)

عن بريدة رضي الله عنه أن رسول الله صلى الله عليه وسلم كان إذا أمَّر أميراً على جيش أو سرية أوصاه بتقوى الله ومن معه من المسلمين خيراً، فقال: (اغزوا بسم الله، في سبيل الله، قاتلوا من كفر بالله، اغزوا ولا تغلوا ولا تغدروا، ولا تمثلوا، ولا تقتلوا وليداً، وإذا لقيت عدوك من المشركين فادعهم إلى ثلاث خصال — أو خلال — فأيتهن ما أجابوك فاقبل منهم وكف عنهم، ثم ادعهم إلى الإسلام فإن هم أجابوك فاقبل منهم، ثم ادعوهم إلى التحول من دارهم إلى دار المهاجرين، وأخبرهم أنهم إن فعلوا ذلك فلهم ما للمهاجرين، وعليهم ما على المهاجرين، فإن أبوا أن يتحولوا منها فأخبرهم أنهم يكونون كأعراب المسلمين، يجري عليهم حكم الله تعالى، ولا يكون لهم في الغنيمة والفيء شيء إلا أن يجاهدوا مع المسلمين، فإن هم أبوا فاسألهم الجزية، فإن هم أجابوك فاقبل منهم وكف عنهم، فإن هم أبوا فاستعن بالله وقاتلهم. وإذا حاصرت أهل حصن فأرادوك أن تجعل ذمة الله وذمة نبيه، فلا تجعل لهم ذمة الله وذمة نبيه، ولكن اجعل لهم ذمتك وذمة أصحابك، فإنكم إن تخفروا ذممكم وذمة أصحابكم أهون من أن تخفروا ذمة الله وذمة نبيه.

وإذا حاصرت أهل حصن فأرادوك أن تنزلهم على حكم الله، فلا تنزلهم على حكم الله، ولكن أنزلهم على حكمك. فإنك لا تدري، أتصيب حكم الله فيهم أم لا) رواه مسلم.

From Buraydah, he said, "When ordering a commander of troops, or expedition, he [the Messenger (ﷺ)] encouraged him to have *taqwā* of Allāh, and to be good to the Muslims that were with him. So he (ﷺ) said,

'Fight in the name of Allāh, killing whoever disbelieves in Allāh. Fight, do not be excessive, nor commit gulūl (stealing from war spoils), nor mutilate. Do not kill a child. When you meet your enemy among the *mushrikīn* then invite him to three things, or three alternatives, if they agree to any of them, then accept it from them and let them be. Invite them to Islām, if they accept this from you, then accept it from them. Then invite them to leave their land to the land of the *muhājirīn*, and inform them that if they do that, then they will have the same rights as the *muhājirīn* do, and will be obliged as the *muhājirīn* are. If they refuse to relocate then inform them that they will be considered as the Muslim bedouins are; they are to conform to the rules of Allāh (ﷻ), they will not share in the prizes or booty of war at all unless they make *jihād* with the Muslims. So if they refuse then they must submit to the *jizyah*. If they accept this then accept it from them and leave them. If they refuse, then seek Allāh's help and fight them.

When you lay siege to a fortress and its people want you to offer them a treaty with Allāh and a treaty with His Messenger, do not agree with them to a treaty with Allāh and a treaty with His Messenger. Rather agree with them to your treaty and your companions' treaty. If you violate your treaty or your companions' treaty it will be easier on you than if you violate Allāh's treaty and His Messenger's treaty. And when you lay siege to a fortress and its people ask you to settle their case with Allāh's judgement, do not give Allāh's judgement on them but give your own judgement on them, for you will not be able to ascertain whether it is Allāh's judgement upon them or not." Recorded by Muslim.

فيه مسائل:

الأولى: الفرق بين ذمة الله وذمة نبيه، وذمة المسلمين.

الثانية: الإرشاد إلى أقل الأمرين خطراً.

الثالثة: قوله: (اغزوا بسم الله في سبيل الله).

الرابعة: قوله: (قاتلوا من كفر بالله).

الخامسة: قوله: (استعن بالله وقاتلهم).

السادسة: الفرق بين حكم الله وحكم العلماء.

السابعة: في كون الصحابي يحكم عند الحاجة بحكم لا يدري أيوافق حكم الله أم لا.

Important Points

1. The difference between a treaty with Allāh, a treaty with His Prophet, and a treaty with the Muslims.
2. Guidance to the lesser of the two possible evils.
3. His saying, "Fight in the name of Allāh."
4. His saying, "Kill whoever disbelieves in Allāh."
5. His saying, "Seek help from Allāh and fight them."
6. The difference between the judgement of Allāh and the judgement of the scholars.
7. That the companion, when necessary, may give a judgement that he cannot be certain whether it agrees with Allāh's judgement or not.

Commentary by ʿ*Allāmah* al-Saʿdī

What is Said About Allāh's Covenant and His Prophet's Covenant

The objective of this section is to beware and be cautious of contracting conditions that it is feared might result in nullifying a treaty or breaching it, after having made a covenant with the enemy to a treaty of Allāh or a treaty with His Messenger. Because when a breach occurs in this situation, then the Muslims will have violated the covenant of Allāh and His Messenger, and forsaken Allāh's honour, and they will have committed the worse of the two atrocities as the Prophet (ﷺ) mentioned. This also disgraces the religion of Islām and aids the disbelievers in thinking less of Islām. Certainly, honouring the covenants made, particularly those where great emphasis and effort are spent, is among the best ways in Islām to invite the enemy to accept it and abide by it.

Chapter 64

ما جاء في الإقسام على الله

What is said about making an oath on behalf of Allāh

عن جندب بن عبد الله رضي الله قال: قال رسول الله صلى الله عليه وسلم: (قال رجل: والله لا يغفر الله لفلان، فقال الله عز وجل: من ذا الذي يتألى عليّ أن لا اغفر لفلان؟ إني قد غفرت له وأحبطت عملك) رواه مسلم.

From Jundab bin 'Abdullāh (ﷺ) who said, "Allāh's Messenger (ﷺ) said, 'A man said, "By Allāh! Allāh will not forgive so and so." So Allāh (ﷻ) said, "Who is the one who swears on my behalf that I will not forgive so and so? I have certainly forgiven him, and nullified your deeds." Recorded by Muslim.

وفي حديث أبي هريرة أن القائل رجل عابد، قال أبو هريرة: تكلم بكلمة أو بقت دنياه وآخرته.

In the ḥadīth of Abū Hurayrah, "That the speaker was a pious man." Abū Hurayrah said, "He spoke a word that ruined his life and his Hereafter."[142]

فيه مسائل:

الأولى: التحذير من التألي على الله.

الثانية: كون النار أقرب إلى أحدنا من شراك نعله.

الثالثة: أن الجنة مثل ذلك.

---

[142] That is, a version of the previous ḥadīth recorded by Abū Dāwūd and Aḥmad.

الرابعة: فيه شاهد لقوله (إن الرجل ليتكلم بالكلمة) الخ..

الخامسة: أن الرجل قد يغفر له بسبب هو من أكره الأمور إليه.

Important Points

1. The warning against swearing for Allāh.
2. That the Fire is closer to each of us than the strap of his sandal.
3. That Paradise is similar to that.
4. This is testified to by his (ﷺ) saying, that "A man may speak words..."
5. That a person may be forgiven just because he was one whom the matter was denied from.

Commentary by *ʿAllāmah* al-Saʿdī

What is Said about making an oath on behalf of Allāh

This behaviour is among the worst of manners regarding Allāh's right, and it is a negation of *tawḥīd*. As for swearing on behalf of Allāh, it is most often done out of self praise, speaking on behalf of Allāh, and out of bad manners with Him. One's faith cannot be complete until he is safe from all of this.

Chapter 65

لا يستشفع بالله على خلقه

Allāh's Intercession may not be sought for His creatures

عن جبير بن مطعم رضي الله عنه قال: جاء أعرابي إلى النبي صلى الله عليه وسلم فقال: يا رسول الله: نهكت الأنفس، وجاع العيال، وهلكت الأموال، فاستسق لنا ربك، فإنا نستشفع بالله عليك وبك على الله، فقال النبي صلى الله عليه وسلم: (سبحان الله! سبحان الله!) فما زال يسبح حتى عرف ذلك في وجوه أصحابه؛ ثم قال النبي صلى الله عليه وسلم: (ويحك، أتدري ما الله؟ إن شأن الله أعظم من ذلك، إنه لا يستشفع بالله على أحد من خلقه) وذكر الحديث. رواه أبو داود.

From Jubayr bin Muṭʿim (ﷺ) who said, "A bedouin came to the Prophet (ﷺ) saying, 'O Messenger of Allāh! Lives are lost, households are starving, wealth is being ruined. So seek rain from your Lord on our behalf. We ask Allāh to intercede with you, and you with Allāh!' The Prophet (ﷺ) said, '*Subḥān Allāh! Subḥān Allāh*!' He did not stop such glorifying until his companions could recognise his anger on his face. Then he said, 'Woe to you, do you know who Allāh is? Allāh's significance is greater than that! Allāh cannot be sought to intercede for anyone.'" And he mentioned the rest of the ḥadīth. Recorded by Abū Dāwūd. [This ḥadīth is weak][143]

فيه مسائل:

الأولى: إنكاره على من قال: نستشفع بالله عليك.

---

[143] This ḥadīth was graded weak by al-Arnā'ūṭ, as well as al-Albānī (*Ḍaʿīf Sunan Abū Dāwūd* no. 1017). The note between brackets is from *al-Qawlus-Sadīd*, although it is not part of *Kitāb al-Tawḥīd*.

الثانية: تغيره تغيراً عرف في وجوه أصحابه من هذه الكلمة.

الثالثة: أنه لم ينكر عليه قوله: (نستشفع بك على الله).

الرابعة: التنبيه على تفسير (سبحان الله).

الخامسة: أن المسلمين يسألونه الاستسقاء.

Important Points

1. Rebuking whoever says "We ask Allāh to intercede with you."
2. His face changing with anger until his companions recognised that from this saying.
3. That he did not rebuke him for saying, "We ask you to intercede with Allāh."
4. Clarifying the meaning of *Subḥān Allāh*.
5. That the Muslims asked him to seek rain.

Commentary by ʿ*Allāmah* al-Saʿdī

Allāh's Intercession may not be sought for His creatures

As far as seeking Allāh to intercede with His creatures, He (ﷻ) is of far greater stature than to be used as a mediator for His creatures. The status of the one used as a mediator is usually less than the status of the one he is asked to mediate with. This is among the worst of behaviours with Allāh, so it must be avoided. For intercession will not be accepted by Him from anyone without His permission, and all who intercede with Him are in awe of Him. So how can the opposite be, and He be made the intercessor! He is the greatest, the magnificent, the one for whom all ability is subjected to, the universe submits to Him entirely.

Chapter 66

ما جاء في حماية النبي صلى الله عليه وسلم حمى التوحيد، وسده طرق الشرك

What has been mentioned about the Prophet's (ﷺ) protection of *tawḥīd* and closing the routes to *shirk*

عن عبد الله بن الشخير رضي الله عنه، قال: انطلقت في وفد بني عامر إلى النبي صلى الله عليه وسلم فقلنا: أنت سيدنا، فقال: (السيد الله تبارك وتعالى). قلنا: وأفضلنا فضلاً، وأعظمنا طولاً؛ فقال: (قولوا بقولكم، أو بعض قولكم، ولا يستجرينكم الشيطان) رواه أبو داود بسند جيد.

From ʿAbdullāh bin al-Shikhkhīr (ﷺ), who said, "I accompanied the delegation of Bani ʿĀmir to Allāh's Messenger (ﷺ). We said, 'You are our Master.' He said, 'Allāh most blessed and most exalted is the master.' We said, 'You are the most virtuous of us and the most revered in speech.' So he said, 'Say what you have to say, and do not let yourselves be used by *shayṭān*.'" Recorded by Abū Dāwūd with a good chain.[144]

وعن أنس رضي الله عنه، أن ناساً قالوا: يا رسول الله: يا خيرنا وابن خيرنا، وسيدنا وابن سيدنا، فقال: (يا أيها الناس، قولوا بقولكم، أو بعض قولكم، ولا يستهوينكم الشيطان، أنا محمد، عبد الله ورسوله، ما أحب أن ترفعوني فوق منزلتي التي أنزلني الله عز وجل). رواه النسائي بسند جيد.

---

[144] Also recorded by Aḥmad, it was graded *ṣaḥīḥ* by al-Arnā'ūṭ, and al-Albānī in *Ṣaḥīḥ al-Jāmiʿ* no. 3700, and *Hidāyah al-Rūwāh* no. 4826.

Anas (🙵) said, "Some people said, 'O Messenger of Allāh! O best of us! Son of the best of us, our master and son of our master.' He said, 'O People! Say what you have to say and do not let yourselves be used by *shayṭān*, I am Muḥammad, the slave of Allāh, and Allāh's Messenger, I do not like for you to raise me above the position that Allāh (🙵) has sent me for." Recorded by al-Nasā'ī with a good chain.[145]

فيه مسائل:

الأولى: تحذير الناس من الغلو.

الثانية: ما ينبغي أن يقول من قيل له: أنت سيدنا.

الثالثة: قوله: (ولا يستجرينكم الشيطان) مع أنهم لم يقولوا إلا الحق.

الرابعة: قوله: (ما أحب أن ترفعوني فوق منزلتي).

Important Points

1. Warning the people from exaggeration.

2. What is required to be said by the one whom it is said, "You are our master."

3. His saying, "Do not let yourselves be used by *shayṭān*" even though they were saying only what was true.

4. His saying, "I do not like for you to raise me above my position."

Commentary by ʿAllāmah al-Saʿdī

What has been mentioned about the Prophet's (🙵) protection of *Tawḥīd* and closing the routes to *Shirk*

This topic was discussed earlier, but the author has returned to it in order to emphasis its importance. *Tawḥīd* will not be complete nor preserved nor fortified, except by avoiding all routes leading to *shirk*. The difference between the two chapters is that the first deals

---

[145] Al-Arnā'ūṭ said, "Perhaps it is with al-Nasā'ī in *al-Kubrā*. It was recorded by Aḥmad in his *Musnad* ... and it is an authentic ḥadīth." See previous note, and the no. in *al-Kubrā* is 100075.

with protecting *tawḥīd* by closing off the routes of actions, and this chapter deals with closing off the routes by manners and protecting sayings.

So every statement that implies some kind of exaggerating which it is feared may result in *shirk*, then it becomes necessary to avoid it, and *tawḥīd* will not be completed without abandoning it.

The result is that *tawḥīd* is fulfilled only by maintaining its conditions, its pillars, its requirements and its rules, and by avoiding what nullifies it, and whatever degrades it outwardly or inwardly, of sayings, actions, intentions and beliefs.

The details that have been mentioned clarify that.

Chapter 67

ما جاء في قول الله تعالى: وما قدروا الله حق قدره

Allāh's (ﷻ) saying "And they have not surmised a status worthy of Allāh."

ما جاء في قول الله تعالى: (وما قدروا الله حق قدره والأرض جميعاً قبضته يوم القيامة) الآية.

Allāh's (ﷻ) saying "And they have not surmised a status worthy of Allāh. And He will grab the entire Earth on the Day of Resurrection...." (*al-Zumar* 39:67)

عن ابن مسعود رضي الله عنه قال: جاء حبر من الأحبار إلى رسول الله صلى الله عليه وسلم فقال: يا محمد! إنا نجد أن الله يجعل السماوات على إصبع، والأرضين على إصبع، والشجر على إصبع، والماء على إصبع، والثرى على إصبع، وسائر الخلق على إصبع، فيقول: أنا الملك. فضحك النبي صلى الله عليه وسلم حتى بدت نواجذه، تصديقاً لقول الحبر، ثم قرأ رسول الله صلى الله عليه وسلم: (وما قدروا الله حق قدره والأرض جميعاً قبضته يوم القيامة) الآية.

From Ibn Masʿūd (ؓ) who said, "A rabbi came to Allāh's Messenger (ﷺ) saying, 'O Muḥammad, we have found it stated that Allāh will place the heavens upon a finger, the earths upon a finger, the trees upon a finger, the water upon a finger, the land upon a finger, and the remainder of creations upon a finger. Then He says, "I am the King."'

The Prophet (ﷺ) laughed until his molars were visible, because of the truth of what the rabbi said. Then he recited, 'And they have not surmised a status worthy of Allāh. And He will grab the entire Earth on the Day of Resurrection....'" (Agreed Upon)

وفي رواية لمسلم: والجبال والشجر على إصبع، ثم يهزهن فيقول: أنا الملك، أنا الله.

In the narration with Muslim, "And the mountains and trees upon a finger, then they tremble as He says, ' I am the King, I am Allāh."

وفي رواية للبخاري: يجعل السماوات على إصبع، والماء والثرى على إصبع، وسائر الخلق على إصبع) أخرجاه.

In the narration with al-Bukhārī, "He places the heavens upon a finger, and the water and land upon a finger, and the remainder of creation upon a finger." Recorded by al-Bukhārī and Muslim.[146]

ولمسلم عن ابن عمر مرفوعاً: (يطوي الله السماوات يوم القيامة، ثم يأخذهن بيده اليمنى، ثم يقول: أنا الملك، أين الجبارون؟ أين المتكبرون؟ ثم يطوي الأرضين السبع ثم يأخذهن بشماله، ثم يقول: أنا الملك، أين الجبارون؟ أين المتكبرون.

Ibn 'Umar relates the Prophet (ﷺ) said; "On the Day of Resurrection Allāh will roll up the heavens, then take them in His right Hand, then He says, I am the King, where are the tyrants? Where are the proud? Then He will roll up the seven earths, then He takes them in His left Hand, then says I am the King, where are the tyrants, where are the proud?" Recorded by Muslim.

وروي عن ابن عباس، قال: (ما السماوات السبع والأرضون السبع في كف الرحمن إلا كخردلة في يد أحدكم).

It is reported from Ibn 'Abbās that he said, "The seven heavens and the seven earths are not in the palm of *al-Raḥmān* but like a mustard seed in one of your hands."

وقال ابن جرير: حدثني يونس، أنبأنا ابن وهب، قال: قال ابن زيد: حدثني أبي، قال: قال رسول الله صلى الله عليه وسلم: (ما السماوات السبع في الكرسي إلا كدراهم سبعة ألقيت في ترس) قال: وقال أبو ذر رضي الله عنه: سمعت رسول الله صلى الله عليه وسلم يقول: (ما الكرسي في العرش إلا كحلقة من حديد ألقيت بين ظهري فلاة من الأرض).

Ibn Jarīr [al-Ṭabari] said, "Yūnus narrated to me, that Ibn Wahb informed us saying, 'Ibn Zayd said, "My father narrated to me; 'Allāh's Messenger (ﷺ) said:

[146] Also recorded by Aḥmad and al-Tirmidhī.

"The seven heavens compared to the *Kursī* are but like seven *dirhāms* tossed in an armoured shield."

He [Ibn Zayd] said, 'Abū Dharr (⌀) said, "I heard Allāh's Messenger (⌀) saying, 'The *Kursī* compared to the Throne is not but like a ring of iron thrown in the midst of a desert of the Earth.'"[147]

وعن ابن مسعود قال: (بين السماء الدنيا والتي تليها خمسمائة عام، وبين كل سماء خمسمائة عام، وبين السماء السابعة والكرسي خمسمائة عام، وبين الكرسي والماء خمسمائة عام، والعرش فوق الماء، والله فوق العرش، لا يخفى عليه شيء من أعمالكم). أخرجه ابن مهدي عن حماد بن سلمة عن عاصم عن زر عن عبدالله ورواه بنحوه عن المسعودي عن عاصم، عن أبي وائل، عن عبد الله. قاله الحافظ الذهبي رحمه الله تعالى، قال: وله طرق.

From Ibn Masʿūd who said, "Between the Earth's heaven and what follows it there are five hundred years, and between every heaven there are five hundred years, and between the seven heavens and the *Kursī* there are five hundred years, and between the *Kursī* and the water there are five hundred years and the Throne is above the water, and Allāh is above the throne, and none of your deeds are hidden from Him." Recorded by Ibn Mahdī from Ḥamād bin Salamah from ʿĀṣim from Zirr from ʿAbdullāh. And al-Masʿūdī recorded similar from ʿĀṣim from Abū Wāʾil from ʿAbdullāh. Al-Ḥāfiẓ al-Dhahabī, may Allāh have mercy upon him said, "And it has other routes."[148]

وعن العباس بن عبد المطلب رضي الله عنه قال: قال رسول الله صلى الله عليه وسلم: (هل تدرون كم بين السماء والأرض؟) قلنا: الله ورسوله أعلم قال: (بينهما مسيرة خمسمائة سنة، ومن كل سماء إلى سماء مسيرة خمسمائة سنة وكثف كل سماء خمسمائة سنة، وبين السماء السابعة والعرش بحر بين أسفله وأعلاه كما بين السماء والأرض، والله سبحانه وتعالى فوق ذلك، وليس يخفى عليه شيء من أعمال بني آدم). أخرجه أبو داود وغيره.

---

[147] It is confirmed from Abū Dharr (⌀) that the Prophet (⌀) said; "The seven heavens are to the *Kursī* but like a ring thrown in a desert land. And the superiority of the Throne compared to that of the *Kursī* is like the superiority of that desert compared to the ring." Recorded by Muḥammad bin Abū Shaybah in *Kitāb al-ʿArsh*, al-Bayhaqī in *al-Asmāʾ wa al-Ṣifāt*, Ibn Marduwyah in his *Tafsīr*, and al-Ṭabarī. Al-Albānī graded it *ṣaḥīḥ* in *al-Ṣaḥīḥah* no.109. And he pointed out that this is the only authentic ḥadīth from the Prophet (⌀) about the virtue of the *Kursī*, however there are others from the companions that are authentic as well. See *Mukhtaṣar al-ʿUlū*.

[148] See *Mukhtaṣar al-ʿUlū*; From Ibn Masʿūd who said, "The Throne is above the water, and Allāh is above the Throne, none of your deeds are hidden from Him." Recorded by al-Bayhaqī in *al-Asmāʾ wa al-Ṣifāt*, Ibn Khuzaymah in *al-Tawḥīd*, and others. Ibn al-Qayyim graded it *ṣaḥīḥ* in *Jayūsh*, and al-Albānī graded it *jayyid* in *Mukhtaṣar al-ʿUlū* no. 48.

From al-ʿAbbās bin ʿAbd al-Muṭṭallib (ﷺ) who said, "Allāh's Messenger (ﷺ) said, 'Do you know how much is between the heavens and the Earth?'" We said, 'Allāh and His Messenger know better.' He said, 'Between them is the distance of five hundred years, and from each heaven to the next heaven is the distance of five hundred years, and the width of each heaven is five hundred years. And between the seven heavens and the Throne is a sea, between its lowest and highest point is as between the heavens and the Earth. Allāh (ﷻ) is above that, and nothing that the children of Ādam do is hidden from Him.'" Recorded by Abū Dāwūd and others.[149]

فيه مسائل:

الأولى: تفسير قوله: (والأرض جميعاً قبضته يوم القيامة) .

الثانية: أن هذه العلوم وأمثالها باقية عند اليهود الذين في زمنه صلى الله عليه وسلم لم ينكروها و لم يتأولوها.

الثالثة: أن الحبر لما ذكر للنبي صلى الله عليه وسلم، صدقه، ونزل القرآن بتقرير ذلك.

الرابعة: وقوع الضحك من رسول الله صلى الله عليه وسلم، لما ذكر الحبر هذا العلم العظيم.

الخامسة: التصريح بذكر اليدين، وأن السماوات في اليد اليمنى، والأرضين في الأخرى.

السادسة: التصريح بتسميتها الشمال.

السابعة: ذكر الجبارين والمتكبرين عند ذلك.

الثامنة: قوله: (كخردلة في كف أحدكم).

التاسعة: عظم الكرسي بالنسبة إلى السماوات.

العاشرة: عظم العرش بالنسبة إلى الكرسي.

---

[149] It was recorded also by Al-Tirmidhī (where al-Albānī graded it weak), and Ibn Mājah. It is apparently weak due to the presence of ʿAbdullāh bin ʿUmayrah whose condition al-Dhahabī claimed is unknown.

الحادية عشرة: أن العرش غير الكرسي والماء.

الثانية عشر: كم بين كل سماء إلى سماء.

الثالثة عشر: كم بين السماء السابعة والكرسي.

الرابعة عشر: كم بين الكرسي والماء.

الخامسة عشر: أن العرش فوق الماء.

السادسة عشرة: أن الله فوق العرش.

السابعة عشر: كم بين السماء والأرض.

الثامنة عشر: كثف كل سماء خمسمائة عام.

التاسعة عشر: أن البحر الذي فوق السماوات بين أعلاه وأسفله مسيرة خمسمائة سنة.

Important Points

1. The explanation of Allāh's (ﷻ) saying, "He will grab the entire Earth on the Day of Resurrection...."
2. That this knowledge, and its like, was among the Jews during his (ﷺ) time, they did not deny it nor give it false interpretations.
3. That what the rabbi said to the Prophet (ﷺ) was true, and the Qur'ān was revealed in approval of it.
4. That Allāh's Messenger (ﷺ) laughed when the rabbi mentioned this great information.
5. The clarity of mentioning the Hands, and that the heavens will be in the right Hand and the earths in the other.
6. The clarification in calling it the left.
7. Mentioning the tyrants and the proud with this.
8. His (ﷺ) saying, "Like a mustard seed in one of your hands."
9. The magnificence of the *Kursī* in comparison to the heavens.

10. The magnificence of the Throne in comparison to the *Kursī*.
11. That the Throne is different than the *Kursī* and the water.
12. The span between each heaven.
13. The distance between the seven heavens and the *Kursī*.
14. The distance between the *Kursī* and the water.
15. That the Throne is above the water.
16. That Allāh is above the Throne.
17. The distance between the Earth and the lowest heaven.
18. The width of each heaven is five hundred years.
19. That the distance between the lowest and highest point of the sea which is above the heavens is five hundred years. And Allāh knows best.

All praise is due to Allāh the Lord of the worlds, and may He mention and send peace upon our master Muḥammad, and upon his family and all of his companions.

Commentary by ʿ*Allāmah* al-Saʿdī

Allāh's (ﷻ) saying "And they have not surmised a status worthy of Allāh. And He will grab the entire Earth on the Day of Resurrection...." (*al-Zumar* 39:67)

The author, may Allāh have mercy upon him ended his book with this topic. He mentioned the texts proving the Lord's magnificence and greatness, His majesty, His glory, and the subjugation of the existence and its creatures to His Might. For these magnificent qualities and perfect attributes are the greatest of evidences and proofs that He alone is to be worshipped, praised, and the one to whom entire submission and the utmost of honour, love and deification is obligatory. Surely He is the Truth and other that He is falsehood, and this is the reality of *tawḥīd*, its heart and spirit, and it is the secret to sincerity.

So we ask Allāh that He guide our hearts upon knowing Him, loving Him, and turning to Him, indeed He is generous and most noble.

And this is the end of the brief notes on *Kitāb al-Tawḥīd* explaining its objectives. In it the highlight of the issues of *tawḥīd* are united, and outlined, and the benefits explained in detail for those who long for this subject, the foundation of foundations upon which all knowledge is established. And I praise Allāh for His facilitation and grace, and may Allāh mention Muḥammad, his family, his companions, and greet him with peace.

Glossary

A

Abī: A form of "Father of".

Abū: A form of "Father of".

Ahl al-Sunnah: The people of the *Sunnah*.

Al-ʿAfu: A Name of Allāh denoting that He is the Pardoner.

Al-Asmā wa l-Ṣifāt: The Names and attributes of Allāh.

ʿAlayhī al-salām: Peace be upon him.

Al-ʿAzīz: A Name of Allāh denoting that He is the Mighty.

Al-Bātin: A Name of Allāh denoting that He is the Most Inner.

Al-Birr: A Name attributed to Allāh, denoting that He is the Compassionate.

Al-Ghafūr: A Name of Allāh denoting that He is the Forgiving.

Al-Ḥakīm: A Name of Allāh denoting that He is the Wise.

Al-Islām: The name of the religion, meaning submission to Allāh.

Al-Karīm: A Name of Allāh denoting that He is the Kind.

Allāhu akbar: "Allāh is most great".

Al-Lāt: The name of a pre-Islamic idol.

Al-Manān: A Name of Allāh denoting that He is the Beneficent.

Al-Masīḥ: The Messiah.

Al-Masīḥ al-Dajjāl: The False Messiah.

Al-Rahīm: A Name of Allāh denoting that He is the Bestower of Mercy.

Al-Raḥmān: A Name of Allāh denoting that He is the Most Merciful.

Al-Razzāq: A Name of Allāh denoting that He is the Provider.

Al-Tawāb: A Name of Allāh denoting that He is the One Who accepts repentance.

Al-ʿUzzā: The name of a pre-Islamic idol.

Al-Wahhāb: A Name of Allāh denoting that He is the One Who Confers.

Al-Ẓāhir: A Name of Allāh denoting that He is Above everything.

Āmīn: A supplication meaning: "O our Lord, let it be so".

Andād: Equals or rivals.

Anṣār: The Helpers. Those who aided and supported the emigrants from Makkah.

ʿArsh: Throne.

Ashʿarī: (Ashʿarīyah) The name of a sect that denies or distorts the meanings of many of Allāh's attributes.

Awliyā': See *walī*.

Āyah: (pl. *Āyāt*) A Quranic phrase or sentance.

Āyāt: See *āyah*.

ʿAzā'im: Incantations, see chapter no. 8.

B

Badr: The first decisive battle in Islam.

Barzakh: The barrier between this life and the Hereafter, and events that occur during that period.

Baṣīrah: Knowledge and clear insight.

Bayt al-Maqdis: "The Holy House" referring to Jerusalem.

D

Ḍaʿīf: Weak. A ḥadīth term.

Dajjāl: Liar or imposter, usually refers to one who claims prophethood.

Dhāṭ al-anwāṭ: "Possessor of the medals of honour" A tree which the idolators used to hang their weapons upon to denote their bravery.

Dhul-mahram: One whom it is unlawful for another to marry.

Dīnār: A silver coin.

Dirham: A gold coin.

Duʿā: Supplication.

Dunyā: The world.

F

fa'l: A good sign or an encouraging indication.

fiqh: Understanding of the religion.

fisq: Wickedness.

Fitnah: (pl. *Fitn*) Trials, turmoil and discord.

H

Ḥadīth: A narration, usually referring to the Prophet (ﷺ).

Ḥajj: The fifth pillar of Islam, the ritual pilgrimage to Makkah and its sacred precincts.

Ḥasan: Good. A ḥadīth term.

Ḥasan gharīb: Good and rare. A ḥadīth term denoting that the ḥadīth is good, but it at a certain point in all of its chain of narration there is only one narrator.

I

ʿIbādah: Worship.

Iblīs: The name of Satan.

Iḥsān: Beneficence, or to worship Allāh as though you see Him.

Ikhlāṣ: Sincerity.

Ilāhiyah: See ulūhiyah.

Ilḥād: Heretical ideas about Allāh's Names.

'Ilm: Knowledge.

Imām: A leader.

Īmān: Faith.

Insān: Man.

Isnād: A chain of narration.

Istaghāthah: Seeking help.

Istawā: To ascend.

Istikhārah: To seek guidance for a decision.

J

Jahannam: Hell.

Jāhilīyyah: The pre-Islamic period of ignorance.

Jahmiyyah: A sect who deny Allah's attributes.

jayyid: Good. A ḥadīth term.

Jibrīl: The name of the angel.

Jibt: See chapter 24.

Jihād: To struggle.

Jinn: Beings created from fire, not normally visible to humans, spirits.

Jizyah: The head tax collected from certain non-Muslims groups living under the protection of an Islamic State.

K

Ka'bah: The Sacred House in Makkah.

Kāfir: (pl. *kuffār*) disbeliever, one who covers the truth.

Kāhin: A fortuneteller or seer.

Khalifah: A successor.

Khamīlah: A type of garment.

Khamīṣah: A type of garment.

Khamr: Wine or intoxicating beverages.

Kufr: Disbelief, blasphemy.

Kunyā: A term attributed to a person which indicates that he or she is the parent of so-and-so. Abū Muḥammad for example; the father of Muḥammad, or Umm Muḥammad, the mother of Muḥammad.

L

Lā ilāha illa Allāh: The statement: "There is no god worthy of worship but Allāh" which is a denial of the right of divinity and all rights due to Allāh from anything that is worshipped besides Him.

M

Makkah: The sacred city located in the *Hijāz* area of the Arabian peninsula.

Manāt: The name of a pre-Islamic idol.

Marfū': A narration that reaches all the way back to the Prophet (ﷺ), meaning that it is a real ḥadīth that he said or did, as opposed to being a statement of someone else.

Masjid: A place of worship.

Mawqūf: A narration that does not reach all the way back to the Prophet (ﷺ), but it stops at someone before him. In most cases it reaches back to a companion.

Millah: Creed or religion.

Mu'alliq: Suspended. A ḥadīth term meaning that there is a gap between the one narrating the narration, and the one it is attributed to.

Mufṭi: One who passes legal rulings.

Muḥkamah: (Pl. *Muḥkamāt*) Decisive, clear, unambiguous.

Mujāhid: A person involved in *jihād*.

Mu'minūn: Believers, the faithful people.

Munāfiq: A hypocrite.

Mursal: A narration that is attributed to the Prophet (ﷺ), but the companion who actually heard it from him is not mentioned in the chain.

Musānīd: See *musnad*.

Mushabihah: The name of the sect that likens Allāh to creatures.

Mushrik: A person that commits *shirk*.

Musnad: (Pl. *Musānīd*) A chain of narration. Normally it is the name of a collection of ḥadīths with their chains.

Muṣṭafā: The selected one, a term used to describe the Prophet Muḥammad (ﷺ).

N

Nabī: Prophet.

Naṣīḥah: Advice and council, the processes of bringing together.

Q

Qadr: The Preordained Divine Order

Qiblah: The direction the worshipper faces while performing of *ṣalāh*.

Qunūt: A type of supplication.

R

Rāfiḍah: The name of the most popular Shiite sect.

Rak'ah: One complete unit of *ṣalāh*.

Raml: Walking quickly.

Riyā’: Showing off.

Rubūbiyah: Lordship.

Rūh: Soul or spirit.

Rukū: The bowing position in *ṣalāh*.

Ruqyā: Recitation of certain phrases to invoke a cure.

S

Ṣadaqah: Charity.

Ṣafar: The name of the second month in the lunar calender.

Ṣaḥīḥ: Correct, genuine. A ḥadīth term denoting authenticity.

Ṣaḥīḥ mawqūf: Correct but stopped. A narration that stops at a companion or someone before the Prophet (ﷺ), and its chain is authentic to that point.

Salaf: Predecessor.

Ṣalāh: The ritual worship most commonly referred to as prayer.

Salām: The greeting of peace and tranquility, or the attribute of being free from danger.

Shahādah: Testimony

Shahādatayn: The two testimonies.

Sharīʿah: Islamic legislation.

Shaykh: Elder or scholar.

Shayṭān: Satan.

Shirk: Association, referring to the act of associating others with Allāh in any of the rights that are His alone.

Subḥān Allāh: “Allāh is free of any imperfection!”

Sunan: Plural for *Sunnah*.

Sunnah: The teachings of the Prophet (ﷺ).

Sūrah: A chapter of the Qur'ān.

Suwā': The name of a pre-Islamic idol.

T

Ta'awudhāt: Talismans.

Tafsīr: Explanation, normally in relation to the Qur'aan.

Ṭāghūt: One who has gone beyond the bounds. It is used to include anyone worshipped besides Allāh, or who is pleased with that worship, or who calls to the worship of others besides Allāh, or one who claims to know the unseen, and it is also used to refer to Satan.

Takbīr: To say: "*Allāhu aḵbar*!"

Takfīr: To claim that another person is not a Muslim after he or she was a Muslim.

Takhrīj: A ḥadīth term that refers to giving references for where to find the ḥadīth and information about its chains of narration.

Talbiyah: A slogan uttered repeatedly during Hajj and 'Umrah.

Tamīmah (pl. Tamā'im) talisman or charm.

Taqwa: To protect oneself from Allāh's punishment by obeying Him.

Tarq: See chapter 25.

Ṭawāghīt: See *ṭāghūt*.

Tawassul: Seeking a means of nearness.

Tawbah: Repentance.

Tawḥīd: Singling out Allāh with all rights due to Him alone.

Ṭiyarah: An omen.

Ṭūbā: "Glad tidings" and it is the name of a tree in Paradise.

U

'Ubūdiyah: Worship, servitude.

Ulūhiyah: Divinity.

Ummah: Community or nation.

ʿUmrah: The ritual visit to the Sacred House in Makkah and the rites that are included in it, such as entering the sacred state of *iḥrām*, encircling the Kaʿbah, going between mounts Safa and al-Marwah, and having the hair shaved or cut.

W

Wadd: The name of a pre-Islamic idol.

Wāhinah: Weakness, or a type of disease that effects the upper arm.

Walī: (pl. *Awliyā'*) It is often used to mean "friend of Allāh", or saint, in which case it refers to the true believer.

Wathin: Idol.

Wilāyah': Friendship, allegiance, protection, also see *Walā*.

Y

Yaghūth: The name of a pre-Islamic idol.

Z

Zakāh: The fourth pillar of Islam, the regular fixed charity.

Zuhd: Doing without that which one has no real need for.